Cantonese

lonely planet

phrasebooks
and
Chiu-yee Cheung & Tao Li

Cantonese phrasebook
4th edition – September 2005

Published by
Lonely Planet Publications Pty Ltd ABN 36 005 607 983
90 Maribyrnong St, Footscray, Victoria 3011, Australia

Lonely Planet Offices
Australia Locked Bag 1, Footscray, Victoria 3011
USA 150 Linden St, Oakland CA 94607
UK 72-82 Rosebery Ave, London, EC1R 4RW

Cover illustration
Far away so close, yet so far by Yukiyoshi Kamimura

ISBN 1 74059 074 0

text © Lonely Planet Publications Pty Ltd 2005
cover illustration © Lonely Planet Publications Pty Ltd 2005

10 9 8 7 6 5 4 3 2

Printed through Colorcraft Ltd, Hong Kong
Printed in China

acknowledgments

Editor Meladel Mistica would like to thank the following people for their contributions to this phrasebook:

Chiu-yee Cheung with the assistance of Tao Li for their well-researched translations and cultural expertise.

Chiu-yee Cheung was born in Hong Kong and studied Chinese language and literature at Jinan University, China. He completed his PhD at the University of Sydney and is currently lecturing in Chinese language and culture at the University of Queensland.

Tao Li was born in Guangzhou, China. She graduated from Zhongshan University, China, majoring in Chinese languages and literature.

Chiu-yee Cheung and Tao Li would like to thank their family for their support and assistance.

Thanks also to layout designer Margie Jung for helping putting the finishing touches to layout and to Mark Germanchis for technical assistance.

Lonely Planet Language Products

Publishing Managers: Chris Rennie & Karin Vidstrup Monk
Commissioning Editor: Ben Handicott
Editor: Meladel Mistica
Assisting Editors: Branislava Vladisavljevic & Jodie Martire
Managing Editor: Annelies Mertens
Layout Designer: Steven Cann
Senior Layout Designer: Sally Darmody
Layout Manager: Adriana Mammarella
Series Designer: Yukiyoshi Kamimura
Cartographer: Wayne Murphy
Project Manager: Annelies Mertens
Production Manager: Jo Vraca

make the most of this phrasebook ...

Anyone can speak another language! It's all about confidence. Don't worry if you can't remember your school language lessons or if you've never learnt a language before. Even if you learn the very basics (on the inside covers of this book), your travel experience will be the better for it. You have nothing to lose and everything to gain when the locals hear you making an effort.

finding things in this book

For easy navigation, this book is in sections. The Tools chapters are the ones you'll thumb through time and again. The Practical section covers basic travel situations like catching transport and finding a bed. The Social section gives you conversational phrases, pick-up lines, the ability to express opinions – so you can get to know people. Food has a section all of its own: gourmets and vegetarians are covered and local dishes feature. Safe Travel equips you with health and police phrases, just in case. Remember the colours of each section and you'll find everything easily; or use the comprehensive Index. Otherwise, check the two-way traveller's Dictionary for the word you need.

being understood

Throughout this book you'll see coloured phrases on each page. They're phonetic guides to help you pronounce the language. You don't even need to look at the language itself, but you'll get used to the way we've represented particular sounds. The pronunciation chapter in Tools will explain more, but you can feel confident that if you read the coloured phrase slowly, you'll be understood.

communication tips

Body language, ways of doing things, sense of humour – all have a role to play in every culture. 'Local talk' boxes show you common ways of saying things, or everyday language to drop into conversation. 'Listen for ...' boxes supply the phrases you may hear. They start with the language (so local people can point out what they want to say to you) and then lead in to the pronunciation guide and the English translation.

CONTENTS

5

social 109

cantonese

CHINA

Guangzhou (Canton)

Macau   Hong Kong
         see enlargement

Laos

Gulf of Tonkin

South China Sea

Thailand

Hong Kong SAR

Shenzhen

Hong Kong Special Administrative Region

Cambodia

Vietnam

Kowloon

Lantau   Hong Kong

Gulf of Thailand

Sulu Sea

Brunei

Malaysia

Celebes Sea

Malaysia

Indonesia   SINGAPORE   Indonesia

☐ official language
☐ widely spoken

For more information, see the **introduction**.

— 'Hey, a new Jackie Chan film has just come out … wanna go see it?'
— 'Excellent! Let's go tonight, and get some dim sum on our way there …'

Next time you have a conversation like this, remember to thank Cantonese speakers for dim sum and kung fu movies (and Jackie Chan). The English-speaking world learnt about Cantonese foods like 'chop suey', cooked in a thing called a 'wok', during Hong Kong's period as a British colony, and over the last century, the success of the Hong Kong action film industry has introduced us to martial arts cinema. So where can you go to experience such a tasty, athletic language for yourself?

Cantonese is used as the official language of Hong Kong and Macau, and within China it's the local language of the mainland's south-east, including most of the province of Guangdong. Elsewhere, the language is spoken by emigrant communities worldwide and minority groups in Southeast Asia, most notably in Singapore. For over 50 years, official Chinese policy has encouraged the use of Mandarin as the one national language of China. However Cantonese speakers have persisted in using their native language, a key part of their pride and cultural

at a glance

language name:
Cantonese

name in language:
gwáwng·dùng·wáa
廣東話
(lit: Guangdong speech)

language family:
Sino-Tibetan

number of speakers:
70 million

close relatives:
Gan, Hakka, Mandarin, Min, Wu, Xiang

donations to English:
cumquat, dim sum, chop suey, typhoon, wok

identity. Not only is the Cantonese film industry thriving, but opera, theatre, literature and popular music continue to have great local and international success. The Cantonese language is now spoken by over 70 million people worldwide.

Today's language can trace its history back over 2000 years to the Qin Dynasty (221–206BC). Both Cantonese and Mandarin, its close relative, developed from the same tongue. Cantonese preserved certain intricate elements of Middle Chinese (581–907) which Mandarin has lost, such as a sophisticated tonal system and sharply clipped consonants at the end of words. Standard Cantonese is based on the language spoken in the city of Guangzhou (Canton), and it's colloquially known as gwáwng·dùng·wáa 廣東話 (Guangdong speech). Its more formal name is yue yu 粤语 (Yue language).

Written Cantonese is mostly ideographic – each symbol represents a concept or object instead of a sound or syllable. Because there aren't pronunciation rules like the ones we're used to in English, you need to memorise the pronunciation of each word when you learn its symbol. To help learners of Cantonese with this process, various 'romanisation' systems have been developed to show Cantonese sounds in Latin script. We've used a slightly simplified version of the widely accepted Yale system.

This book will help you buy tickets, get directions and assist you in your day-to-day communication. The translations we've provided will be understood both in Hong Kong and mainland China – where that isn't the case, a phrase has been marked HK for Hong Kong and China for the mainland. There's a world of Cantonese food, culture and people to discover, so don't just stand there, open the pages of this book and say something!

abbreviations used in this book

a	adjective	n	noun
China	used in Cantonese-speaking areas of China	pl	plural
		pol	polite
HK	used in Hong Kong	sg	singular
inf	informal	v	verb

Cantonese sounds aren't that different to English ones, although there are some unique vowel combinations. The biggest challenge for English speakers is the tonal system, but with a bit of practice you'll find Cantonese quite easy to pronounce.

The pronunciation of Cantonese words in mainland China and Hong Kong is essentially the same.

vowel sounds

Most Cantonese vowel sounds are similar to ones you use in English.

symbol	english equivalent		cantonese example
a	but	七	chàt
aa	father (long vowel sound)	單	dàan
aw	saw	歌	gàw
e	ten	蛇	sè
eu	fern	長	cheung
ew	blew (short with tightened lips)	書	sèw
i	deep	知	jì
o	foe	嘈	cho
u	put	富	fu

The next sounds are also vowels but they combine two sounds from the previous table.

symbol	english equivalent	cantonese example	
ai	**ai**sle (short sound)	雞	**gài**
aai	l**ie**	太	**taai**
au	**ou**t	走	**jáu**
aau	sc**ou**t (long sound)	交	**gàau**
ay	**pay**	飛	**fày**
eui	as in French *feuille* (eu sound with i)	去	**heui**
iu	**yu**letide	橋	**kiu**
oy	b**oy**	袋	**dóy**
ui	as in French *oui*	會	**wuí**

consonant sounds

There are only a few differences between consonant sounds in English and Cantonese. Firstly, the ng sound can appear at the start of the word. Practise by saying 'sing along' slowly and then do away with the 'si' at the beginning. After a few tries, it should come easily.

Note that words ending with the consonant sounds p, t, and k must be clipped in Cantonese. This happens in English as well – say 'pit' and 'tip' and listen to how much shorter the p sound is in 'tip'.

Many Cantonese speakers, particularly young people, re-place an n sound with an l if it begins the word – náy (you), is often heard as láy. This change has been made where appropriate throughout this book.

symbol	english example	cantonese example	
b	bill	北	bàk
ch	cheese	茶	chaa
d	dill	打	dàa
f	fan	肥	fày
g	ago	金	gàm
h	how	黑	hàak
j	catch	仔	jái
k	kick	橋	kiù
l	like	零	lìng
m	man	貓	màau
n	now (see note on page 12)	嬲	nàu
ng	sing	牛	ngàu
p	pat	皮	páy
s	sing	山	sàan
t	top	睇	tái
y	yes	人	yàn
w	wish	雲	wàn

tones

The use of tones in Cantonese can be quite tricky for an English speaker. 'Tone' is the pitch and melody of a syllable when you pronounce it. The same word, pronounced with different tones can have a very different meaning, eg gw<u>a</u>t 掘 means 'dig up' and gwàt 骨 means 'bones'.

Cantonese has between six and ten tones, depending on which definition you use. In our pronunciation guide they've been simplified to five tones: high, high rising, level, low falling, low rising and low. They can be divided into two groups: high and low pitch. High pitch tones involve tightening your

pronunciation

vocal muscles to get a higher sounding note, whereas lower pitch tones are made by relaxing the vocal chords to get a lower note. These tones are represented as accents and diacritics as shown in the table below.

symbol	description	cantonese example	
à	high	睇	tái
á	high rising	嬲	nàu
a	level	角	gawk
à	low falling	人	yàn
á	low rising	被	páy
a	low	問	man

Tones in Cantonese fall on vowels (a, e, i, o, u) and on 'n'. Use the chart below as a guide to help you pronounce the different tones.

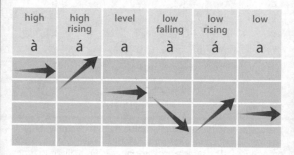

high	high rising	level	low falling	low rising	low
à	á	a	à	á	a

Bear in mind that tones are not absolute in pitch, but relative to your natural vocal range. Don't feel inhibited – just experiment with the contours of your natural voice. English speakers do this anyway to a small extent. When you pronounce 'What?' you're getting close to a Cantonese high rising tone, and when you say 'Damn!' you're approximating a high tone.

contents

The list below shows which grammatical structures you can use to say what you want. Look under each function – in alphabetical order – for information on how to build your own phrases. For example, to tell the taxi driver where your hotel is, look for **giving directions/orders** and you'll be directed to information on **imperatives** and **verbs**. A glossary of grammatical terms is included at the end of this chapter.

making a statement

naming things/people

negating

pointing things out

possessing

glossary

adjectives

describing things

Adjectives come directly before the noun in Cantonese. If the
adjective has two or more syllables, then add ge 嘅 between
the noun and the adjective.

| a big house | 大屋 | d<u>a</u>ai ng<u>ù</u>k
(lit: big house) |
| a clean house | 乾淨嘅屋 | g<u>à</u>wn·j<u>e</u>ng ge ng<u>ù</u>k
(lit: clean ge house) |

adverbs

doing things

Adverbs are formed by adding the suffix ·dì 啲 to the end of
an adjective.

slow	慢	m<u>aa</u>n
slowly	慢啲	m<u>aa</u>n·dì
quick	快	faai
quickly	快啲	faai·dì

Adverbs can also convey when an action takes place. These adverbs of time are important because tense is not indicated on
verbs in Cantonese (see **verbs**). Adverbs of time can indicate
whether an action has already taken place (past time adverb),
is taking place (present time adverb) or is about to take place
(future time adverb). Adverbs normally come directly after the
subject.

We will have lunch tomorrow.
我地听日食晏。   ng<u>á</u>w·day tìng·y<u>a</u>t s<u>i</u>k·ng<u>aa</u>n
(lit: we tomorrow eat-lunch)

adverbs of time			
past	before (like 'used to')	以前	yí·chìn
	yesterday	寢日	kàm·yat
present	now	宜家	yì·gàa
	for the time being/ temporarily	暫時	jaam·sì
future	in a moment	一陣 (間)	yàt·jan(·gàan)
	tomorrow	听日	tìng·yat

be

describing things • making a statement • negating

The Cantonese equivalent of 'be' is h<u>a</u>i 係.

This bag is mine.
呢個袋係我嘅。   l<u>à</u>y·gaw dóy h<u>a</u>i ng<u>á</u>w ge
                      (lit: this bag is mine)

This is my brother.
佢係我哥哥。   k<u>é</u>ui h<u>a</u>i ng<u>á</u>w g<u>à</u>w·g<u>à</u>w
                      (lit: he is my older-brother)

When you're describing something using an adjective, you can omit the verb h<u>a</u>i (be).

This bag is cheap.
呢個袋好平。   l<u>à</u>y·gaw dóy hó pèng
                      (lit: this bag very cheap)

I am cold.
我凍   ng<u>á</u>w dung
                      (lit: I cold)

If you want to negate a sentence, see **negation**.

classifiers

counting things • naming things

In Cantonese, when you talk about quantities of any noun, you'll need to use a classifier or 'measure word' after the number. English has words that are similar to classifiers, like 'head' in 'a head of cattle'. Classifiers indicate specific properties of a noun as shown in the next table.

packets or parcels	包	bàau
things bound together, eg books	本	bún
rooms & some buildings	間	gàan
a generic classifier, also used for people & small objects	個	gaw
rooms & some buildings	間	gàan
articles of clothing (worn on upper part of body)	件	gin
boxes or cases	盒	hap
animals & parts of the body	隻	jek
leaves or sheets of something, eg paper	張	jèung
long thin, flexible or winding objects, eg roads, snakes & clothing worn on the legs, like trousers or skirts	條	tiu

I would like three first-class tickets.

我想要三
張軟座飛。

ngáw séung yiu sàam
jèung yéwn·jaw·fày
(lit: I think want three
jèung soft-seat-ticket)

Classifiers are also used with demonstratives, like in 'these three books' and in that case go after the demonstrative in Cantonese (see **demonstratives**).

Classifiers are not used when you're talking about non-specific things:

People here are friendly.

呢度啲人幾友善。

lày·do dì yàn gáy yáu·sin
(lit: here people rather friendly)

demonstratives

indicating location • pointing things out

To point things out, you can use the demonstratives in the table below. The may be used on their own (as pronouns), as in '**that** is mine' or before a noun, as in '**this bag** is mine'.

demonstrative	cantonese	transliteration
this	呢個	lày·gaw
that	嗰個	gáw·gaw
these	呢啲	lày·dì
those	嗰啲	gáw·dì

I want to buy this.
我要買呢個。

ngáw yiu máai lày·gaw
(lit: I want buy this)

I want to buy this.
我要買嗰個。

ngáw yiu máai gáw·gaw
(lit: I want buy that)

That bag is mine.
嗰個袋係我嘅。

gáw·gaw dóy hai ngáw·ge
(lit: that bag is mine)

Note that gaw 個 and dì 啲 are actually classifiers (see **classifiers**) and would normally change according to the type of thing you're pointing to. In spoken Cantonese you'll still be understood if you use the forms from page 20 – just be sure you also point out the object in question to avoid confusion.

Also see **classifiers**.

imperatives

giving directions/orders

To make a command, simply leave out the subject in a regular sentence.

The particle làa 啦 is often added to make the command more polite.

You came here yesterday.
你寢日過嚟。

láy kàm·yat gaw·lày
(lit: you yesterday over-come)

Come here please!
過嚟（啦）！

gaw·lày(·làa)
(lit: over-come-làa)

negation

To negate a sentence add ǹg· 唔 (not) before the verb.

I'm a student.
我唔係學生。 ngáw hai hawk·sàng
(lit: I am student)

I'm not a student.
我唔係學生。 ngáw ǹg·hai hawk·sàng
(lit: I not-am student)

This prefix can also be added to adjectives.

I'm happy.
我唔開心。 ngáw hòy·sàm
(lit: I open-heart)

I'm not happy.
我唔開心。 ngáw ǹg·hòy·sàm
(lit: I not-open-heart)

nouns

Cantonese nouns are very simple – they have the same form for singular and plural. You can specify plurality by using a number, with a classifier (see **classifiers**), or you can use one of the 'approximate' numbers in the next table.

english	cantonese	transliteration
ten-and-a-few (13-19)	一十幾	sap·gáy
a-few-tens (30-90)	一幾十	gáy·sap
hundred-something (130-199)	一百幾	baak·gáy
thousand-odd (1300-1999)	一千零	chin·léng

There were a thousand odd people at the concert.

音樂會有千幾人。

yàm·ngawk·wuí yáu chìn gáy yan
(lit: concert has thousand
odd people)

Note that you should use a classifier if a noun is accompanied by a number or demonstrative. The classifier should go directly after the demonstrative or number, but even if you don't get this right, you'll still be understood. See **classifiers** and **demonstratives**.

compound nouns

In Cantonese, there are many nouns that are actually made up of two or more simpler nouns – the word 'refrigerator' is formed with two words in combination: 'snow' and 'cupboard'.

refrigerator	雪櫃 sewt·gw<u>a</u>i	snow + cupboard
rooster	雞公 gài·gùng	chicken + male
jasmine tea	香片 hèung·pín	fragrant + leaf

personal pronouns

naming things/people • making a statement

There is only one word for 'he', 'him', 'she', 'her' and 'it' in Cantonese. Plural pronouns are formed by adding d<u>a</u>y 地 after the singular pronouns.

He/She looks like dad.

佢似爸爸。

kéui chí b<u>aa</u>·bàa
(lit: he/she look-like dad)

pronoun	cantonese	transliteration
I/me	我	ngáw
you sg	你	láy
he/she/ him/her/it	佢	kéui
you pl	你地	láy·day
we/us	我地	ngáw·day
they/them	佢地	kéui·day

possessive pronouns

naming things/people · possessing

To form possessive pronouns such a 'my', 'your', 'her', 'his' etc, add ge 嘅 after the personal pronouns outlined in **personal pronouns**. These come directly before the object or thing that's owned.

My bags have been stolen.

我嘅個袋俾人
偷咗。

ngáw·ge gaw dóy báy yàn
tàu·jáw
(lit: my gaw bag by people stolen)

To say 'mine', 'yours', 'theirs' etc in Cantonese, simply omit the thing or object that is owned.

Those are my bags.

嗰啲係我嘅個袋。

gáw·dì hai ngáw·ge gaw dóy
(lit: those are my gaw bag)

Those are mine.

嗰啲係我嘅。

gáw·dì hai ngáw·ge
(lit: those are mine)

possessive pronoun	cantonese	transliteration
my/mine	我嘅	ngáw·ge
your/ yours sg	你嘅	láy·ge
his/her/ hers/its	佢嘅	kéui·ge
our/ours	我地嘅	ngáw·d̯ay·ge
your/ yours pl	你地嘅	láy·d̯ay·ge
their/ theirs	佢地嘅	kéui·d̯ay·ge

prepositions

indicating location • pointing things out

Prepositions in Cantonese function in much the same way as English prepositions. They come before the noun and they express notions of position and direction like 'to', 'at', 'in' etc.

My girlfriend is at the bar.
我女朋友宜家
喺酒吧。

ngáw léui·pàng·yáu yì·gàa
hái jáu·bàa
(lit: my female-friend now
at bar)

The only way Cantonese prepositions differ from English prepositions is that they can take the same endings as verbs (verb suffixes), like ·gán 緊 in the example below. These verb suffixes indicate 'aspect'. See **verbs** for more on aspect and verb endings.

I'm dining with my boyfriend.

我同緊
男朋友食晚飯。

ngáw tùng·gán
làam·pàng·yáu sik máan·faan
(lit: I with-gán boyfriend eat dinner)

preposition	cantonese	transliteration
at	喺	hái
in	喺……裡面	hái … léui·min
on	喺	hái
to/towards (away from the speaker)	去	heui
to/towards (closer to the speaker)	嚟	lày
with	同	tùng
without	之外	jì·ngoy

questions

A simple way to form yes/no questions is by doubling the verb and inserting ·ǹg· 唔 (not) between them in a regular sentence:

You are going to Hong Kong.
你去香港？
láy heui hèung·gáwng
(lit: you go Hong-Kong)

Are you going to Hong Kong?
你去唔去香港？
láy heui·ǹg·heui hèung·gáwng
(lit: you go-not-go Hong-Kong)

To sound more 'authentic', you can add aa 啊 at the end of your question.

Are you cold?
你係唔係凍(呀)？
láy hai·ǹg·hai dung (aa)
(lit: you be-not-be cold (aa))

To answer 'yes' to a question such as 'Are you cold?', simply repeat back the verb. To answer 'no' use the word for 'not' ǹg· 唔 followed by the verb:

Yes.	係。	hai
No.	唔係。	ǹg·hai

You can also form questions by using a question word – it's the same as forming a regular sentence except you replace the object, person or thing you are asking about with a question word.

You were speaking to my friend.
你同我朋友講嘢。
láy tung ngáw pàng·yáu gáwng yé
(lit: you to my friend speak something)

Who were you speaking to?
你同邊個講嘢？
láy tung bìn·gaw gáwng yé
(lit: you to who speak something)

question words		
who	邊個	bìn·gaw

Who's your favourite sportsperson?
你最鍾意嘅球星
係邊個？
láy jeui jùng·yi ge kàu·sìng hai bìn·gaw
(lit: you most love ge soccer-star is who)

what	乜嘢	màt·yé

What are you doing tonight?
你今晚做緊乜嘢？
láy gàm·máan jo·gán màt·yé
(lit: you tonight doing what)

where	邊度	bìn·do

Where shall we go?
我地應該去邊度？
ngáw·day yìng·gòy heui bìn·do
(lit: we should go where)

when*	幾時	gáy·sì

When's the next tour?
下個旅遊團係幾時？
haa·gaw léui·yàu·tèwn hai gáy·sì
(lit: next tour is when)

why *	點解	dím·gáai

Why do you use chopsticks?
你點解用筷子？
láy dím·gáai yung faai·jí
(lit: you why use chopsticks)

how *	點樣	dím·yéung

How do you eat with chopsticks?
你點樣用筷子食嘢？
láy dím·yéung yung faai·jí sik yé
(lit: you how use chopsticks eat something)

* These question words go after the subject of the sentence

requests

Making a request is very simple. Just state what you want and add ng·gòy 唔該, which roughly means 'please', before or after the sentence. See also **word order**.

I want a cup of coffee.
我要杯咖啡。

ngáw yiu buì gaa·fè
(lit: I want cup coffee)

May I have a cup of coffee?
唔該，我要杯咖啡。

ng·gòy ngáw yiu buì gaa·fè
(lit: please I want cup coffee)

May I have a cup of coffee?
我要杯咖啡，唔該。

ngáw yiu buì gaa·fè ng·gòy
(lit: I want cup coffee please)

verbs

Cantonese verbs don't change according to tense (eg 'walk' vs 'walked') or person (eg 'I walk' vs 'he walks'). Verbs can, however, have additional suffixes (an extra syllable or two at the end) to indicate, what is known as, aspect. Aspect can indicate whether an action has been completed or is still ongoing. Because verbs don't change for tense in the same way as English verb, adverbs can be used to indicate time. See also **adverbs**.

description	verb suffix	trans- literation	example
completed action	一咗	·jáw	開咗 hòy·jáw has (already) opened
unchanging state of things	一住	·jew	掛住 gwaa·jew miss (someone)
ongoing and habitual (done regularly but not continuously)	一開	·hòy	食開 sik·hòy eat (type of food)
happening now (like the -ing ending in English)	一緊	·gán	歎緊 taan·gán enjoying

word order

making a statement

The basic word order of Cantonese resembles English: subject followed by verb then object. Word order is the only thing in Cantonese that tells us which is the subject and which is the object.

I saw a panda.
我見到一隻熊貓。 ngáw gin·dó yàt jek hùng·màau
(lit: I saw one jek panda)

The panda saw me.
熊貓見到我。 hùng·màau gin·dó ngáw
(lit: panda saw I)

In sentences without an object, the subject can follow the verb:

I walked all day.

行咗我成日。 hàang·jáw ngáw sèng·yat
(lit: walked I whole-day)

With verbs such as 'give' and 'make' where the sentence has a direct object (the thing given or made) as well as an indirect object (the person that the thing was given to or made for), the indirect object always comes after the direct object in Cantonese.

I gave him five dollars.

我俾咗五蚊佢。 ngáw báy·jáw ńg màn kéui
(lit: I gave five dollars him)

The basic word order remains unchanged in questions and negative sentences (see **negation** and **questions**).

---

colour me happy

What's your power colour? If you're in a Cantonese-speaking region, your favourite colour may have a very different meaning from what you expect.

- Yellow (wàwng·sìk 黃色) is the symbol of royalty and the colour of the imperial dragon. It pays respect to the dead, promotes prosperity and luck, but oddly enough pornographic movies are 'yellow' (not 'blue' as in the West).
- Red (hung·sìk 紅色) is a highly auspicious colour which represents joy, warmth, happiness, fame and wealth. In Peking Opera, red represents loyalty and bravery.
- Blue (làam·sìk 藍色) is the colour of wealth and self-cultivation, and it also symbolises depth and cleanliness. It's the traditional colour for little girls.
- White (baak·sìk 白色) represents peace, purity and innocence – a key colour of funerals and mourning. In Peking Opera, it's a code for treachery.
- Black (hàak·sìk 黑色) is associated with evil, guilt and death. A little ominously, it's the clichéd colour for little boys.

glossary

adjective	a word that describes something – '**delicious** food'
adverb	a word that explains how an action was done – 'he ate **slowly**'
aspect	shows whether an action is completed or not
classifier	a counting word like a **pair** of pants
demonstrative	a word that means 'this' or 'that'
direct object	the thing or person in the sentence that has the action directed to it – 'I read the **menu**'
indirect object	the person in the sentence that benefits from an action – 'I gave **him** the specials'
imperative	a type of sentence or verb that tells someone to do something – 'give me the bill'
noun	a thing, person or idea – 'rice'
personal pronoun	a word that means 'I', 'you', etc
preposition	a word like 'for' or 'before' in English
possessive pronoun	a word that means 'mine', 'yours', etc
subject	the thing or person in the sentence that does the action – '**the chef** made his specialty'
suffix	extra syllable(s) added to the end of a word, eg -ly is added to 'slow' to make 'slowly'
tense	marking on the verb that tells you whether the action is in the present, past or future
transliteration	pronunciation guide for words and phrases
verb	the word that tells you what action happened – 'I **ate** the fried rice'

language difficulties

語言障礙

Do you speak (English)?
你識唔識講
(英文)啊？
láy sìk·ǹg·sìk gáwng
(yìng·mán) aa

Does anyone speak (English)?
邊個識講
(英文)啊？
bìn·gaw sìk gáwng
(yìng·mán) aa

Do you understand?
你明唔明啊？
láy mìng·ǹg·mìng aa

Yes, I do understand.
明白。
mìng·baak

No, I don't understand.
我唔明。
ngáw ǹg mìng

I speak (English).
我識講(英文)。
ngáw sìk gáwng (yìng·mán)

I don't speak Cantonese.
我唔識講
廣東話。
ngáw ǹg sìk gáwng
gwáwng·dùng wáa

I speak a little.
我識講一啲。
ngáw sìk gáwng yàt·dì

I (don't) understand.
我 (唔)明。 ngáw (ǹg) mìng

Could you write that in Pinyin for me?
唔該用拼音寫 ǹg·gòy yung ping·yàm sé
俾我。 báy ngáw

Could you write that in Chinese characters for me?
唔該幫我用 ǹg·gòy bàwng ngáw yung
中文寫落嚟。 jùng·màn sé lawk lài

What does 'hung·màau' mean?
"熊貓"係乜嘢意思？ hung·màau hai màt·yé yi·sì

How do you ...? 點樣……？ dím·yéung …
   pronounce this 讀呢個 duk lày gaw
   write 'hùng·màau' 寫"熊貓" sé hùng·màau

Could you please ...? 唔該你……？ ǹg·gòy láy …
   repeat that 再講一次 joy gáwng yàt chi
   speak more slowly 講慢啲 gáwng maan dì
   write it down 寫落嚟 sé lawk lài

---

mah jong

The game of *mah jong* mà jēuk 麻雀 (lit: sparrow) is popular within the Cantonese community, and it has spread to most Chinese and Japanese communities internationally. Typically, there are four mà jēuk gēuk 麻雀腳 (*mah jong* players) who each receive 13 páai 牌 (tiles). Each turn they pick up a new tile and surrender one, holding 13 throughout the game. The tiles are marked with symbols or drawings such as fà 花 (flowers), sei gwei 四季 (seasons), tùng 筒 (dots) and three kinds of dragons. The first person to use all their tiles, plus the new one, in a specified series wins the game. People play to kill time, for fun, as a social or business activity, or to gamble – in Hong Kong, some mà jēuk gwóon 麻雀館 (gambling dens) are even called ma jēuk hok haau 麻雀學校 (*mah jong* school).

cardinal numbers

基數

Counting in Cantonese is easy once you've mastered the numbers from 1 to 10. To form numbers between 11 and 19, add sap 十 (ten) before the single-digit number. To form multiples of ten, use sap· as a prefix before the number.

Note that you may also find English numerals used in Cantonese script but they're pronounced as Cantonese.

0	零	lìng
1	一	yàt
2	二	yi
3	三	sàam
4	四	say
5	五	ńg
6	六	luk
7	七	chàt
8	八	baat
9	九	gáu
10	十	sap
11	十一	sap·yàt
12	十二	sap·yi
13	十三	sap·sàam
14	十四	sap·say
15	十五	sap·ńg
16	十六	sap·luk
17	十七	sap·chàt
18	十八	sap·baat
19	十九	sap·gáu
20	二十	yi·sap

21	二十一	yi·sap·yàt
22	二十二	yi·sap·yi
30	三十	sàam·sap
40	四十	say·sap
50	五十	ńg·sap
60	六十	luk·sap
70	七十	chàt·sap
80	八十	baat·sap
90	九十	gáu·sap
100	一百	yàt·baak
200	兩百	léung·baak
1,000	一千	yàt·chìn
10,000	一萬	yàt·maan
1,000,000	一百萬	yàt·baak·maan

ordinal numbers

序數

1st	第一	dai·yàt
2nd	第二	dai·yi
3rd	第三	dai·sàam
4th	第四	dai·say
5th	第五	dai·ńg

fractions

百分比

a quarter	四分之一	say·fan·ji·yàt
a third	三分之一	sàam·fan·ji·yàt
a half	一半	yàt·bun
three-quarters	四分之三	say·fan·ji·sàam
all	所有	sáw·yáu
none	冇	mó

counters/classifiers

量詞

These are the most commonly used classifiers or 'counters' which are used when counting things. For an explanation of how they work see the **phrasebuilder**, page 19.

generic classifer (also used for people)
個   gaw

animals & body parts
隻   jek

rooms & buildings
間   gàan

packets & parcels
包   bàau

leaves or sheets (paper)
張   jèung

clothing (worn on the upper part of body)
件   gin

it sounds like it ...

In Cantonese, special attention is paid to the pronunciation of particular words. Certain numbers are seen as bringing good or bad luck, not because of any numerological reason but because they sound like words of good or bad fortune.

The number 4 (say 四) is considered bad luck because it sounds like sái 死 (death). The number 8 (baat 八) is associated with good luck because it rhymes with faat 發 (prosperous), while 28 (yi·sap·baat 二十八) is doubly lucky because 2 (yi 二) sounds just like yi 易 (easy).

useful amounts

How much?	幾多？	gáy·dàw
How many?	幾個？	gáy·gaw
Please give me ...	唔該俾……我。	ǹg·gòy báy... ngáw
(50) grams	(50)克	(ńg·sap) hàak
half a dozen	半打	bun dàa
half a kilo	半公斤	bun gùng·gàn
a kilo	1公斤	yàt gùng·gàn
a bottle	一樽	yàt jèun
a jar/tin	一罐	yàt gun
a packet	一盒	yàt hap
a slice	一塊	yàt faai
a few	一啲	yàt dì
less	少啲	siú dì
(just) a little	一啲啲	yàt dì dì
a lot	好多 好多	hó dàw hó dàw
many	好多	hó dàw
more	多啲	dàw dì
some	一啲	yàt dì

a catty of 16 taels

It can be a little tricky to work out 'how much' of something you have, as a few a different measuring systems are used. The Chinese system – with gàn 斤 (*catties*) and léung 兩 (*taels*) – is widely used, as are the bawng 鎊 (pound), ngòn·sí 安士 (ounce), gùng·gàn 公斤 (kilogram) and hàak 克 (gram).

1 *catty*	= 16 *taels*	
3 *catties*	= 4 pounds	= 1.82Kg
1 *tael*	= 1.34 oz	= 38.5g
1 lb	= 12 *taels*	
1 oz	= 28.4g	= 0.75 *tael*
1Kg	= 26 *taels*	
100g	= 4.8 *taels*	

telling the time

時間同日期

幾點鐘

Telling the time in Cantonese is quite straightforward once you get the hang of it. For 'o'clock' add ·dím·jùng 點鐘 to the end of the number. For one to ten minutes past the hour, add 點 ·dím to the number to show the hour then lìng 零 (zero), then the number of minutes to the number followed by fàn 分, as seen in 'five past ten' below.

For minutes past the hour that are multiples of five (5, 10, 15 etc), add ·dím 點 as described above then the number of minutes divided by 5. The example 'quarter past ten' below is sap·dím sàam 十點三 (literally: ten-o'clock three).

Instead of thirty minutes say bun 半 (half), as in 'half past ten' below.

What time is it?	而家幾點鐘？	yì·gàa gáy·dím·jùng
It's (ten) o'clock.	(十)點鐘。	(sap)·dím·jùng
Five past (ten).	(十)點零五分。	(sap)·dím lìng ńg fàn
Quarter past (ten).	(十)點三。	(sap)·dím sàam
Half past (ten).	(十)點半。	(sap)·dím bun
Quarter to (ten).	九點九。	gáu·dím gáu
Twenty to ten.	九點八。	gáu·dím baat
am	上晝	seung·jau
pm	下晝	haa·jau
At what time?	幾時開始？	gáy·sì hòy·chí
At ten.	十點鐘開始。	sap·dím·jùng hòy·chí
At (7.57pm).	夜晚 (7點 57分 開始)。	ye·máan (chàt dím ńg·sap·chàt fàn hòy·chí)

days

To say the days of the week, all you do is count the days and add sìng·kày 星期 (week) – Monday is sìng·kày·yàt 星期一 (lit: week one), Tuesday is sìng·kày·yi 星期二 (lit: week two), etc.

Monday	星期一	sìng·kày·yàt
Tuesday	星期二	sìng·kày·yi
Wednesday	星期三	sìng·kày·sàam
Thursday	星期四	sìng·kày·say
Friday	星期五	sìng·kày·ńg
Saturday	星期六	sìng·kày·luk
Sunday	星期日	sìng·kày·yat

months

For the months, use the numbers from one to twelve followed by yewt 月 (month).

January	一月	yàt·yewt
February	二月	yi·yewt
March	三月	sàam·yewt
April	四月	say·yewt
May	五月	ńg·yewt
June	六月	luk·yewt
July	七月	chàt·yewt
August	八月	baat·yewt
September	九月	gáu·yewt
October	十月	sap·yewt
November	十一月	sap·yàt·yewt
December	十二月	sap·yi·yewt

dates

What date is it today?
今日幾號？　　　　　　　　　gàm·yat gáy ho

It's (18 October).
（十月十八）號。　　　　　　(sap·yewt sap·baat) ho

seasons

spring	春天	chèun·tìn
summer	夏天	haa·tìn
autumn/fall	秋天	chàu·tìn
winter	冬天	dùng·tìn

present

現在時

now	而家	yì·gàa
today	今日	gàm·yat
tonight	今晚	gàm·máan
this year	今年	gàm·lín
this …	呢個……	làv·gaw …
morning	早晨	jó·sàn
afternoon	下晝	haa·jau
week	星期	sìng·kày
month	月	yewt

time will tell

When dynastic periods or important eras are talked about in Chinese culture, the Christian abbreviations BC and AD aren't used. Instead, you'll hear gùng·yèwn·chìn 公元前 (BCE – Before Common Era) and gùng·yèwn 公元 (CE – Common Era).

past

(three days) ago	(三日)前	(sàam yạt) chìn
day before yesterday	前日	chìn yạt
since (May)	從(五月)	chụng (ńg·yẹwt)
last ...		
night	寢晚	kàm·máan
week	上個星期	sẹung·gaw sìng·kày
month	上個月	sẹung·gaw yẹwt
year	舊年	gạu·lín
yesterday ...	寢日……	kàm·yạt …
morning	朝早	jiù·jó
afternoon	下畫	hạa·jau
evening	晚	máan

future

tomorrow morning	听朝	tìng·jiù
tomorrow afternoon	听日下畫	tìng·yạt hạa·jau
tomorrow evening	听晚	tìng·máan
next week	下個星期	hạa·gaw sìng·kày
next month	下個月	hạa·gaw yẹwt
next year	出年	chèut·lín
day after tomorrow	後日	hạu·yạt
until (June)	到(六月)	do (lụk·yẹwt)
in (six days)	(六日)後	lụk yạt hạu

TOOLS

42

When Hong Kong reunited with China In 1997 they kept the British public holidays and also introduced the Chinese ones, which means they get a double dose.

These are the public holidays recognised in the Hong Kong Special Administration Region:

New Year's Day	新年	sàn·lìn
Chinese New Year	農曆新年	lùng·lìk sàn·lìn
Clear and Bright Festival (Ching Ming Festival)	清明節	chìng·mìng·jit
Good Friday	耶穌	yè·sò
	受難日	sau·laan·yat
Day after Good Friday	耶穌	yè·sò
	受難日	sau·laan·yat
	第二日	dai·yì·yat
Easter Monday	復活節	fuk·wut·jit
International Labour Day	國際	gawk·jai
	勞動節	lò·dung·jit
Buddha's Birthday	浴佛節	yuk·fat·jit
Dragon Boat Festival	端午節	dèun·ńg·jit
Hong Kong Special Administrative Region Establishment Day	香港	hèung·gáwng
	特別	dak·bìt
	行政區	hang·jing·kèui
	成立	sìng·lap
	紀念日	gáy·lìm·yat
Mid-Autumn Festival	中秋節	jùng·chàu·jit
Chinese National Day	國慶節	gawk·hing·jit
Double Nine Festival (Chung Yeung Festival)	重陽節	chùng·yèung·jit
Christmas	聖誕節	sing·daan·jit
Boxing Day	節禮日	jit·lái·yat

during the day

afternoon	下晝	haa·jau
dawn	天光	tìn·gwàwng
day	日頭	yat·táu
evening	夜晚	ye·máan
midday	中午	jùng·ńg
midnight	深夜	sàm·ye
morning	朝早	jiù·jó
night	晚黑	máan·hàak
sunrise	日出	yat·chèut
sunset	日落	yat·lawk

rest days

Besides the general public holidays recognised in Hong Kong, there are also Chinese holidays when certain people get a whole or half day off.

International Women's Day
(women get a half day off)
   國際婦女節   gawk·jai fú·léui·jit
Youth Day
(people aged 14-20 get a half day off)
   青年節   chìng·lìn·jit
Children's Day
(children 13 years old and under get a full day off)
   兒童節   yì·tùng·jit
Army Day
(entitles all armed forces personnel time off)
   建軍節   gin·gwàn·jit

How much is it?
幾多錢？　　　　　　　　gáy·dàw chín

Can you write down the price?
唔該寫低個價錢。　　　　ng·gòy sé dài gaw gaa·chìn

Can I pay in (Hong Kong dollars)?
收唔收 (港紙) 啊？　　　　sàu·ng·sàu gáwng·jí aa

What's the ...?	…… 係幾多？	... hai gáy·dàw
exchange rate	兌換率	deui·wun·léut
charge for that	手續費	sáu·juk·fai

It's ...	係 ……	hai ...
free	免費嘅	mín·fai ge
(1200) RMB	(一千二百)	(yàt chìn yi baak)
	蚊人民幣	màn yàn·màn·bai
(1200) HK dollars	(一千二百)	(yàt chìn yi baak)
	港元	gáwng·yuàn

Do you accept ...?	你地收唔收 …… 呀？	láy·day sàu·ng·sàu ... aa
credit cards	信用卡	seun·yung·kàat
debit cards	提款卡	tài·fún·kàat
travellers cheques	旅行支票	léui·hàng jì·piu

I'd like ..., please.	我可唔可以 …… 呀？	ngáw háw·ng·háw·yí ... aa
a refund	退錢	teui·chín
my change	找錢	jáau·chín
to return this	退番呢個	teui·fàan láy·gáw

I'd like to ...	我要……	ngáw yiu ...
cash a cheque	兑現一	deui·yìn yàt
	張支票	jèung jì·piu
change a	換張	wun jèung
travellers cheque	旅行支票	léui·hàng jì·piu
change money	換錢	wun chín
get a cash advance	透支現金	tau·jì yìn·gàm
withdraw money	攞現金	láw yìn·gàm

Where's ...?	…… 喺邊度？	... hái bìn·do
an automatic teller machine	自動提款機	jì·dung tài·fún·gày
a place to change foreign money	換外幣 嘅地方	wun ngoy·bai ge day·fàwng

talking about money money

In Hong Kong (Special Administration Region), the unit of currency is the gáwng·yuàn 港元 (HK dollar), which is divided into 100 cents. In Macau, it's the pò·bai 葡幣 (*Pataca*). On the mainland it's the *Renminbi* (RMB), or 'People's Money'. The units of the RMB are shown below:

yuan (official term) – the basic unit of RMB
元   yuàn

man – colloquial term for a yuan
蚊   màn

jiao (official term) – 10 jiao make up one yuan
角   gawk

ho – colloquial term for a jiao
毫   hò

fen (official term) – 10 fen make up one jiao
分   fàn

getting around

點樣去

Is this the ... to (Guangzhou)?	呢班……係唔係去(廣州)喋？	lày bàan ... hai·ǹg·hai heui (gwáwng·jàu) gaa
Which ... goes to (Guangzhou)?	去(廣州)坐邊班……？	heui (gwáwng·jàu) cháw bìn·bàan ...
boat	船	sèwn
bus	巴士	bàa·sí
ferry	渡輪	do·lèun
minibus	小巴	siú·bàa
plane	飛機	fày·gày
shuttle bus	穿梭巴士	chèwn·sàw bàa·sí
train	火車	fáw·chè
tram	電車	din·chè
When's the ... (bus)?	……(巴士)幾點開？	... (bàa·sí) gáy dím hòy
first	頭班	tàu·bàan
last	尾班	máy·bàan
next	下一班	haa·yàt·bàan

What time does it leave?
幾點鐘出發？
gáy·dím jùng chèut·faa

What time does it get to (Shunde)?
幾點鐘到(順德)？
gáy·dím jùng do (seun·dàk)

How long will it be delayed?
推遲幾耐？
tèui·chì gáy·loy

Is this seat free?
呢個位有冇人喋？
lày·gaw wái yáu·mó yàn gaa

That's my seat.
呢個係我個位。
lày·gaw hai ngáw gaw wái

Please tell me when we get to (Guangzhou).
到 (廣州) 嘅時候，   do (gwáwng·jàu) ge sí·hau
唔該叫聲我。   ǹg·gòy giu sèng ngáw

Please stop here.
唔該落車。   ǹg·gòy lawk·chè

How long do we stop here?
喺度停幾耐？   hái·do tìng gáy·loy

tickets

買飛

Where do I buy a ticket?
去邊度買飛？   heui bìn·do máai fày

Where can I buy an Octopus card?
去邊度買   heui bìn·do máai
"八達通"？   baat·daat·tùng

I'd like an Octopus card.
我要張   ngáw yiu jèung
"八達通"。   baat·daat·tùng

Do I need to book?
駛唔駛定飛先呀？   sái·ǹg·sái deng·fày sìn a

A ... ticket to (Panyu).	一張去 (番禺) 嘅……飛。	yàt jèung heui (pùn·yèw) ge ... fày
1st-class	頭等	tàu·dáng
2nd-class	二等	yi·dáng
3rd-class	三等	sàam·dáng
child's	小童	siú·tùng
one-way	單程	dàan·chìng
return	雙程	sèung·chìng
student	學生	hawk·sàang

I'd like a/an ... seat.	有冇……位？	yáu·mó ... wái
aisle	路邊	lo·bìn
nonsmoking	不吸煙	bàt·kàp·yìn
smoking	吸煙	kàp·yìn
window	窗口	chèung·háu

I'd like a ... berth.	我想坐……	ngáw séung cháw ...
hard-seat	硬座	ngaan·jaw
hard-sleeper	硬臥	ngaan·ngaw
soft-seat	軟座	yéwn·jaw
soft-sleeper	軟臥	yéwn·ngaw

I'd like a/an ... berth.	我想瞓……	ngáw séung fan ...
upper	上鋪	seung·pò
middle	中鋪	jùng·pò
bottom	下鋪	haa·pò

I'd like to travel by ...	我想坐……	ngáw séung cháw ...
direct train	直快	jik·faai
express train	特快	dak·faai
fast train	快車	faai·chè
local train	本地車	bún·day·chè
slow train	慢車	maan·chè

listen for ...		
月台	yéwt·tòy	platform
押後	ngaat·hau	delayed
取消	chéui·sìu	cancelled
呢個	lày·gaw	this one
時間表	si·gaan·bíu	timetable
旅行社	léui·hàng·sé	travel agent
售票處	sau·piu·chew	ticket window
嗰個	gáw·gaw	that one
滿	mún	full
罷工	baa·gùng	strike n

Is there (a) …?	有冇……呀？	yáu·mó … aa
air conditioning	冷氣 HK	láang·hay
	空調 China	hùng·tìu
blanket	氈	jìn
sick bag	衛生袋	wai·sàng·dóy
toilet	廁所	chi·sáw

How much is it?
幾多錢？ gáy·dàw chín

How much is a (soft-seat) fare to …?
去……嘅(軟座飛) heui … ge (yéwn·jaw fày)
幾多錢？ gáy·dàw chín

---

when push comes to shove

Buying tickets in mainland China can be quite challenging for foreigners. You could try finding an English speaker to get you to the front of the queue, and maybe even translate your request to the ticket seller. Ask around:

Do you speak English?
你識唔識講 láy sìk·ǹg·sìk gáwng
英文啊？ yìng·mán aa

Does anyone speak English?
邊個識講 bìn·gaw sìk gáwng
英文啊？ yìng·mán aa

You could also ask your new translator to help you by writing out your request in Chinese characters.

Could you write down the ticket details in Cantonese characters?
唔該你用中文 ǹg·gòy láy yung jùng·mán
寫低我要買嘅飛。 sé·dài náw yiu máai ge fày

Could you write down (Kowloon) in Chinese characters?
唔該你用中文 ǹg·gòy láy yung jùng·mán
寫低(九龍)。 sé·dài (gáu·lùng)

Hand your piece of paper through the ticket window and you'll be able to get your ticket to ride.

How long does the trip take?
幾多個鐘頭到？   gáy·dàw qaw jùng·tàu do

Is it a direct route?
係唔係直達嘅？   hai·ǹg·hai jik·daat ge

Can I get a stand-by ticket?
可唔可以買張
後補飛呀？   háw·ǹg·háw·yí máai jèung
hau·bó fày aa

Can I get a platform ticket?
可唔可以買張
月台飛呀？   háw·ǹg·háw·yí máai jèung
yeut·tòy fày aa

What time should I check in?
幾點鐘入閘？   gáy·dím jùng yap·jaap

I'd like to … my ticket, please.	唔該，我想 ……飛。	ǹg·gòy ngáw séung … fày
cancel	退	teui
change	改	góy
confirm	確定張	kawk·dìng jèung

luggage

行李

Where can I find …?	……喺邊度？	… hái bìn·do
the baggage claim	行李 領取處	hàng·láy líng·chéui chew
the left-luggage office	行李 寄存處	hàng·láy gay·chèwn chew
a luggage locker	行李 locker	hàng·láy làwk·káa
a trolley	行李車	hàng·láy chè

My luggage has been …	我嘅 行李……	ngáw ge hàng·láy …
damaged	爛咗	laan·jáw
lost	唔見咗	ǹg·gin·jáw
stolen	俾人偷咗	báy·yàn tàu·jáw

That's (not) mine.
嗰個(唔)係我嘅。 gáw·gaw (ǹg) hai ngáw ge

Can I have some coins?
我想換啲硬幣飛。 ngáw séung wun dì ngaang·bai fày

Can I have some tokens?
我想換啲行李飛。 ngáw séung wun dì hàng·láy fày

listen for ...		
登機卡	dàng·gày·kàat	**boarding pass**
手提行李	sáu·tài hàng·láy	**carry-on baggage**
過重行李	gaw·chúng hàng·láy	**excess baggage**
護照	wu·jiu	**passport**
行李飛	hàng·láy fày	**token**
過境	gaw·gíng	**transit**
轉機	jewn·gày	**transfer**

plane

飛機

Where does flight (12) arrive/depart?
(十二)號飛機喺邊度 (sap·yi) ho fày·gày hái bìn·do
起飛／降落？ háy·fày/gawng·lawk

Where's ...?	…… 喺邊度 ?	... hái bìn·do
the airport	機場	gày·chèung
shuttle	巴士	bàa·sí
arrivals	入境口	yap·gíng·háu
departures	出境口	chèut·gíng·háu
duty-free	免稅店	mín·seui·dim
gate (8)	(八號)	(bàat ho)
	登機口	dàng·gày·háu

bus & coach

How often do buses come?
呢度嘅巴士幾耐一班？　　làay·d̯o ge bàa·sí gáy loy yàt bàan

Which number bus goes to …?
幾號巴士去……？　　gáy h̯o bàa·sí heui …

Which bus goes to (Mong Kok) subway station?
幾號巴士去
(旺角)地鐵站？　　gáy h̯o bàa·sí heui
(w̯awng·gawk) d̯ay·t̯it·jaam

Does it stop at (Mong Kok)?
會唔會喺
(旺角)停呀？　　wuí·ng·wuí hái
(w̯awng·gawk) t̯ìng aa

What's the next stop?
下個站叫乜名？　　h̯aa·gaw jaam giu màt méng

I'd like to get off at (Panyu).
我要喺(番禺)落車。　　ngáw yiu hái (pùn·y̯èw) l̯awk·chè

Please stop pushing!
唔好逼啦！　　ng·hó bìk làa

city a	市區	sí·kèui
inter-city	長途	chèung·t̯ò
local	本地	bún·d̯ay
airport bus	機場巴士	gày·chèung bàa·sí
bus	公共汽車 China	gùng·g̯ung hay·chè
	巴士 HK	bàa·sí
city bus	城巴	sìng·bàa
double-decker bus	雙層巴士	sèung·chàng bàa·sí
First Bus (company)	新巴	sàn·bàa
maxicab	小巴	siú·bàa
public light bus	公共小巴	gùng·g̯ung siú·bàa
shuttle bus	穿梭巴士	chèwn·sàw bàa·sí
sightseeing bus	旅遊巴士	léui·y̯àu bàa·sí
sleeper bus	長途巴士	chèung·t̯ò bàa·sí
trolley bus	無軌電車	mó·gwái d̯im·chè
tunnel bus	隧道巴士	s̯eui·d̯o bàa·sí

subway, train & tram

Which platform for train ...?
……火車喺邊個月台？ … fó·chè hái bìn·gaw yewt·tòy

What station is this?
呢個係乜野站？ lày·gaw hai màt·yé jaam

What's the next station?
下個係邊個站？ haa·gaw hai bìn·gaw jaam

How many stations to (Hong Kong Terminal)?
去(香港總站) heui (hèung·gáwng júng·jaam)
仲有幾多個站？ jung·yáu gáy·dàw gaw jaam

Does it stop at (New Territory)?
可唔可以喺 háw·ǹg·háw·yí hái
(新界)落車呀？ (sàn·gaai) lawk·chè aa

Do I need to change?
需唔需要轉車呀？ sèui·ǹg·sèui·yiu jewn·chè aa

At which station should I change?
喺邊個站轉車？ hái bìn·gaw jaam jewn·chè

Which carriage do I get on?
上幾號車廂？ séung gáy ho chè·sèung

Is it ...?	係唔係……車呀？	hai·ǹg·hai … chè aa
direct	直通	jik·tùng
express	特快	dak·faai
Which carriage is (for) ...?	……喺幾號車廂？	… hái gáy ho chè·sèung
Kowloon	去九龍	heui gáu·lùng
soft sleeper	軟臥	yéwn·ngaw
dining	餐卡	chàan·kàa

electrical train	電動火車	dim·dung fó·chè
funicular railway	纜車	laam·chè
KCR East Rail (Kowloon-Canton Railway)	九廣鐵路東線	gáu·gwáwng tlt·lo dùng·sin
LRT (Light Rail Transit)	輕鐵	hìng·tit
MTR (Mass Transit Railway)	地鐵	day·tit
Octopus card	八達卡	bàat·daat·kàat
subway station	地鐵站	day·tit·jaam
subway	地鐵	day·tit
tramway	電車	din·chè

boat

船

How long is the trip to …?
幾耐到⋯⋯？　　　　gáy·loy do …

Is there a fast boat?
有冇快艇？　　　　　yáu·mó faai·téng

How long will we stop here?
呢度停幾耐？　　　　làry·do tìng gáy·loy

What time should we be back on board?
幾點鐘再返上船？　　gáy dím·jùng joy fàan séung sèwn

What's the sea like today?
今日浪大唔大？　　　gàm·yat lawng daai·ǹg·daai

What island is this?
呢個係乜嘢？　　　　làry·gaw hai màt·yé dó

What beach is this?
呢個係乜嘢海灘？　　làry·gaw hai màt·yé hóy·tàan

I feel seasick.
我有啲暈船浪。　　　ngáw yáu dì wan·sèwn·lawng

Can I dine at the captain's table?
我想同船長
共進晚餐。　　　　　ngáw séung tùng sèwn·jéung gùng jeun máan·chàan

I'd like to do a sightseeing cruise.

我想參加
遊艇觀光團。

ngáw séung chàam·gàa
yàu·téng gùn·gwàwng tèwn

Is/Are there ... on the boat?	船上 有冇……呀？	sèwn seung yáu·mó ... aa
a toilet	廁所	chi·sáw
karaoke	卡拉OK	kàa·làa ò·kày
life jackets	救生衣	gau·sàng·yì

cabin	船艙	sèwn·chàwng
car deck	車艙	chè·chàwng
captain	船長	sèwn·jéung
China Ferry terminal	中國客運 碼頭	jùng·gawk haak·wan máa·tàu
deck	甲板	gaap·báan
ferry (across harbour)	渡海小輪	do·hóy siú·lèun
ferry (to China/Macau)	渡船	do·sèwn
hoverferry	氣墊船	hay·din·sèwn
hydrofoil	飛翔船	fày·chèung·sèwn
jetfoil	飛翼船	fày·yìk·sèwn
jolly roger	海盜船	hóy·do sèwn
junk	帆船	fàan·sèwn
local village ferry	街渡	gàai·dó
lifeboat	救生艇	gau·sàng·téng
life jacket	救生衣	gau·sàng·yì
Macau ferry	澳門渡船	ngo·mún do·sèwn
ocean terminal	海運碼頭	hóy·wan máa·tàu
speedboat	快艇	faai·téng
Star Ferry	天星小輪	tìn·sìng siú·lèun
yacht	游艇	yàu·téng

taxi

的士

I'd like a taxi …	我想坐的士……	ngáw séung cháw dìk·sí …
now	而家	yì·gàa
tomorrow	听日	tìng·yat

I'd like a taxi at (9am).
我想(9點鐘)
坐的士。
ngáw séung (gáu dím·jùng)
cháw dìk·sí

I'd like an English-speaking driver.
唔該, 我想要個
識講英文嘅司機。
ng·gòy ngáw séung yiu gaw
sìk gáwng yìng·mán ge sì·gày

Where's the taxi rank?
的士站喺邊度?
dìk·sí·jaam hái·bìn·do

Is this taxi free?
呢架的士有冇人㗎?
làoy gaa dìk·sí yáu·mó yàn gaa

Please put the meter on.
唔該打咪表。
ng·gòy dáa mài·biù

How much is it to …?
去……幾多錢?
heui … gáy·dàw chín

Please take me to (this address).
唔該帶我去
(呢個地址)。
ng·gòy daai ngáw heui
(làoy gaw day·jí)

How much is it?
幾多錢?
gáy·dàw chín

Can you write down the price?
唔該寫低個價錢。
ng·gòy sé dài gaw gaa·chìn

Keep the change.
唔駛找。
ng·sái jáau

Please …	唔該……	ng·gòy …
slow down	慢啲	maan dì
stop here	喺呢度停	hái làoy·do tìng
wait here	喺呢度等	hái làoy·do dáng

car & motorbike hire

I'd like to hire a/an ...	我想租架……	ngáw séung jò gaa ...
4WD	4WD (四輪傳動)	fàw·wiù·jàai·fù (say·lùn·chèwn·dung)
automatic	自動波	ji·dung·bàw
car	車	chè
manual	手動波	sáu·dung·bàw
motorbike	電單車	din·dàan·chè
with ...	有……	yáu ...
air conditioning	冷氣	láang·hay
a driver	司機	sì·gày
How much for ... hire?	租…… 幾多錢？	jò ... gáy·dàw chín
daily	一日	yàt yat
weekly	一個禮拜	yàt gaw lái·baai

road signs

Travellers to the Special Administration Region (SAR) – the former British colony which includes Hong Kong Island and Kowloon – will find that most street and road signs are in both English and Cantonese.

入口	yap·háu	Entrance
不可進入	bàt·háw jeun·yap	No Entry
收費	sàu·fai	Toll
停	tíng	Stop
高速公路	gò·chùk gùng·lo	Exit Freeway
出口	cheut·háu	
單程	dàan·ching	One-way
讓路	yeung·lo	Give Way

PRACTICAL

58

Does that include insurance/mileage?
包唔包保險／汽油？ bàau·ǹg·bàau bó·hím/hay·yàu

How much to hire a car with a driver to …?
請個司機租車 chéng gaw sì·gày jò chè
去……要幾多錢？ heui … yiu gáy·dàw chín

That's too expensive.
太貴啦。 tàai gwài laa

Is it air-conditioned?
有冇冷氣？ yáu·mó láang·hay

Is petrol included?
包唔包汽油？ bàau·ǹg·bàau hay·yàu

Are tolls included?
包唔包過路費？ bàau·ǹg·bàau gaw·lo·fai

Could I have a receipt for the toll?
唔該俾張過路費 ǹg·gòy báy jèung gaw·lo·fai
收據我。 sàu·geui ngáw

Do you have a guide to the road rules in English?
你有冇英文嘅 láy yáu·mó yìng·màn ge
駕駛規則呀？ gaa·sái kwài·jàk aa

Do you have a road map?
你有冇街道圖呀？ láy yáu·mó gàai·do·tò aa

on the road

What's the speed limit?
時速限制係幾多？ sì·chùk haan·jai hai gáy·dàw

Is this the road to (Mong Kok)?
呢條路係唔係去 lày tiu lo hai·ǹg·hai heui
(旺角)㗎？ (wàwng·gawk) gaa

Where's a petrol station?
油站喺邊度？ yàu·jaam hái·bìn·do

Please fill it up.
唔該入滿佢。 ǹg·gòy yap mún keui

I'd like … litres.
我要……公升。 ngáw yiu … gùng·sìng

diesel	柴油	chàai·yàu
leaded	含鉛汽油	hàm·yewn hay·yàu
LPG	石油氣	sek·yàu·hay
regular	標準汽油	biù·jéun hay·yàu
(premium)	(優質)	(yàu·jàt)
unleaded	不含鉛汽油	bàt·hàm·yewn hay·yàu

Can you check the …?
你可唔可以睇下啲……? láy háw·ǹg·háw·yí tái háa dì …

oil	油	yáu
tyre pressure	車胎氣壓	chè·tàai hay·ngaat
water	水	séui

---

listen for …

(國際) 車牌	(gawk·jai) chè·pàai	(international) drivers licence
公里	gùng·láy	kilometres
免費	mín·fai	free
停車咪錶	tìng·chè mài·biù	parking meter

Can I park here?
呢度泊唔泊得車㗎? là:y·do paak·ǹg·paak·dàk chè gaa

How long can I park here?
我喺呢度可以停 ngáw hái làiy·do háw·yí tìng
幾耐? gáy·loy

Do I have to pay?
我係唔係要 ngáw hai·ǹg·hai yiu
俾錢呀? báy·chín aa

problems

I need a mechanic.
我要個整車師傅。 ngáw yiu gaw jíng·chè sì·fú

I've had an accident.
我撞咗車。 ngáw jawng·jáw chè

The car has broken down at (Mong Kok).
架車係(旺角) gaa chè hái (wàwng·gawk)
壞咗。 wāai jáw

The motorbike has broken down at (Mong Kok).
架電單車係 gaa dìn·dàn·chè hái
(旺角)壞咗。 (wàwng·gawk) wāai jáw

The car won't start.
架車撻唔著。 gaa chè tàat·n̄g·jeuk

The motorbike won't start.
架電單車 gaa dìn·dàn·chè
撻唔著。 tàat·n̄g·jeuk

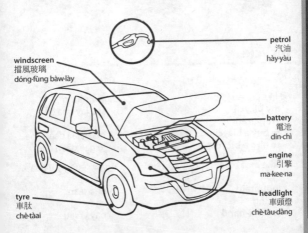

petrol
汽油
hày·yàu

windscreen
擋風玻璃
dóng·fūng bàw·làiy

battery
電池
dìn·chìh

engine
引擎
ma·kee·na

tyre
車肽
chè·tàai

headlight
車頭燈
chè·tàu·dàng

I have a flat tyre.
我爆咗肽。 — ngáw baau·jáw tàai

I've lost my car keys.
我唔見咗車匙。 — ngáw ǹg·gin·jáw chè·sì

I've locked the keys inside.
我鎖咗車匙喺
裡邊。 — ngáw sáw·jáw chè·sì hái léui·bin

I've run out of petrol.
我冇晒油。 — ngáw mó saai yáu

Can you fix it (today)?
你可唔可以
(今日)搞掂佢呀？ — láy háw·ǹg·háw·yí (gàam·yat) gáau·dim kéui aa

How long will it take?
要等幾耐？ — yiu dáng gáy·loy

When will it be ready?
幾時嚟攞？ — gáy·sì lày láw

bicycle

單車

I'd like ...	我想……	ngáw séung ...
my bicycle repaired	修呢架車	sàu lày gaa chè
to buy a bicycle	買架單車	máai gaa dàan·chè
to hire a bicycle	租架單車	jò gaa dàan·chè
I'd like a ... bike.	我想要架…… 單車。	ngáw séung yiu gaa ... dàan·chè
mountain	爬山	páa·sàan
racing	賽	choy
second-hand	比二手	báy·yi·sáu

How much is it per ...? 幾多錢⋯⋯? gáy·dàw chín ...

    day 一日 yàt yat

    hour 一個鐘 yàt gaw jùng

Do I need a helmet?
要唔要帶
安全帽呀?
yiu·ǹg·yiu daai
ngàwn·chewn·mó aa

Do I have to pay a deposit?
駛唔駛落訂先啊? sái·ǹg·sái lawk·deng sìn aa

How much is the deposit?
幾多錢押金? gáy·dàw chín ngaat·gàm

Could you pump up my tyres please?
可唔可以幫我
砵氣呀?
háw·ǹg·háw·yí bàwng
ngáw bàm·hay aa

I have a puncture.
穿咗窿。 chèwn·jáw lùng

How much to have this repaired?
修呢度幾多錢? sàu lày·dò gáy·dàw·chín

That's too expensive.
太貴啦。 tàai gwài laa

Where's the bicycle parking lot?
喺邊度停單車? háy·bìn·dò ting dàan·chè

My bicycle has been stolen.
我架單車俾人
偷咗。
ngáw gaa dàan·chè báy yàn
tàu·jáw

handlebars	把手	báa·sáu
helmet	頭盔	táu·kwài
pedal n	腳踏	geui·daap
spoke n	車輻	chè·fùk
tube (tyre)	內肽	loy·tàai

Are you waiting for more people?

仲要等人呀？　　　　　　　jung yiu dáng yàn aa

Can you take us around the city please?

唔該帶我入　　　　　　　　ǹg·gòy daai ngáw yap
城兜個圈。　　　　　　　　sèng dàu gaw hèwn

How many people can ride on this?

架車可以坐　　　　　　　　gaa chè háw·yí cháw
幾多人？　　　　　　　　　gáy·dàw yàn

| rickshaw | 人力車 | yàn·lìk·chè |
| pedicab | 三輪車 | sàam·lèun·chè |

---

one, two, buckle my shoe ...

If you're at a loss for what to say, try a few lines from this Cantonese nursery rhyme. It starts like this ...

落雨大，水浸街。
láwk·yéw dáai, séui jam gàai
The rain is heavy. The street is flooded.

阿哥擔柴上街賣，
a·gàw dàam chàai séung gàai maai
A lad carries fire woods to sell on the street.

阿嫂出街著花鞋。
a·só chèut gàai jeuk fàa hàai
A dame goes out wearing colourful shoes.

花鞋花襪花腰帶，
fàa hàai fàa mat fàa yiù·dáai
Wearing colourful shoes, socks, and waistband.

珍珠蝴蝶兩邊排。
làn·jèw wù·díp léung bìn paai
Pearls and butterflies are on two sides.

border crossing

過境

I'm ...	我係……	ngáw hai ...
in transit	過境	gaw·gíng
on business	出差嚟嘅	chèut·chàai lái ge
on holiday	嚟度假嘅	lái do·gaa ge
on a student visa	攞學生	láw hawk·sàang
	簽證嘅	chìm·jing ge

I'm here for ...	我要住……	ngáw yiu jew ...
one days	二天	yi yat
four weeks	四個星期	say gaw sìng·kày
three months	三個月	sàam gaw yewt

I'm going to (Shenzhen).
我要去(深圳)。 ngáw yiu heui (sàm·jan)

I'm staying at (China Hotel).
我住(中國大 ngáw jew (jùng·gawk daai
酒店)。 jáu·dim)

listen for ...		
簽證	chìm·jing	visa
團體	tewn·tái	group
護照	wu·jiu	passport
一家人	yàt gàa yàn	family
一個人	yàt gaw yàn	alone

The children are on this passport.
細佬仔喺呢個護照度。   sai·lo·jái hái lày·gaw wu·jiu do

My visa is in order.
我個簽證辦好啦。   ngáw gaw chìm·jing baan hó la

Do I have to pay extra for that?
要俾手續費呀？   yiu báy sáu·juk·fai aa

at customs

報關

I have nothing to declare.
我冇嘢報。   ngáw mó yé bo

I have something to declare.
我有嘢報。   ngáw yáu yé bo

Do I have to declare this?
呢樣嘢要報關呀？   lày·yeung yé yiu bo·gwàan à

That's (not) mine.
(唔)係我嘅。   (ǹg) hai ngáw ge

I didn't know I had to declare it.
我唔知道呢樣   ngáw ǹg·jì·do lày·yeung
嘢要報關。   yé yiu bo·gwàan

signs		
海關	hóy·gwàan	Customs
免稅	mín·seui	Duty-Free
入境	yap·gíng	Immigration
護照檢查	wu·jiu gím·chà	Passport Control
檢疫	gím·yik	Quarantine

Where's a/the ...? ……喺邊度？ ... hái·bìn·do
  bank 銀行 ngàn·hàwng
  tourist office 旅行社 léui·hàng·sé

How do I get there?
點樣去？ dím·yéung heui

How far is it?
有幾遠？ yáu gáy yéwn

Can you show me (on the map)?
你可唔可以（喺地圖度） láy háw·ǹg·háw·yí (hái day·to do)
指俾我睇我喺邊度？ jí báy ngáw tái ngáw hái bìn·do

It's ... 喺…… hái ...
  behind ... ……嘅後面 ... ge hau·mìn
  here 呢度 lày·do
  near ... ……附近 ... fu·gan
  nearby 離呢度有幾遠 lày lày·do mó gáy·yéwn
  next to ... ……旁邊 ... pàwng·bìn
  on the corner 十字路口 sap·ji·lo·háu
  opposite ... ……嘅對面 ... ge deui·mìn
  straight ahead 前面 chìn·mìn
  there 嗰度 gáw·do

Turn at ... 喺……轉彎 hái ... jewn·wàan
  the corner 十字路口 sap·ji·lo·háu
  the traffic lights 紅綠燈 hùng·luk·dàng

Turn ... 向……轉。 heung ... jewn
  left 左 jáw
  right 右 yau

listen for ...		
公里	gùng·láy	**kilometres**
公尺	gùng·chek	**metres**
分鐘	fàn·jùng	**minutes**

By ...	……去。	... heui
bus	坐車	cháw·chè
foot	行路	hàang·lo
train	坐地鐵	cháw dai·tit

What ... is this?	呢條……叫乜嘢？	lày tiù ... giu màt·yé
street	路	lo
village	村	chèun

north	北	bàk
south	南	làam
east	東	dùng
west	西	sài

typical addresses

What's the address?	地址係？	day·jí hai
alleyway	巷仔	háwng·jái
avenue	街	gàai
lane	巷	háwng
street	路	lo

traffic lights
紅綠燈
hùng·luk·dàng

intersection
十字路口
sap·ji·lo·háu

bus
巴士
bàa·sí

shop
鋪頭
po·táu

taxi
的士
dìk·sí

corner
路口
lo·háu

pedestrian overpass
行人天橋
hàng·yàn tìn·kìu

finding accommodation

撳地方住

Where's a ...?	邊度有……？	bìn·do yáu …
dormitory	宿舍	sùk·se
four-star hotel	四星級酒店	say·sìng·kàp jáu·dim
guesthouse	賓館	bàn·gún
hotel	酒店	jáu·dim
hostel	招待所	jiù·doy·sáw
inn	旅館	léui·gún
luxury hotel	豪華酒店	hò·wàa jáu·dim

Can you recommend somewhere ...?	你可唔可以推薦個……嘅地方住呀？	láy háw·ǹg·háw·yí tèui·jin gaw … ge day·fawng jew a
cheap	平	peng
clean	乾淨	gàwn·jeng
good	好	hó
luxurious	舒服	sèw·fuk
nearby	比較近	báy·gaau kán
romantic	有情調	yáu chìng·diù

What's the address?
地址係？   day·jí hai

Can you show me on the map where it is?
可唔可以幫我喺   háw·ǹg·háw·yí bàwng ngáw hái
地圖度撳下喺邊度？   day·to do wán háa hái bìn·do

For responses, see **directions**, page 67.

local talk		
dive n	爛屋	laan ngùk
rat-infested	老鼠竇	ló·séw·dau
top spot	好地方	hó day·fàwng

booking ahead & checking in

定房與登記

Can foreigners stay here?
外國人可唔可以
住呢度呀？
ngoy·gawk yàn háw·ǹg·háw·yí
jew lày·do gaa

I'd like to book a room, please.
我想定房。
ngáw séung deng fàwng

I have a reservation.
我預定咗。
ngáw yew·deng jáw

My name is …
我叫……
ngáw giu …

For (three) nights/weeks.
住（三）日／個星期。
jew (sàam) yat/gaw sìng·kày

From (July 2) to (July 6).
由（7月2號）到
（7月6號）。
yàu (chàt yewt yi ho) do
(chàt yewt luk ho)

Do you have a ... room?	有冇……房？	yáu·mó ... fáwng
double	雙人	sèung·yàn (to)
single	單人	dàan·yàn
twin	雙人	sèung·yàn

How much is it per ...?	一……幾多錢？	yàt ... gáy·dàw chín
night	晚	máan
person	個人	gaw yàn
week	個星期	gaw sìng·kày

PRACTICAL

That's too expensive.
太貴啦。 tàai gwai laa

Do you have a suite?
有冇套房呀？ yáu·mó to·fáwng aa

Do you have a room with a bathroom?
有冇有沖涼房 yáu·mó yáu chùng·lèung·fáwng
嘅房㗎？ ge fáwng gaa

Can I see it?
可唔可以睇下間 háw·ǹg·háw·yí tái háa gàan
房呀？ fáwng aa

I'll take it.
我要呢間。 ngáw yiu lày gàan

Do I need to pay upfront?
預先要俾幾多錢呀？ yew·sìn yiu báy gáy·dàw chín aa

Do you give student discounts?
有冇學生折扣？ yáu·mó hawk·sàang jit·kau

Can I pay by …?	可唔可以用	háw·ǹg·háw·yí yung
	……埋單呀？	… maai·dàan aa
credit card	信用卡	seun·yung·kàat
travellers cheque	旅行支票	léui·hàng jì·piu

For other methods of payment, see **shopping**, page 79.

listen for …		
幾多晚？	gáy·dàw máan	How many nights?
住滿	jew mún	full
鑰匙	sáw·sì	key
護照	wu·jiu	passport
接待處	jip·doy·chew	reception

accommodation

71

signs		
廁所	chi·sáw	Bathroom
出口	chèut·háu	Exit
入口	yap·háu	Entry
女	léui	Female
男	laam	Male
冇房	mó fáwng	No Vacancy
有房	yáu fáwng	Vacancy

requests & queries

請求與疑問

When is breakfast served?
幾點鐘有早餐？　　　gáy·dím jùng yáu jó·chàan

Where is breakfast served?
幾點邊度有早餐？　　gáy·dím bìn·do yáu jó·chàan

Please wake me at (seven).
唔該(朝早七點鐘)　　ng·gòy (jiù·jó chàt·dím jùng)
叫醒我。　　　　　　giu séng ngáw

Please fill up the flask with hot water.
唔該入滿個熱水樽。　ng·gòy yap mún gaw yit·séui jèun

Is there hot water all day?
全日有熱水呀？　　　chewn·yat yáu yit·séui aa

Is there heating?
有暖氣呀？　　　　　yáu léwn·hay aa

What times does the ... come on?	幾點鐘有……？	gáy·dím jùng yáu ...
heating	暖氣	léwn·hay
hot water	熱水	yit·séui

Can I use the ...?	可唔可以用下……呀？	háw·ng·háw·yí yung háa ... aa
kitchen	廚房	chew·fáwng
laundry	洗衣房	sái·yì·fáwng
telephone	電話	din·wáa

Do you have a/an ...?	有冇……？	yáu·mó ...
elevator	電梯	dīn·tāi
laundry service	洗衣服務	sái·yì fuk·mo
message board	通告欄	tùng·go·làan
safe	甲萬	gàap·maan
swimming pool	游泳池	yàu·wìng·chì

Do you ... here?	你地可唔可以……呀？	láy·day háw·n̄g·háw·yí ... aa
arrange tours	安排旅行團	ngàwn·pàai léui·hàng·tèwn
change money	換錢	wun chín

Could I have ..., please?	可唔可以俾……我？	háw·n̄g·háw·yí báy ... ngáw
an extra blanket	多張氈	dàw jèung jìn
a mosquito net	張蚊帳	jèung màn·jeung
a receipt	張發票	jèung faat·piu
a towel	條毛巾	tiù mo·gàn
my key	條門匙	tiù mùn sì
some soap	塊番鹼	faai fàan·gáan

Is there a message for me?
有冇人留言呀？　　　　yáu·mó yàn làu·yìn aa

Can I leave a message for someone?
我可唔可以留　　　　ngáw háw·n̄g·háw·yí làu
個字條呀？　　　　gaw ji·tiù aa

I'm locked out of my room.
我入唔到我　　　　ngáw yap n̄g dó ngáw
間房。　　　　gàan fáwng

a knock at the door ...		
Who is it?	邊個？	bìn·gaw
Just a moment.	等陣。	dáng·jan
Come in.	入嚟。	yap·lày
Come back later, please.	唔該等陣再嚟。	n̄g·gòy dáng·jan joy lày

complaints

The room is too ...	間房太……啦	gàan fáwng taai ... laa
bright	光	gwàwng
cold	凍	dung
dark	暗	ngam
dirty	污糟	wù·jò
expensive	貴	gwai
noisy	嘈	chò
small	細	sai

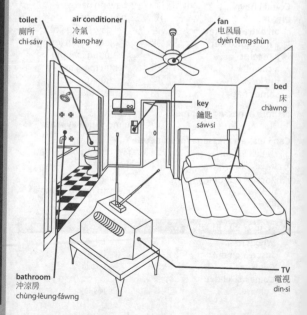

toilet
廁所
chi·sáw

air conditioner
冷氣
láang·hay

fan
电风扇
dyèn fērng·shùn

key
鑰匙
sáw·sì

bed
床
chàwng

bathroom
沖涼房
chùng·lèung·fáwng

TV
電視
din·si

The ... doesn't work.	……壞咗。	... waai·jáw
air conditioning	冷氣 **HK**	láang·hay
	空調 **China**	hùng·tìu
electrical outlet	插座	chaap·jaw
fan	風扇	fùng·sin
light	電燈	dìn·dàng
shower	花洒	fàa·sáa
tap (faucet)	水喉	séui·hàu
toilet	廁所	chi·sáw
window	窗	chèung

The ... is blocked.	……塞咗。	... sàk·jáw
bath	浴缸	yuk·gàwng
sink	洗碗盆	sái·wún·pùn
toilet	廁所	chi·sáw

I saw ... in my room.	我間房有……	ngáw gàan fáwng yáu ...
cockroaches	甲由	gaat·jáat
mice	老鼠	ló·séw
a big rat	隻大老鼠	jek daai ló·séw

Can I get an extra (blanket)?
我可唔可以攞
多張(氈)呀？
ngáw háw·ǹg·háw·yí láw
dàwe jèung (jìn) aa

This (pillow) isn't clean.
呢個(枕頭)唔乾淨。
lày gaw (jám·tàu) ǹg gàwn·jeng

checking out

退房

What time is checkout?
幾點鐘退房？
gáy dím·jùng teui·fáwng

Can I have a late checkout?
我可唔可以遲
啲退房啊？
ngáw háw·ǹg·háw·yí chì
dì teui·fáwng aa

Can you call a taxi for me (for 11 o'clock)?
唔該幫我叫
架的士
（朝早十一點嚟）。
ṅg·gòy bàwng ngáw giu
gaa dìk·sí
(jiù·jó sap·yàt dím lày)

Tomorrow is my last day here.
听日我就走啦。
tìng·yat ngáw jau jáu laa

I'm leaving now.
我而家走啦。
ngáw yì·gàa jáu laa

Can I leave my bags here?
可唔可以放低啲
行李喺度啊？
háw·ṅg·háw·yí fawng dài dì
hàng·láy hái·do aa

I had a great stay, thank you!
我喺呢度住得好
開心，多謝！
ngáw hái lày·do jew dàk hó
hòy·sàm dàw·je

I'll recommend it to my friends.
我會推薦呢度俾
朋友。
ngáw wuí tèui·jin lày·do báy
pàng·yáu

There's a mistake in the bill.
帳單錯咗。
jeung·dàan chaw jáw

What's that ... for?
呢筆……
係做乜嘅？
lày bàt ...
hai jo màt ge

amount	數	so
charge	收費	sàu·fai
deposit	存款	chèwn·fún

**Could I have my ...,
please?**
唔該，我嚟
攞……
ṅg·gòy ngáw lày
láw ...

deposit	押金	ngaat·gàm
passport	護照	wu·jiu
valuables	貴重物品	gwai·jung mat·bán

I'll be back ...
我……會再嚟
ngáw ... wuí joy lày

in (three) days	（三）日後	(sàam) yat hau
on (Tuesday)	下個
（星期二）	haa gaw
(sìng·kày·yi)
next year	出年	chèut·lín

camping

露營

Where can we camp?
喺邊度紮營好啊？
hái bìn·do zàat-yìng hó aa

Can we camp here?
喺呢度可唔可以
露營啊？
hái làly·do háw·ǹg·háw·yí
lo·yìng aa

Can we light a fire here?
喺呢度可唔可以
燒嘢㗎？
hái làly·do háw·ǹg·háw·yí
siù·yé gaa

Is it safe to sleep in this place?
喺呢度
安唔安全㗎？
hái làly·do
ngàwn·ǹg·ngàwn·chewn gaa

renting

租房

I'm here about the ... for rent.	我係嚟租……嘅。	ngáw hai làly jò ... ge
Do you have a/an ... for rent?	有冇……出租呀？	yáu mó ... chèut·jò aa
apartment	單位	dàan·wái
house	屋	ngùk
room	房	fáwng
serviced apartment	包服務嘅單位	bàau fuk·mo ge dàan·wái
villa	別墅	bit·séui
furnished	包傢俬嘅	bàau gàa·sì ge
partly furnished	有啲傢俬嘅	yáu dì gàa·sì ge
unfurnished	冇傢俬嘅	mó gàa·sì ge

staying with locals

Can I stay at your place?
我可唔可以喺
你屋企住啊？
ngáw háw·ṅg·háw·yí hái
láy ngùk·káy jew aa

Is there anything I can do to help?
有乜嘢可以幫
你㗎？
yáu màt·yé háw·yí bàwng
láy gaa

I have my own ... 我帶咗自己 ngáw daai·jáw ji·gáy
嘅…… ge ...

mattress 床褥 chàwng·yúk
sleeping bag 睡袋 seui·dóy

Can I ...? 駛唔駛我 sái·ṅg·sái ngáw
……啊？ ... aa

bring anything 買啲嘢加餸 máai dì yé
for the meal gàa·sung
clear the table 執好張檯 jàp·hó jèung tóy
do the dishes 幫你洗碗 bàwng láy sái·wún
set the table 擺好張檯 báai·hó jèung tóy
take out the 擺走啲 láw·jáu dì
rubbish 垃圾 laap·saap

Thanks for your hospitality.
多謝你嘅款待。
dàw·je láy ge fún·doy

The food was delicious.
啲嘢好好食。
dì yé hó·hó sik

For more dining-related expressions, see **food**, page 161.

looking for ...

摱地方

Where's a/the ...?	⋯⋯喺邊度？	... hái·bìn·dọ
department store	百貨公司	baak·faw gùng·sí
market	街市	gàai·sí
shopping centre	商場	sèung·chèung
supermarket	超級市場	chiù·kàp sí·chèung

Where can I buy (a padlock)?
邊度可以買倒(鎖)？　　　bìn·dọ háw·yí máai dó (sáw)

For phrases on directions, see **directions**, page 67.

making a purchase

買嘢

I'm just looking.
睇下。　　　　　　　　　tái hạa

I'd like to buy (an adaptor plug).
我想買(一個　　　　　　ngáw séung máai (yàt gaw
轉換插頭)。　　　　　　jéwn·wụn chaap·tàu)

How much is it?
幾多錢？　　　　　　　　gáy·dàw chín

Can you write down the price?
唔該寫低個价錢。　　　　ǹg·gòy sé dài gaw gaa·chìn

Do you have any others?
仲有冇其他嘅？　　　　　jụng yáu·mó kày·tàa ge

Can I look at it?
我可唔可以睇下？　　　　ngáw háw·ǹg·háw·yí tái hạa

Do you accept …?	你地收唔收 ……呀？	láy·day sàu·ǹg·sàu … aa
credit cards	信用卡	seun·yung·kàat
debit cards	提款卡	tài·fún·kàat
travellers cheques	旅行支票	léui·hàng jì·piu

Could I have a …, please?	唔該俾 ……我。	ǹg·gòy báy … ngáw
bag	個袋	gaw dóy
receipt	張單	jèung dàan

Could I have it wrapped?
可唔可以包一下啊？   háw·ǹg·háw·yí bàau yàt·háa aa

Does it have a guarantee?
有冇保養啊？   yáu mó bó·yéung aa

Can I have it sent abroad?
可唔可以寄出
國外啊？   háw·ǹg·háw·yí gay chèut
gawk·ngoy aa

Can I take this out of the country?
我可唔可以帶
出境啊？   ngáw háw·ǹg·háw·yí daai
chèut·gíng aa

Can you order one for me?
可唔可以幫我
定一個呀？   háw·ǹg·háw·yí bàwng ngáw
deng yàt gaw aa

Can I pick it up later?
我等一陣嚟攞，
得唔得？   ngáw dáng yàt·jan làuy láw
dàk·ǹg·dàk

It's faulty.
壞咗。   waai·jáw

This item is fake.
假嘢嚟嘅。   gáa·yé làuy ge

I'd like … please.	唔該，我要……	ǹg·gòy ngáw yiu …
my change	找錢	jáau·chín
a refund	退錢	teui·chín
to return this	退番呢個	teui·fàan làuy gaw

PRACTICAL

local talk		
bargain n	講價	gáwng·gaa
rip-off	搵笨	wún ban
sale	大減價	daai gáam·gaa
specials	特價	dak·gaa

bargaining

講價

That's too expensive!
太貴啦！　　　　　　　taai gwai laa

You're kidding!
講笑！　　　　　　　　gáwng·siú

Can you lower the price?
可唔可以平啲呀？　　　háw·ng·háw·yí pèng dì aa

Do you have something cheaper?
有冇平啲㗎？　　　　　yáu·mó pèng dì gaa

I'll give you (five RMB).
俾(五百蚊　　　　　　　báy (ńg baak màn
人民幣)你。　　　　　　yàn·màn·bai) láy

That's my final offer.
一口价。　　　　　　　yàt háu gaa

books & reading

書與讀

Do you have a/an ...?	有冇……？	yáu mó ...
book by (Lu Xun)	(魯迅)嘅書	(ló·seun) ge sèw
entertainment guide	娛樂指南	yew·lawk jí·laam

Is there an English-language ...?	附近有冇 英文……呀？	fu·gan yáu·mó yìng·man ... aa
bookshop	書店	sèw·dim
section	書架	sèw·gáa

I'd like (a/an) …	我想買本……	ngáw séung máai …
dictionary	本字典	bún ji·dín
newspaper (in English)	份（英文）報紙	fan (yìng·màn) bo·jí
notepad	本筆記簿	bún bàt·gay·bó

Can you recommend a book for me?
你可唔可以推薦
本好書俾我呀？
láy háw·ǹg·háw·yí tèui·jin
bún hó sèw báy ngáw aa

Do you have Lonely Planet guidebooks?
有冇 Lonely Planet 嘅
旅行指南？
yáu mó lùng·lì pèng·lɐt ge
léui·yàu jí·làam

clothes

衫

My size is …	我著……號。	ngáw jeuk … ho
40	40	say·sap
small	細	sai
medium	中	jùng
large	大	daai
extra-large	加大	gàa daai

Can I try it on?
可唔可以試下？
háw·ǹg·háw·yí si háa

Is there a mirror?
有冇鏡呀？
yáu·mó gèng aa

It doesn't fit.
唔啱身。
ǹg ngàam·sàn

Where can I find a tailor?
邊度可以搵個
裁縫？
bìn·do háw·yí wún gaw
choy·fúng

For clothing items, see the **dictionary**.

electronic goods

電子器材

Will this work on any DVD player?
係唔係乜嘢DVD
機都放得㗎？
hai·ǹg·hai màt·yé dì·wì·dì
gày dò fawng dàk gaa

Is this a (PAL/NTSC) system?
係唔係(PAL／NTSC)？
hai·ǹg·hai (pàau/èn·tì·è·si·tì)

Is this the latest model?
係唔係最新款嘅？
hai·ǹg·hai jeui sàn·fún ge

Is this (240) volts?
係唔係(240)
伏嘅？
hai·ǹg·hai (yi·baak sai·sap)
fuk ge

Where can I buy duty-free electronic goods?
喺邊度可以買倒
免稅嘅電子器材？
hái bìn·do háw·yí máai·dó
mín·seui ge din·jí hay·chòy

hairdressing

飛髮

I'd like (a) ...	我想……	ngáw séung ...
blow wave	電髮	din·faat
colour	染髮	yím·faat
haircut	剪髮	jín·faat
my beard trimmed	修鬚	sàu·sò
shave	剃鬚	tai·sò
trim	剪短啲	jín déwn dì

Don't cut it too short.
唔好剪得太短。
ǹg·hó jín dàk taai déwn

Please use a new blade.
唔該用塊新刀片。
ǹg·gòy yung faai sàn dò·pín

Shave it all off!
剃光晒佢！
tai gwàwng saai kéui

shopping

83

music

I'd like a ...	我想買……	ngáw séung máai ...
blank tape	餅空嘅	béng hùng ge
	錄音帶	luk·yàm·dáai
CD	張 CD	jèung sì·dì
DVD	張 DVD	jèung dì·wì·dì

I'm looking for something by (Dāng Lāi·gùn).
我要搵 (鄧麗君)　　ngáw yiu wán (dang lai·gùn)
嘅歌。　　　　　　ge gàw

What's their best recording?
佢地最好嘅CD係　　kéui·day jeui·hó ge sì·dì hai
邊張？　　　　　　bìn jèung

Can I listen to this?
我可唔可以試聽呀？　ngáw háw·ǹg·háw·yí si·tèng aa

photography

I need ... film for this camera.	我想買呢架相機嘅……菲林。	ngáw séung máai lày gaa séung·gày ge ... fày·lám
APS	APS	ày·pì·è·si
B&W	黑白	hàak·baak
colour	彩色	chóy·sìk
slide	幻燈	waan·dàng
... speed	……感光度	... gám·gwàwng·do
Do you have ... for this camera?	你有冇啱呢部相機嘅……？	láy yáu·mó ngàam làybo séung·gày ge ...
batteries	電池	din·chi
memory cards	儲存卡	chéw·chèwn·kàat

我有乜嘢可以幫倒你？ ngáw yáu màt·yé háw·yí bàwng dó láy	**Can I help you?**
仲要啲乜嘢呀？ jung·yiu dì màt·yé a	**Anything else?**
冇晒啦。 mó saai laa	**No, we don't have any.**

Can you ...?	可唔可以……呀？	háw·ng·háw·yí ... aa
develop	沖晒呢	chùng·saai lày
this film	筒菲林	tung fày·lám
develop digital photos	晒數碼相	saai so·máa séung
load my film	裝呢筒菲林	jàwng lày tung fày·lám
recharge the battery for my digital camera	幫我架數碼相機電池沖電	bàwng ngáw gaa so·máa séung·gày dìn·chì chùng·dìn
transfer photos from my camera to CD	幫我將相機啲相轉落CD	bàwng ngáw jèung séung·gày dì séung jewn làwk sì·dì

When will it be ready?

幾時嚟攞？　　　　　　　gáy·sí lày láw

How much is it?

幾多錢？　　　　　　　　gáy·dàw chín

I need a cable to connect my camera to a computer.

我要條線將部　　　　　　ngáw yiu tiù sin jèung bo
相機駁落部電腦度。　　　séung·gày bawk làwk bo dìn·ló do

I need a cable to recharge this battery.

我要條線沖電。　　　　　ngáw yiu tiù sin chùng·dìn

I need a video cassette for this camera.

我要呢架相機　　　　　　ngáw yiu lày gaa séung·gày
嘅錄影帶。　　　　　　　ge luk·yíng·dáai

I need a passport photo taken.
我要影張護照相。　　　ngáw yiu yíng jèung wu·jiu·séung

I'm not happy with these photos.
啲相晒得好差。　　　　dì séung saai dàk hó chàa

I don't want to pay the full price.
唔該俾個折扣。　　　　ǹg·gòy báy gaw jit·kau

repairs

修理

Can I have my ...	你可唔可以修好	láy háw·ǹg·háw·yí sàu·hó
repaired here?	我個……呀？	ngáw gaw ... aa
When will my ...	我嘅……幾時	ngáw ge ... gáy·si
be ready?	有得攞？	yáu dàk láw
backpack	背囊	beui·làwng
camera	相機	séung·gày
(sun)glasses	(黑)眼鏡	(hàak) ngáan·géng
shoes	鞋	haai

souvenirs		
calligraphy	書法	sèw·faat
carpets	地氈	day·jìn
chinaware	瓷器	chì·hày
curios	古玩	gú·wún
embroidery	刺繡	chi·sau
jade	玉器	yuk·hày
lacquerware	漆器	chàt·hày
painting	畫	wáa
paper cut outs	剪紙	jín·jí
personal seal	圖章	to·jèung
porcelain	瓷器	chì·hày
pottery	陶器	tò·hày
scroll (calligraphy)	國書	gawk·wáa
silk	絲綢	sì·chàu

the internet

上網

Where's the local Internet café?
附近有冇網吧？　　　fu·gan yáu·mó máwng·bàa

I'd like to ...	我想……	ngáw séung ...
check my email	睇下我嘅電子信箱	tái háa ngáw ge dìn·jí yàu·sèung
get Internet access	上網	séung·máwng
use a printer	打印	dáa·yan
use a scanner	掃描	so·miù

Do you have ...?	有冇……呀？	yáu·mó ... aa
PCs	個人電腦	gaw·yàn dìn·ló
Macs	蘋果電腦	ping·gwáw dìn·ló
a Zip drive	ZIP盤	sìp pún

How much per ...?	每……幾多錢？	muí ... gáy·dàw chín
hour	個鐘	gaw jùng
(five) minutes	（五）分鐘	(ńg) fàn·jùng
page	頁	yip

CD	CD	sì·dì
email n	電子郵件	dìn·jí yàu·gín
Internet	互聯網	wu·lèwn·máwng
keyboard	鍵盤	gin·pún
printer	打印機	dáa·yan·gày

Is it possible to get an account with a local Internet provider?
我可唔可以開個　　ngáw háw·ǹg·háw·yí hòy gaw
本地IP賬戶呀？　　bún·day àai·pì jeung·wu aa

How do I log on?
我點樣上網？　　ngáw dím·yéung séung·máwng

Please change it to the English-language setting.
唔該幫我換成　　ǹg·gòy bàwng ngáw wun·sìng
英文格式。　　yìng·màn gaak·sìk

This connection is really slow.
網速太慢啦。　　máwng·chùk taai maan laa

It's crashed.
死咗機。　　sáy·jáw gày

I've finished.
上完啦。　　séung yèwn laa

mobile/cell phone

手機

I'd like a ...	我想買個……	ngáw séung máai gaw ...
charger for my phone	手機 充電器	sáu·gày chùng·dìn·hay
mobile/cell phone for hire	出租手機	chèut·jò sáu·gày
prepaid mobile/ cell phone	預付手機	yew·fu sáu·gày
SIM card for your network	你地網絡 用嘅SIM卡	láy·day máwng·làwk yung ge sím·kàat

What are the rates?
電話費點計？ dìn·wáa·fai dím gai

(30 jiao) per (30) seconds.
每(三十)秒鐘 muí (sàam·sap) fàn·jùng
(三十毫子)。 (sàam·sap ho·jí)

phone

打電話

What's your phone number?
你嘅電話號碼 láy ge dìn·wáa ho·máa
係幾多號？ hai gáy·dàw ho

Where's the nearest public phone?
呢度附近有冇 làay·do fu·gan yáu·mó
公眾電話呀？ gùng·jung dìn·wáa aa

Can I look at a phone book?
有冇電話簿呀？ yáu·mó dìn·wáa·bó aa

Can you help me find the number for ...?
唔該幫我揾 ǹg·gòy bàwng ngáw wán
下……嘅號碼。 háa ... ge ho·máa

communications

89

I want to ...	我想……	ngáw séung ...
buy a	買張	máai jèung
phonecard	電話卡	dịn·wáa·kàat
call (Singapore)	打電話去	dáa dịn·wáa heui
	(新加坡)	(sàn·gaa·bàw)
make a	打(市區)	dáa (sí·kèui)
(local) call	電話	dịn·wáa
reverse the	打對方付款	dáa deui·fàwng
charges	嘅電話	fụ·fún ge dịn·wáa
speak for (three)	講(三)	gáwng (sàam)
minutes	分鐘	fàn·jùng

How much does ... cost?	……幾多錢？	... gáy·dàw chín
a (three)-	講(三)	gáwng (sàam)
minute call	分鐘	fàn·jùng
each extra	每多一	méui dàw yàt
minute	分鐘	fàn·jùng

The number is ...
號碼係……   họ·máa hại ...

What's the country code for (New Zealand)?
(新西蘭)嘅區號   (sàn·sài·làan) ge kèui·họ
係幾多號？   hại gáy·dàw họ

It's engaged.
佔咗綫。   jim·jáw sin

I've been cut off.
斷咗綫。   téwn·jáw sin

The connection's bad.
電話綫接得唔好。   dịn·wáa·sin jip·dàk ǹg·hó

Hello.
喂。   wáy

Can I speak to ...?
我搵……   ngáw wán ...

It's ...
我係……   ngáw hại ...

Is … there?
……喺唔喺度？　　　　　… hái·ṇg·hái do

Please tell him/her I called.
唔該話俾佢聽我　　　　　ṇg·gòy waa báy kéui tèng ngáw
打過電話俾佢。　　　　　dáa gaw dịn·wáa báy kéui

Can I leave a message?
我可唔可以留言呀？　　　ngáw háw·ṇg·háw·yí làu·yịn aa

My number is …
我嘅號碼係……　　　　　ngáw ge họ·máa hại …

I don't have a contact number.
我冇聯絡電話。　　　　　ngáw mó lẹwn·lawk dịn·wáa

I'll call back later.
我遲啲再打過嚟。　　　　ngáw chì·dì joy dáa gaw lày

listen for …		
打錯咗。	dáa chaw·jáw	**Wrong number.**
你係邊個？	láy hại bìn·gaw	**Who's calling?**
你搵邊個？	láy wán bìn·gaw	**Who do you want to speak to?**
等陣。	dáng·jạn	**One moment.**
佢唔喺度。	kéui ṇg·hái·do	**He/She is not here.**

post office

郵局

I want to send a …	我想……	ngáw séung …
fax	發傳真	faat chèwn·jàn
letter	寄信	gay seun
parcel	寄包裹	gay bàau·gwáw
postcard	寄明信片	gay mịng·seun·pín

I want to buy a/an ...	我想買……	ngáw séung máai ...
aerogram	個航空郵束	gaw hàwng·hùng yàu·gáan
envelope	個信封	gaw seun·fùng
stamp	張郵票	jèung yàu·piu
customs declaration	海關報稅	hóy·gwàan bo·seui
domestic	國內	gawk·loy
fragile	易碎	yi·seui
international	國際	gawk·jai
mail n	信件	seun·gín
mailbox	信箱	seun·sèung
postcode	郵政編碼	yàu·jing pìn·máa

Please send it by airmail to (Australia).
唔該寄航空
去(澳大利亞)。
ǹg·gòy gay hàwng·hùng heui (ngo·daai·lay·a)

Please send it by surface mail to (Australia).
唔該寄平郵去
(澳大利亞)。
ǹg·gòy gay pìng·yàu heui (ngo·daai·lay·a)

It contains (souvenirs).
裡面有(紀念品)。
léui·min yáu (gáy·lim·bán)

Where's the poste restante section?
領取指示寫喺邊度？
léng·chéui jí·si sé hái bìn·do

Is there any mail for me?
有冇我嘅信？
yáu·mó ngáw ge seun

snail mail		
air	航空	hàwng·hùng
express	速遞	chùk·dai
registered	掛號	gwaa·ho
sea/surface	平郵	pìng·yàu

In Hong Kong, all bank staff speak English. However, you'll find the following phrases useful for the rest of Southeast China.

What time does the bank open?
銀行幾時開門？   ngàn·hàwng gáy·sì hòy·mùn

Where can I ...?	我喺邊度 可以⋯⋯？	ngáw hái bìn·do háw·yí ...
I'd like to ...	我要⋯⋯	ngáw yiu ...
cash a cheque	兑一張 支票	deui yàt jèung jì·piu
change a travellers cheque	換旅行 支票	wun léui·hàng jì·piu
change money	換錢	wun chín
get a cash advance	現金透支	yin·gàm tau·jì
withdraw money	攞現金	láw yin·gàm

Where's a/an ...?	⋯⋯喺邊度？	... hái bìn·do
automatic teller machine	自動 提款機	ji·dung tài·fún·gày
foreign exchange office	換外幣 嘅地方	wun ngoy·bai ge day·fàwng
What's the ...?	⋯⋯係乜嘢？	... hai gáy·dàw
charge for that	手續費	sáu·juk·fai
exchange rate	兑換率	deui·wun·léut

The automatic teller machine took my card.

提款機食咗我   tài·fún·gày sik·jáw ngáw
張卡   jèung kàat

I've forgotten my PIN.

我唔記得咗   ngáw ǹg·gay·dàk·jáw
我嘅密碼。   ngáw ge mat·máa

Can I use my credit card to withdraw money?

我可唔可以用   ngáw háw·ǹg·háw·yí yung
信用卡攞現金呀？   seun·yung·kàat láw yin·gàm aa

Has my money arrived yet?

我嘅匯款到咗未？   ngáw ge wui·fún do·jáw may

How long will it take to arrive?

仲要等幾耐？   jung·yiu dáng gáy·lóy

listen for ...		
證件	jing·gín	identification
護照	wu·jiu	passport
簽字。 chìm ji		Sign here.
你嘅帳戶冇錢。 láy ge jeung·wu mó chín		You have no funds left.
呢度有問題。 làay·do yáu man·tài		There's a problem.
我地辦唔倒。 ngáw·day baan·ǹg·dó		We can't do that.

I'd like a/an ...	我想買……	ngáw séung máai ...
audio set	錄音導	luk·yàm do·yàu
catalogue	目錄	muk·luk
guide	指南	jí·làam
guidebook	英文旅遊	yìng·màn léui·yàu
in English	指南	jí·làam
(local) map	本地地圖	bún·day day·tò
pass	入場券	yap·chèung·gewn

Do you have information on ... sites?	有冇關于 ……嘅資料？	yáu·mó gwàan·yèw ... ge jì·liú
cultural	文化	màn·faa
historical	歷史	lik·sí
religious	宗教	jùng·gaau

I'd like to see ...
我想睇下……　　　　ngáw séung tái háa ...

What's that?
喇啲係乜嘢？　　　　gáw dì hai màt·yé

Who made it?
係邊個做嘅？　　　　hai bìn·gaw jo ge

How old is it?
有幾舊？　　　　　　yáu gáy gau

Can I take photos?
我可唔可以
影相呀？　　　　　　ngáw háw·ǹg·háw·yí
　　　　　　　　　　yíng·séung aa

Could you take a photo of me?
你可唔可以幫
我影相呀？　　　　　láy háw·ǹg·háw·yí bàwng
　　　　　　　　　　ngáw yíng·séung aa

Can I take a photo (of you)?
我可唔可以影 　　　　　　ngáw háw·ǹg·háw·yí yíng
(你)嘅像呀？ 　　　　　　(láy) ge séung aa

I'll send you the photo.
我會寄相俾你。 　　　　　ngáw wuí gay séung báy láy

Please write down your name and address.
唔該記低你個 　　　　　　ǹg·gòy gay·dài láy gaw
名同埋地址。 　　　　　　méng tung·maai day·jí

---

east, west, home's best

When you're asked to recite the four compass points in
China, say dùng làam sài bàk 東南西北 (east, south, west,
north). Perhaps the east is given prominence because it's
synonymous with the Orient, or perhaps not – traditionally,
the thrones of Chinese emperors faced south, as this
symbolised sovereignty. The west represents the heavenly
paradise -- to say that someone has gwài·sài 歸西 (returned
to the western paradise) means that they've passed away.

---

getting in

What time does it open?
幾點開？ 　　　　　　　　gáy dím hòy

What time does it close?
幾點關門？ 　　　　　　　gáy dím gwàan·mùn

What's the admission charge?
入場券幾多錢？ 　　　　　yap·chèung· gewn gáy·dàw chín

Is there a	有冇……	yáu·mó …
discount for …?	折扣呀？	ji·kau aa
children	小童	siú·tùng
families	家庭	gàa·tìng
groups	團體	tèwn·tái
older people	長者	jéung·jé
students	學生	hawk·sàang

tours

Can you recommend a ...?	你可唔可以推薦……呀？	láy háv·n̄g·háw·yí tèui·jin … aa
When's the next ...?	下個……係幾時？	haa·gaw … hai gáy·sì
boat trip	遊船團	yàu·sewn·tèwn
bus tour	巴士團	bàa·sí·tèwn
day trip	一日遊	yàt·yat·yàu
night tour	夜遊	ye·yàu
tour	旅遊團	léui·yàu·tèwn
walking tour	步行團	bo·hàng·tèwn

Is ... included?	包唔包……呀？	bàau·ǹg·bàau … aa
accommodation	住宿	jew·sùk
food	飲食	yúm·sik
transport	交通	gàau·tùng

The guide will pay.
嚙導會俾錢。
do·yàu wuí báy chín

The guide has paid.
嚙導已經俾咗錢。
do·yàu yí·gìng báy·jáw chín

How long is the tour?
呢團要幾長時間？
lày tèwn yiu gáy chèung sì·gaan

What time should we be back?
幾點要返嚟？
gáy dím yiu fàan·lài

I'm with them.
我同佢地喺一齊嘅。
ngáw tùng kéui·day hái yàt·chài ge

I've lost my group.
我搵唔到我個團。
ngáw wán ǹg dó ngáw gaw tèwn

chinese dynasties

You may see some of these Chinese dynastic periods written on plaques when touring around museums. The abbreviations BCE and CE stand for 'Before Common Era' and 'Common Era', the non-Christian equivalents to the terms BC and AD.

Xia dynasty (2070-1600BCE)
夏朝   haa·chiù

Shang dynasty (1600-1046BCE)
商朝   sèung·chiù

Zhou dynasty (1046-256BCE)
周朝   jàu·chiù

Spring & Autumn period (770-476BCE)
春秋時期   chèun·chàu sì·kày

Warring States period (475-221BCE)
戰國時期   jin·gawk sì·kày

Qin dynasty (221-207BCE)
秦朝   chȩun·chiù

Han dynasty (206BCE-220CE)
漢朝   hawn·chiù

Tang dynasty (618-907CE)
唐朝   tàwng·chiù

Song dynasty (960-1279CE)
宋朝   sung·chiù

Yuan dynasty (1279-1368CE)
元朝   yȩwn·chiù

Ming dynasty (1368-1644CE)
明朝   mìng·chiù

Qing dynasty (1644-1911CE)
清朝   chìng·chiù

Republic of China (1911-1949CE)
民國時期   màn·gawk sì·kày

People's Republic ('Liberated era') (1949-present)
公和國時期   gùng·wàw·gawk sì·kày

looking for a job

搵工

Where are jobs advertised?
邊度登廣告請人？　　　　bin·do dàng gwáwng·go chéng·yàn

I'm enquiring about the position advertised.
我樣問下賣　　　　　　　ngáw séung man háa maai
廣告嗰份工。　　　　　　gwáwng·go gáw fan gùng

I'm looking	我搵緊……	ngáw wán gán …
for … work.	嘅工。	ge gùng
bar	酒吧	jáu·bàa
casual	臨時	làm·sì
English-teaching	教英文	gaau yìng·màn
fruit-picking	摘生果	jaak sàang·gwáw
full-time	全職	chèwn·jìk
labouring	體力勞動	tái·lìk lò·dung
office	辦公室	baan·gùng·sàt
part-time	半職	bun·jìk
waitering	侍應	si·ying

I've had experience.
我有經驗。　　　　　　　ngáw yáu gìng·yim

What's the wage?
工資幾多？　　　　　　　gùng·jì gáy·dàw

Do I need	我需唔需	ngáw sèui·ng·sèui
(a) …?	要…… ？	yiu …
contract	份合同	fan hap·tùng
insurance	保險	bó·hím
my own	自己嘅	ji·gáy ge
transport	交通工具	gàau·tùng gùng·geui
uniform	件制服	gin jai·fuk
work permit	工作簽證	gùng·jawk chìm·jing

Here is/are my ...	呢個係我	lày gaw hai ngáw
	嘅……	ge ...
bank account	銀行賬戶	ngàn·hàang jeung·wu
details	資料	jì·liú
CV	簡歷	gáan·lìk
visa	簽證	chìm·jing
work permit	工作簽證	gùng·jawk chìm·jing
What time	我幾點鐘……？	ngáw gáy dím·jùng ...
do I ...?		
finish	收工	sàu·gùng
have a break	休息	yàu·sìk
start	開始	hòy·chí
Can you	你可唔可以……	láy háw·ǹg·háw·yí ...
start ...?	開工呀？	hòy·gùng aa
I can start ...	我可以……	ngáw háw·yí ...
	開工。	hòy·gùng
at (8) o'clock	（八）點	(baat) dím
next week	下個禮拜	haa gaw lái·baai
today	今日	gàm·yat
tomorrow	听日	tìng·yat

doing business

傾生意

I'm attending a ...	我參加個……	ngáw chàam·gàa gaw ...
conference	研討會	yìn·tó·wuí
course	培訓班	puì·fan·bàan
meeting	會議	wuí·yí
trade fair	交易會	gàau·yìk·wuí
I'm with ...	我同……	ngáw tung ...
	一齊嚟嘅。	yàt·chài lai ge
China Travel	中國	jùng·gawk
Service	旅行社	léui·hang·sé
my colleague(s)	（幾個）同事	(gáy gaw) tung·si
(two) others	（兩個）人	(léung gaw) yàn

I'm alone.
我一個人嚟嘅。 ngáw yàt gaw yàn lai ge

I have an appointment with …
我約咗…… ngáw yeuk·jáw …

I'm staying at the (China Hotel), room (100).
我住喺(中國大 ngáw jew hái (jùng·gawk daai
酒店),(一百)房。 jáu·dim), (yàt·baak) fáwng

I'm here for (two) days/weeks.
我要喺呢度住 ngáw yiu hái lày·do jew
(兩)日／個星期。 (léung) yat/gaw sìng·kày

Here's my business card.
俾我嘅卡片你。 báy ngáw ge láy kàat·pín

Here's my …	俾我嘅……你。	báy ngáw ge … láy
What's your …?	你有冇……呀？	láy yáu·mó … aa
address	地址	day·jí
email address	電子郵箱	dìn·jí yáu·sèung
fax number	傳真號碼	chèwn·jàn ho·máa
mobile number	手機號碼	sáu·gày ho·máa
pager number	傳呼機號碼	chèwn·fù·gày ho·máa
work number	公司電話	gùng·sì dìn·wáa

Where's the …?	……喺邊度？	… hái·bìn·do
business centre	商務中心	sèung·mo jùng·sàm
conference	研討會	yìn·tó·wuí
meeting	會議	wui·yí

I need (a/an)…	我要……	ngáw yiu …
computer	個電腦	gaw dìn·ló
Internet connection	上網	séung·máwng
interpreter	位翻譯	wái fàan·yik
more business cards	多印啲卡片	dàw yan dì kàat·pín
some space to set up	啲地方 辦公	dì day·fàwng baan·gùng
to send a fax	發個傳真	faat gaw chèwn·jàn

That went very well.
會開得好好。
wuí hòy dàk hó·hó

Thank you for your time.
唔該晒。
ǹg·gòy saai

Shall we go for a drink/meal?
我地去飲杯／
食飯呢？
ngáw·day heui yám·buì/
sik·faan lè

It's on me.
我請客。
ngáw chéng haak

showing your cards

If you're doing business deals in Hong Kong and Southeastern China, make sure your business card is translated into Cantonese. Include your business title and any noteworthy qualities about your company, such as being the largest or oldest in the industry. When you actually exchange your business cards:

- hold your card with both hands when you offer it – never give it out with only one hand
- offer your card with the English side facing up – if you have the Cantonese side facing up, this may be seen as an assumption that the recipient can't read English
- don't write on someone else's card even to jot down extra details, unless asked to do so

senior & disabled travellers
老年及殘疾旅客

In China older people are revered. To be called 老伯 **ló·baak** (old man) or 老太太 **ló·taai·táai** (old woman) is seen as a compliment and a tribute to your maturity and wisdom. Disabled people, on the other hand, will not find China easy as there are few facilities available for them.

I have a disability.
我行動不便。
ngáw hàng·dung bàt bin

I need assistance.
我需要幫助。
ngáw sèui·yiu bàwng·màwng

What services do you have for people with a disability?
有冇特別照顧傷殘
人士嘅服務呀？
yáu·mó dak·bit jiu·gu sèung·chàan yàn·si ge fuk·mo aa

Are there disabled toilets?
有冇傷殘人士專用
嘅廁所呀？
yáu·mó sèung·chàan yàn·si jèwn·yung ge chi·sáw aa

Are there disabled parking spaces?
有冇傷殘人士
專用嘅泊車位呀？
yáu·mó sèung·chàan yàn·si jèwn·yung wái aa

Is there wheelchair access?
輪椅入唔入得㗎？
léun·yí yap·ng·yap·dàk gaa

How wide is the entrance?
門口有幾闊？
mùn·háu yáu gáy fut

I'm deaf.
我耳仔聾咗。
ngáw yí·jái lùng·jáw

I have a hearing aid.
我帶咗助聽器。
ngáw daai·jáw jaw·ting·hay

Are guide dogs permitted?
盲公狗
入唔入得㗎呀？
màang·gùng·gáu yap·ng·yap·dàk lài aa

How many steps are there?

有幾級樓梯？ yáu gáy kàp làau·tài

Is there a lift/elevator?

有冇電梯呀？ yáu·mó dịn·tài aa

Are there rails in the bathroom?

沖糧房有冇 chùng·lèung·fáwng yáu·mó
扶手呀？ fù·sáu aa

Could you call me a disabled taxi?

唔該叫架輪椅 ǹg·gòy giu gaa léun·yí
上得嘅的士。 séung dàk ge dìk·sí

Could you help me cross the street safely?

唔該，可唔可以幫 ǹg·gòy háw·ǹg·háw·yí bàwng
我安全過馬路呀？ ngáw ngàwn·chèwn gaw máa·lọ aa

Is there somewhere I can sit down?

邊度可以坐下？ bìn·dọ háw·yí cháw háa

guide dog	盲公狗	màang·gùng·gáu
older person	老人	ló·yàn
person with	傷殘人士	sèung·chàan yàn·sị
a disability	殘疾人	chàan·jạt yàn
ramp	斜道	chẹ·dọ
walking frame	柺架	gwáai·gáa
walking stick	柺杖	gwáai·jéung
wheelchair	輪椅	léun·yí

travelling with children

帶細佬仔旅遊

Are children allowed?
可唔可以帶細路去啊？　　háw·ǹg·háw·yí daai sai·lo̯ heui aa

Are there any good places to take children around here?
附近有冇細路仔
玩嘅地方呀？
fu·ga̯n yáu·mó sai·lo̯·jái
wáan ge da̯y·fàwng aa

Is there a …?	呢度有冇……？	là̯y·do̯ yáu mó …
baby change room	嬰兒設施	yìng·yì chit·sì
child-minding service	保姆服務	bó·mó fu̯k·mo̯
child-sized portion	小童份量	siú·tu̯ng fa̯n·le̯ung
children's menu	小童菜單	siú·tu̯ng choy·dàan
discount for children	小童折扣	siú·tu̯ng jit·kau
family ticket	家庭套票	gàa·tìng to·piu

I need a/an …	我要……	ngáw yiu …
baby seat	BB座	bi̯·bì ja̯w
(English-speaking) babysitter	（識講英文嘅)保姆	(sìk gáwng yìng·mán ge) bó·mó
booster seat	幼兒車座	yau·yì chè·ja̯w
cot	BB床	bi̯·bì chàwng
highchair	高凳	gò·dang
plastic sheet	塑膠布	sawk·gàau·bo
plastic bag	塑膠袋	sawk·gàau·dóy
potty	BB坐廁	bi̯·bì cháw·chi
pram	BB車	bi̯·bì chè
sick bag	衛生袋	wa̯i·sàng·dóy

Where's the nearest ...?	呢度附近有冇……啊？	làydo fugan yáumó ... aa
drinking fountain	飲水噴泉	yámséui panchèun
park	公園	gùngyéwn
playground	遊樂場	yàulawkchèung
swimming pool	游泳池	yàuwingchì
tap/faucet	水喉	séuihàu
theme park	主題公園	jéwtài gùngyéwn
toyshop	玩具店	wungeuidim

Do you sell ...?	你地有冇……啊？	láyday yáumó ... aa
baby wipes	嬰兒紙巾	yìngyì jígàn
disposable nappies/diapers	一次性尿片	yàtchising liupín
painkillers for infants	嬰兒止痛藥	yìngyì jítung yeuk
tissues	紙巾	jígàn

Do you hire prams/strollers?
你地有冇BB車出租啊？   láyday yáumó bibì chè chèutjò aa

Is there space for a pram?
有冇地方放BB
車啊？   yáumó dayfàwng fawng bibì chè aa

Where can I change a nappy?
去邊度可以換尿片？   heui bìndo háwyí wun liupín

Do you mind if I breast-feed here?
我喺呢度喂奶你
唔介意啊嗎？   ngáw hái làydo wailáai láy ng gaaiyi àmaa

Could I have some paper and pencils please?
可唔可以借紙筆用下？   háwnghawyí je jí bàt yung háa

Is this suitable for (two)-year-old children?
(兩)歲嘅細路
啱唔啱㗎？   (léung) seui ge sailo ngaannngngaan gaa

Do you know a (dentist/doctor) who is good with children?
有冇識睇細路嘅
(牙醫／醫生)？   yáumó sik tái sailo ge (ngaayì/yìsàng)

If your child is sick, see **health**, page 193.

同細路仔傾偈

What's your name?
你叫乜嘢名？
láy giu màt·yé méng aa

How old are you?
細路，你幾歲啊？
sai·lo láy gáy seui aa

Do you go to school?
你返學未啊？
láy fàan·hawk may aa

Do you go to kindergarten?
你返幼稚園
未啊？
láy fàan·yau·ji·yéwn
may aa

What grade are you in?
讀幾年級？
duk gáy lìn·kàp

Do you like ...?　你鍾唔鍾意　láy jùng·ǹg·jùng·yi
　　　　　　　……啊？　　... aa

school　　返學　　fàan·hawk
sport　　運動　　wan·dung
your teacher　你個先生　láy gaw sìn·sàang

What do you do after school?
下晝放咗學　haa·jau fawng·jáw·hawk
鍾意做乜嘢？　jùng·yi jo màt·yé

Do you learn (English)?
開始學(英文)未啊？　hòy·chí hawk (yìng·màn) may aa

I come from very far away.
我喺好遠嚟嘅。　ngáw hái hó yéwn lài ge

Are you lost?
你係唔係蕩失路啊？　láy hai·ǹg·hai dawng·sàt·lo aa

talking about children

How many months pregnant are you?
有咗幾多個月啦？   yáu·jáw gáy·dàw gaw yewt laa

Have you thought of a name?
諗好個名未啊？   lám·hó gaw méng may aa

Is this your first child?
係你第一個細路啊？   hai láy dai·yàt gaw sai·lo aa

How many children do you have?
你有幾個細路？   láy yáu gáy gaw sai·lo

What a beautiful child!
呢個細路真得意！   lày·gaw sai·lo jàn dàk·yi

Is it a boy or a girl?
係男仔定係女仔？   hai làam·jái ding·hai léui·jái

How old is he/she?
呢個細路幾歲啦？   lày·gaw sai·lo gáy seui laa

Does he/she go to school?
佢讀書未呀？   kéui duk·sèw may aa

What's his/her name?
佢叫乜嘢名啊？   kéui giu màt·yé méng aa

Is he/she well-behaved?
佢乖唔乖？   kéui gwàai·ǹg·gwàai

He/She …	佢……	kéui …
has your eyes	雙眼好似你	sèung ngáan hó chí láy
looks like dad	似爸爸	chí baa·bàa
looks like mum	似媽媽	chí màa·màa

交流

basics

開頭

Requests usually start with the word ǹg·gòy 唔該. See the **phrasebuilder**, page 15 for more on this.

Yes.	係。	hai
No.	不係。	ǹg·hai
Please ...	唔該……	ǹg·gòy …
Thank you (very much).	多謝(你)。	dàw·je (láy)
You're welcome.	唔駛客氣。	ǹg·sái haak·hay
Excuse me. (to get attention)	對唔住。	deui·ǹg·jew
Excuse me. (to get past)	唔該借借。	ǹg·gòy je·je
Sorry.	對唔住。	deui·ǹg·jew
I wish you well.	你好。	láy hó

actions speak louder than words

In Hong Kong and China, people shake hands or nod when greeting each other. On some formal occassions it's customary to bow. Kissing in public should be avoided – even a friendly kiss on both cheeks can be seen as a little too forward.

greetings & goodbyes

打招呼

If you think people show too much concern about your eating habits when they greet you, you needn't be too worried – asking if you've had something to eat yet is a common way of greeting in Cantonese.

Hello.	哈佬。	hàa·ló
Hi.	嗨。	hày
Good morning.	早晨。	jó·sàn
Good afternoon.	午安。	ńg·ngàwn
Good evening.	晚安。	máan·ngàwn

Have you eaten?
食咗飯未？
sik·jáw faan may

Have you had *yum-cha*?
飲咗茶未？
yám·jáw chàa may

How are you?
你幾好啊嗎？
láy gáy hó à maa

Fine.
幾好。
gáy hó

And you?
你呢？
láy lè

Not too bad.
仲可以。
jung háw·yi

I'm very busy.
我好忙。
ngáw hó·màwng

What's your name?
你叫乜嘢名？
láy giu màt·yé méng aa

If you're invited out to yám·chàa 飲茶 (yum cha), it's customary to allow your host to order the food, even if you're asked what you'd like to have.

What will you have?
你想食乜野？   làuy séung sìk màt·yè

Anything you recommend.
你定啦。   làuy dìng làa

My name is …
我叫……   ngáuw giu …

I'm pleased to meet you.
幸會！   hang·wui

I'd like to introduce you to …
介紹……你識。   gaai·siu … láy sìk

This is my …	呢個係我 嘅……	làuy gaw hai ngáuw ge …
child	仔	jái
colleague	同事	tung·si
friend	朋友	pàng·yáu
husband	老公	ló·gùng
partner (intimate)	伴	pún
wife	老婆	ló·pò

For family members, see **family**, page 116.

See you later.	再見。	joy·gin
Goodbye.	再見。	joy·gin
Bye.	拜拜。	bàai·baai
Good night.	晚安。	máan·ngàwn
Bon voyage!	一路平安。	yàt lo ping·ngàwn

addressing people

In Cantonese, titles are used to either indicate your relationship with the person you're addressing or to show respect to someone older than you – they're attached to the end of the surname.

When you're first introduced to someone, address them by their full name, including their surname. If you're speaking to someone older than you, call them by their surname followed by a title, such as 'Sir' or 'Madam', eg Madame Li would be li·éui·sí.

Mr/Ms	先生／小姐	·sìn·sàang/·siú·jé
Sir/Madam	先生／女士	·sìn·sàang/·léui·sí
Mrs	太太	·taai·táai

---

what's in a name ...

The titles below can be used in informal settings to show what type of relationship you have with the person you're talking to.

老友	·ló·yáu	'mate' or 'buddy' – for people you don't know who are the same age as you
仔	·jái	male friends or colleagues who are younger than you
叔	·sùk	males who are younger than your father (lit: uncle)
伯	·baak	males who are older than your father (lit: uncle)
姐	·jè	to females older than yourself

SOCIAL

112

making conversation

What a beautiful day!
今日幾好天。 gàm·yat gáy·hó tìn

Nice weather, isn't it?
今日天氣幾好。 gàm·yat tìn·hay gáy·hó

Awful weather, isn't it?
今日天氣好差。 gàm·yat tìn·hay hó chàa

Do you live here?
你住呢度啊？ láy jew lày·do àa

Where are you going?
你去邊度啊？ láy heui bìn·do aa

What are you doing?
你做緊乜嘢？ láy jo·gán màt·yé

Do you like it here?
你鍾唔鍾意呢度啊？ láy jùng·ǹg·jùng·yi lày·do aa

What's this called?
呢個叫乜嘢？ lày gaw giu màt·yé

Can I take a photo (of you)?
我可唔可以影 ngáw háw·ǹg·háw·yí yíng
(你嘅) 相啊？ (láy ge) séung aa

That's (beautiful), isn't it?
真係 (靚)。 jàn hai (leng)

How long are you here for?
你喺呢度留幾耐？ láy hái lày·do làu gáy loy

I'm here for (four) weeks.
我留 (四個) 星期。 ngáw làu (say gaw) sìng·kày

Are you here on holiday?
你嚟呢度渡假啊？ láy lài lày·do do·gaa aa

I'm here ...	我嚟呢度……	ngáw lài lày·do …
for a holiday	旅遊	léui·yàu
on business	出差	chèut·chàai
to study	留學	làu·hawk

國籍

Where are you from?
你係邊度人？ láy hai bin·do yàn

I'm from ... 我係喺…… ngáw hai hái …
嚟嘅。 lài ge

   Australia 澳大利亞 ngò·daai·lay·aa
   Canada 加拿大 gàa·làa·daai
   Singapore 新加坡 sàn·gaa·bàw

For more countries, see the **dictionary**.

age

年齡

How old ...? ……幾大啊？ … gáy daai aa
   are you 你 láy
   is your son 你個仔 láy gaw jái
   is your daughter 你個女 láy gaw léui

I'm ... years old.
我……歲。 ngáw … seui

He/She is ... years old.
佢……歲。 kéui … seui

Too old!
太老啦！ tàai ló laa

I'm younger than I look.
我其實仲好 ngáw kày·sat jung hó
後生。 hau·sàang

For your age, see **numbers & amounts**, page 35.

occupations & studies

What's your occupation?
你做邊行㗎？　　　　láy jo bìn hàwng gaa

I'm a/an ...	我係……	ngáw hai ...
accountant	會計	wui·gai
chef	廚師	chèw·sì
engineer	工程師	gùng·chìng·sì
journalist	記者	gay·jé
teacher	先生	sìn·sàang

I do...	我……	ngáw ...
casual work	打散工	dáa sáan·gùng
business	做生意	jo sàang·yi

I work in ...	我做……	ngáw jo ...
administration	行政工作	hàng·jing gùng·jàwk
health	衛生工作	wai·sàng gùng·jàwk
sales & marketing	推銷	tèui·siù

---

local talk

Beautiful!	靚啊！	jeng aa
Excellent!	冇得頂！	mó·dàk·díng
Great!	冇得頂！	mó·dàk·díng
Hey!	喂！	way
It's OK.	OK。	ò·kày
Just a minute.	等陣。	dáng·jan
Just joking.	開玩笑。	hòy wàan·siu
Maybe.	可能。	háw·làng
No way!	無得傾！	mó·dàk·kìng
No problem.	無問題。	mó·man·tài
Sure, whatever.	一定，一定。	yàt·dìng yàt·dìng
That's enough!	夠啦，夠啦。	gau laa gau laa

meeting people

115

I'm ...	我……	ngáw …
retired	退咗休	teui·jáw·yàu
self-employed	自己做老細	ji·gáy jo ló·sai
unemployed	失咗業	sàt·jáw·yip

What are you studying?
你學乜嘢㗎？ láy hawk màt·yé gaa

I'm studying ...	我……	ngáw …
Cantonese	廣東話	gwáwng·dùng·wáa
Chinese	中文	jùng·mán
humanities	讀文科	duk màn·fàw
science	讀理科	duk láy·fàw

say 'aa'

The character aa 阿 can come before kinship terms to
show closeness. When addressing your younger sister, for
example, you can call her muí 妹 (little sister) or aa muí
阿妹, which is like calling her 'lil' sis'.

family

家庭

Family has always been a fundamental part of Chinese culture
and its importance is reflected in the detailed naming conven-
tions for family members. Names are based on gender, the age
and the generation gap between the speaker and the family
member, and whether they're related through maternal or paternal lines. The 'kinship' terms in Cantonese are used both to
address family members and to refer to them.

Do you have a/an ...?
你有冇 ……呀？ láy yáu·mó … aa

I have a/an ...
我有…… ngáw yáu …

I don't have a/an ...
我有冇…… ngáw yáu mó …

aunt (mother's sister)	阿姨	aa·yì
aunt (father's sister)	姑姐	gù·jè
brother	兄弟	hìng·dai
daughter	女	léui
father	爸爸	baa·bàa
grandchildren	孫	sèwn
grandfather	阿爺	aa·yè
grandmother	阿嫲	aa·màa
husband	丈夫 pol	jeung·fù
	老公 inf	ló·gùng
mother	媽媽	màa·màa
older brother	哥哥	gàw·gàw
partner (intimate)	伴	pún
sister/older sister	家姐	gàa·jè
son	仔	jái
uncle (father's younger brother)	叔	sùk
uncle (father's older brother)	伯	baak
wife	太太 pol	táai·táai
	老婆 inf	ló·pò
younger brother	細佬	sai·ló
younger sister	妹妹	mui·muí

Are you (married)?
你係唔係(結咗婚)啊？ láy hai·ǹg·hai (git·jáw·fàn) aa

I live with someone.
我有個伴。 ngáw yáu gaw pún

I'm ... 我…… ngáw ...
　married 結咗婚 git·jáw·fàn
　separated 分咗手 fàn·jáw·sáu
　single 單身 dàan·sàn

farewells

Tomorrow is my last day here.
听日我就走啦。　　　　tìng·yat ngáw jau jáu laa

If you come to (Scotland), you can stay with me.
有機會嚟(蘇克蘭)，　　yáu gày·wui lài (sò·gak·làan)
可以嚟搵我。　　　　　háw·yí lài wán ngáw

Keep in touch!
保持聯系！　　　　　　bó·chì lèwn·hai

It's been great meeting you.
識倒你真係好高興。　　sìk·dó láy jàn·hai hó gò·hing

Here's my ...	呢個係我	lày·gaw hai ngáw
	嘅……	ge ...
What's your ...?	你嘅……呢？	láy ge ... lè
address	地址	day·jí
email address	電子郵箱	din·jí yàu·sèung
phone number	電話號碼	din·wáa ho·máa

well wishing

Bless you!
祝你好運！　　　　　　jùk láy hó·wan

Bon voyage!
一路平安！　　　　　　yàt·lo ping·ngàwn

Congratulations.
恭喜，恭喜。　　　　　gùng·háy gùng·háy

Good luck.
祝你好運。　　　　　　jùk láy hó·wan

Happy birthday.
生日快樂。　　　　　　sàang·yat faai·lawk

Happy New Year.
新年快樂。　　　　　　sàn·lin faai·lawk

May you make lots of money!
恭喜發財！　　　　　　gùng·háy faat·chòy

common interests

共同興趣

What do you do in your spare time?
你有乜嘢愛好啊？ | láy yáu màt·yé ngoy·ho aa

Do you like ...?	你鍾唔鍾意 ……啊？	láy jùng·ńg·jùng·yi … aa
I (don't) like ...	我(唔)鍾意……	ngáw (ńg·jùng·yi …
calligraphy	書法	sèw·faat
computer games	電腦游戲	dìn·ló yàu·hay
cooking	煮飯	jéw·faan
dancing	跳舞	tiu·mó
drawing	畫畫	waak·wáa
drinking	飲酒	yám·jáu
eating	食飯	sik·faan
films	睇戲	tái·hay
gardening	種花	jung·fàa
mountain climbing	爬山	pàa·sàan
music	聽音樂	tèng yàm·ngawk
photography	影相	yíng·séung
reading	睇書	tái·sèw
sport	體育	tái·yuk
surfing the Internet	上網	séung·máwng
talking	傾偈	kìng·gái
travelling	旅遊	léui·yàu
walking	散步	saan·bo
watching TV	睇電視	tái·dìn·si
window shopping	行公司	hàang gùng·sì

For sporting activities, see **sport**, page 145 and the **dictionary**.

music

音樂

Do you ...?	你鍾唔鍾意 ……啊？	láy jùng·n̄g·jùng·yi ... aa
dance	跳舞	tiu·mó
go to concerts	聽音樂會	tèng yàm·ngawk·wúi
listen to music	聽音樂	tèng yàm·ngawk
play an instrument	玩樂器	wáan ngawk·hay
sing	唱歌	cheung·gàw

What ... do you like?	你鍾意邊……？	láy jùng·yi bìn ...
bands	個樂隊	gaw ngawk·déui
music	種音樂	júng yàm·ngawk
singers	個歌手	gaw gàw·sáu

alternative music	非主流音樂	fày jéw·làu yàm·ngawk
Beijing opera	京劇	gìng·kek
blues	傷感爵士樂	sèung·gám jeuk·si ngawk
Cantonese opera	粵劇	yewt·kek
Cantopop (Cantonese pop)	粵語 流行曲	yewt·yéw làu·hàng·kùk
classical music	古典音樂	gú·dín yàm·ngawk
easy listening	輕鬆音樂	hìng·sùng yàm·ngawk
electronic music	電子音樂	din·jí yàm·ngawk
folk	民間音樂	màn·gàan yàm·ngawk
hip hop	霹靂舞音樂	pìk·lìk·mó yàm·ngawk
heavy metal	重金屬 音樂	chúng·gàm·suk yàm·ngawk
jazz	爵士樂	jeuk·si ngawk
pop	流行音樂	làu·hàng yàm·ngawk
rock	滾石音樂	gún·sek yàm·ngawk
traditional music	中樂	jùng·ngawk
world music	世界各地 音樂	sai·gaai gawk·day yàm·ngawk

Planning to go to a concert? See **buying tickets**, page 48 and
going out, page 129.

cinema & theatre

電影與戲劇

I feel like going to a ...	我想去睇……	ngáw séung heui tái …
Did you like the ...?	呢……好唔好睇呀？	lày … hó·ǹg·hó tái aa
ballet	場芭蕾舞	chèung bàa·lèui·mó
film	出電影	chèut din·yíng
play	出話劇	chèut wáa·kek

What's showing at the cinema tonight?
今晚戲院
有乜嘢節目？
gàm·máan hay·yéwn
yáu màt·yé jit·muk

What's showing at the theatre tonight?
今晚劇院
有乜嘢節目？
gàm·máan kek·yéwn
yáu màt·yé jit·muk

Is it in English?
係唔係講英文㗎？
hai·ǹg·hai gáwng yìng·mán gaa

Does it have (English) subtitles?
有無(英文)字幕㗎？
yáu·mó (yìng·mán) ji·mawk gaa

Is this seat taken?
呢個位有人㗎？
láy·gaw wái yáu yàn gàa

Have you seen ...?
你睇過……未啊？
láy tái·gaw … may aa

Who's in it?
有邊個演？
yáu bìn·gaw yín

It stars ...
主角係……
jéw·gawk hai …

I thought it was …	我覺得……	ngáw gawk·dàk …
excellent	好好睇	hó·hó tái
long	有啲長	yáu dì chèung
OK	OK	ò·kày

I (don't) like …	我(唔)鍾意……	ngáw (ǹg) jùng·yi …
action movies	動作片	dung·jawk·pín
animated films	卡通片	kàa·tùng·pín
Bruce Lee films	李小龍嘅戲	láy siú·lùng ge hay
Chinese cinema	中國電影	jùng·gawk din·yíng
comedies	笑片	siu·pín
documentaries	記錄片	gay·luk·pín
drama	戲劇片	hay·kek·pín
Hong Kong cinema	香港電影	hèung·gáwng din·yíng
horror movies	恐怖片	húng·bo·pín
Jackie Chan films	成龍嘅戲	sìng·lùng ge hay
kung fu movies	武俠片	mó·hap·pín
martial arts	武術	mó·seut
sci-fi	科幻片	fò·waan·pín
short films	短片	déwn·pín
thrillers	緊張	gán·jèung
	刺激片	chi·gìk pín
war movies	戰爭片	jin·jàng·pín

---

the language of *fùng séui*

Also known as 'geomancy', fùng séui 風水 (lit: wind water) was originally a form of divination used to select good sites for buildings and burials. It later became an artform practised to create harmony between humans and their environments, especially mountains and water-bodies. A fùng séui ló 風水佬 (lit: *fùng séui* guy) or fùng séui sìn sàng 風水先生 (geomancer master) will test your space with a lò gàng 羅更 (*fùng séui* compass) and arranges your furniture, mirrors, plants and water features to give your work or living space lung yuet 龍穴 ('the dragon's den', meaning good *fùng séui*).

感覺與見解

feelings

感覺

Are you ...?	你係唔係……呀？	láy hai·ǹg·hai ... aa
I'm ...	我……	ngáw ...
I (don't) feel ...	我(唔)覺得……	ngáw (ǹg·)gawk·dàk ...
cold	凍	dung
disappointed	失望	sàt·mawng
embarrassed	唔好意思	ǹg·hó yi·sì
happy	開心	hòy·sàm
hot	熱	yit
hungry	肚餓	tó·ngaw
in a hurry	忙	màwng
sad	唔開心	ǹg·hòy·sàm
surprised	驚訝	gìng·ngaa
thirsty	頸渴	géng·hawt
tired	攰	gwui
worried	心急	sàm·gàp

If you're feeling unwell, see **health**, page 189.

feelings & opinions

go with the flow

Even though people in Hong Kong speak English, they still adhere to Chinese cultural rules.

Chinese culture places a greater emphasis on the collective whole rather than the individual – if you're too outspoken or express opinions too strongly this may be seen as disturbing the harmony of the group.

mixed emotions		
a little 有啲		yáu dì
I'm a little sad. 我 有啲 唔 開心 。		ngáw yáu dì ǹg·hòy·sàm
very 好		hó
I'm very surprised. 我好驚訝。		ngáw hó gìng·ngaa
extremely 極之		gìk·jì
I'm extremely happy. 我 極之開心 。		ngáw gìk·jì hòy·sàm

opinions

見解

Did you like it?
你覺得好唔好啊？ láy gawk·dàk hó·ǹg·hó a

What do you think of it?
你覺得點樣？ láy gawk·dàk dím·yéung

I thought it	我以為	ngáw yí·wài
was …	佢……	kéui …
It's …	佢……	kéui …
awful	好差	hó jáa
beautiful	好靚	hó leng
boring	好冇聊	hó mò·liù
good	好	hó
great	好精彩	hó jìng·chóy
interesting	好得意	hó dàk·yi
OK	OK	ò·kày
strange	奇怪	kày·gwaai
too expensive	太貴啦	taai gwai laa

politics & social issues

興論與社會問題

Who do you vote for?
你投邊個黨嘅票？   láy tàu bìn·gaw dáwng ge piu

I support the ...	我支持……	ngáw jì·chì ...
party.	黨。	dáwng
I'm a member of	我係……	ngáw hai ...
the ... party.	黨員。	dáwng·yèwn
communist	共產黨	gung·cháan·dáwng
conservative	保守派	bó·sáu·paai
democratic	民主派	màn·jéw·paai
green	環保分子	wàan·bó fan·jí
liberal	自由派	ji·yáu·paai
social democratic	社會民主黨	sé·wuí màn·jéw dáwng
socialist	社會主義者	sé·wuí·jéw·yi·jé

---

party on

These are some of the major political parties in China's Cantonese-speaking regions:

Communist Party (China)
共產黨   gung·cháan·dáwng

Democratic Alliance (for the Betterment of Hong Kong)
民主黨民建聯   màn·jéw·dáwngmàn·gin·lèwn

Kuomintang (China)
國民黨   gawk·màn·dáwng

Liberal Party (Hong Kong)
自由黨   ji·yàu·dáwng

People's Progressive Party (Taiwan, China)
民進黨   màn·jeun·dáwng

feelings & opinions

Did you hear about …?
你有冇聽過……啊？ — láy yáu·mó tèng·gaw … aa

Do you agree?
你同唔同意呀？ — láy tùng·ǹg·tùng·yi aa

I (don't) agree with …
我（唔）同意…… — ngáw (ǹg·)tùng·yi …

How can we protest against …?
我地點樣
可以抗議……？ — ngáw·day dím·yéung háw·yí kàwng·yí …

How can we support …?
我地點樣
可以支持……？ — ngáw·day dím·yéung háw·yí jì·chì …

abortion	墮胎	daw·tòy
animal rights	動物權利	dung·mat kèwn·lay
crime	犯罪活動	faan·jeui wut·dung
discrimination	歧視	kày·si
drugs	毒品	duk·bán
the economy	經濟	gìng·jai
education	教育	gaau·yuk
the environment	環境	wàan·gíng
equal opportunity	平等待遇	pìng·dáng doy·yew
euthanasia	安樂死	ngàwn·lawk·sái
globalisation	全球化	chèwn·kàu·faa
human rights	人權	yàn·kèwn
immigration	移民	yì·màn
inequality	不平等	bàt pìng·dáng
party politics	黨派鬥爭	dáwng·paai dau·jàng
political reform	政制改革	jing·jai góy·gaap
privatisation	私有化	sì·yáu·faa
racism	種族歧視	júng·juk kày·si
sexism	大男人主義	daai·laam·yán·jéw·yi
social welfare	社會福利	sé·wuí fùk·lay
the war in …	……戰爭	… jin·jàng
terrorism	恐怖主義	húng·bo·jéw·yi
unemployment	失業問題	sàt·yip man·tài
unification	統一	túng·yàt

the environment

環保

Is this a protected …?	呢個……係 受保護㗎？	làay·gaw … hai sau bó·wu gaa
forest	森林	sàm·làm
park	公園	gùng·yéwn
species	物種	màt·júng

Is there a … problem here?
本地有……問題呀？　　bún·day yáu … man·tài aa

What should be done about …?
……應該點樣處理？　　… yìng·gòy dím·yéung chéw·láy

How do people feel about …?
人地對……點㗎？　　yàn·day deui … dím lám

conservation	環保	wàan·bó
deforestation	斬伐樹林	jáam·fat sew·làm
drought	乾旱	gàwn·háwn
ecosystem	生態系統	sàng·taai hai·túng
endangered species	瀕臨滅絕物種	pàn·làm mit·jewt mat·júng
genetically modified food	基因改良食品	gày·yàn góy·lèung sik·bán
hunting	打獵	dáa·lip
hydroelectricity	水力發電	séui·lik faat·din
irrigation	農田水利	lùng·tin séui·lay
nuclear energy	核能	hat·làng
nuclear testing	核試驗	hat si·yim
ozone layer	臭氧層	chau·yéung·chàng
pesticides	農藥	lùng·yeuk
pollution	污染	wù·yím
poverty	貧困問題	pàn·kun man·tài
recycling programme	回收措施	wuì·sàu cho·sì
toxic waste	有毒廢物	yáu·duk fai·mat
water supply	供水	gùng·séui

where to go

去邊度

What's there to do in the evenings?
夜晚有乜嘢好 ye·máan yáu màt·yé hó
玩㗎? wáan gaa

Where can I get the latest copy of 'South China City Talk'?
去邊度可以攞到 South heui bìn·do háw·yí láw·dó sàu·fù
China City Talk? chàai·nàa sìt·tì tàwk

What's on …?	……有乜嘢 活動?	… yáu màt·yé wut·dung
locally	呢度附近	làiy·do fu·gan
this weekend	呢個週末	làiy·gaw jàu·mut
today	今日	gàm·yat
tonight	今晚	gàm·máan

Where can I find …?	邊度有……?	bìn·do yáu …
clubs	夜總會	ye·júng·wúi
gay venues	同志吧	tung·ji·bàa
places to eat	食飯嘅地方	sik·faan ge day·fàwng
pubs	酒吧	jáu·bàa

Is there a local …	有冇本地……	yáu mó bún·day …
guide?	指南?	jí·làam
entertainment	娛樂	yèw·lawk
film	電影	din·yíng
gay	同性戀	tung·sing·léwn
music	音樂	yàm·ngawk

I feel like going to (a/the) ...	我想去……	ngáw séung heui …
ballet	睇芭蕾舞	tái bàa·lèui·mó
bar/pub	酒吧	jáu·bàa
café	咖啡屋	gaa·fè·ngùk
concert	聽音樂會	tèng yàm·ngawk·wúi
film	睇電影	tái dìn·yíng
karaoke bar	唱卡拉OK	cheung kàa·làa ò·kày
nightclub	夜總會	ye·júng·wúi
party	party	pàat·tì
performance	睇表演	tái biú·yín
puppet theatre performance	睇木偶戲	tái muk·ngàu·hay
restaurant	餐廳	chàan·tèng

For more on eateries, bars and drinks, see **romance**, page 135, and **eating out**, page 161.

SOCIAL

130

invitations

What do you feel like doing tonight?

今晚有乜節目啊？　　　　gàm·máan yáu màt jit·muk aa

What are you doing …?	你⋯⋯做緊乜嘢？	láy … jo·gán màt·yé
now	而家	yì·gàa
this weekend	呢個週末	lày·gaw jàu·mut
tonight	今晚	gàm·máan

| **Would you like to go (for a) …?** | 你想唔想去⋯⋯啊？ | láy séung·ǹg·séung heui … aa |
I feel like going (for a) …	我想去⋯⋯	ngáw séung heui …
banquet	大食會	daai·sik·wúi
coffee	飲咖啡	yám gaa·fè
dancing	跳舞	tiu·mó
drink	飲酒	yám jáu
gambling	賭番舖	dó·fàan·pò
meal	食飯	sik·faan
out somewhere	出去玩	chèut·heui wáan
to the races	跑馬	páau·máa
walk	散散步	saan·saan·bo
yum cha	飲茶	yúm·chàa

Do you know a good restaurant?

你知唔知邊間酒樓好啊？　láy jì·ǹg·jì bìn gàan jáu·làu hó aa

Do you want to come to the concert with me?

你想唔想同我　　　　　　láy séung·ǹg·séung tùng ngáw
去听音樂會啊？　　　　　heui tèng yàm·ngáwk·wúi aa

We're having a party/banquet.

我地要開 party／　　　　ngáw·day yiu hòy pàat·tì/
大食會　　　　　　　　　daai·sik·wúi

You should come.

你應該㗎。　　　　　　　láy yìng·gòy lài

responding to invitations

Sure!
好！ hó

Yes, I'd love to.
好，我去。 hó ng<u>á</u>w heui

That's very kind of you.
你太客氣啦。 l<u>á</u>y taai haak·hay laa

That sounds like fun!
幾好喎。 gáy hó waw

Where shall we go?
我地應該去邊度？ ng<u>á</u>w·d<u>a</u>y yìng·gòy heui bìn·d<u>o</u>

No, I'm afraid I can't.
唔得，我可能嚟唔倒。 <u>ǹ</u>g·dàk ngáw háw·l<u>à</u>ng l<u>à</u>y·<u>ǹ</u>g·dó

Maybe another time.
下次先啦。 haa·chi sìn làa

What about tomorrow?
听日得唔得？ tìng·yat dàk·ǹg·dàk

Sorry, I can't sing/dance.
唔好意思，我唔識 ǹg·hó yi·sì ngáw ǹg sìk
唱歌／跳舞。 cheung·gaw/tiu·mó

I (don't) like ... 我唔鍾意…… ngáw (ǹg·)jùng·yi …
   dancing 跳舞 tiu·mó
   drinking 飲酒 yám·jáu
   films 睇戲 tái·hay
   karaoke 卡拉OK kàa·làa ò·kày

arranging to meet

約人

What time will we meet?
幾點見？ gáy dím gin

Where will we meet?
喺邊度見？ hái bìn·do gin

Let's meet at (eight) o'clock.
我地喺(八)點鐘見。 ngáw·day hái (baat) dím·jùng gin

Let's meet at the entrance.
我地喺門口見。 ngáw·day hái mùn·háu gin

I (don't) know where that is.
我 (唔) 知道嗰度 ngáw (ǹg·)jì·do gáw·do
喺邊度。 hái bìn·do

How do I get there?
嗰度點樣去㗎？ gáw·do dím·yéung heui gaa

Is that a safe area?
嗰度安唔安全 gáw·do ngàwn·ǹg·ngàwn·chèwn
㗎？ gaa

I'll pick you up.
我嚟接你。 ngáw láy jip láy

Are you ready?
準備好未？ jéun·bay hó may

I'm ready.
準備好了。 　　　　　　　jéun·bay hó la

I'll be coming later.
我會遲啲嚟。 　　　　　　ngáw wuí chì dì làay

Where will you be?
你會喺邊度？ 　　　　　　láay wuí hái bìn·dọ

If I'm not there by (nine), don't wait for me.
如果(九)點鐘我 　　　yèw·gáw (gáu) dím·jùng ngáw
仲未到，就唔好等我。 jung·may do jau ǹg·hó dáng ngáw

I'll see you then.
到時見。 　　　　　　　　do·sì gin

See you later.
遲啲見。 　　　　　　　　chi dì gin

See you tomorrow.
遲听日見。 　　　　　　　chi tìng·yat gin

Sorry I'm late.
唔好意思，嚟晚啦。 ǹg·hó yi·sì làay chì·jáw

Never mind.
唔緊要。 　　　　　　　　ǹg·gán·yiu

drugs

毒品

Do you want to have a smoke?
想唔想食枝煙啊？ séung·ǹg·séung sik jì yìn aa

Do you have a light?
有冇火啊？ 　　　　　　yáu·mó fáw aa

I take ... occasionally.
我偶然食…… 　　　　ngáw ngáu·yìn sik ...

I'm high.
我好 high。 　　　　　　ngáw hó hàai

I don't feel like taking anything.
我唔想食。 　　　　　　ngáw·ǹg séung sik

I don't take drugs.
我唔吸毒。 　　　　　　ngáw·ǹg kàp·duk

asking someone out

約人出去玩

Would you like to do something (tomorrow)?
(听日) 想唔想
出去玩啊？
(tìng·yat) séung·ǹg·séung
chèut·heui wáan aa

Yes, I'd love to.
好啊，好想去。
hó aa hó séung heui

I'm busy.
對唔住，我有事。
deui·ǹg·jew ngáw yáu si

Where would you like to go (tonight)?
(今晚) 想去
邊度玩？
(gàm·máan) séung heui
bìn·do wáan

pick-up lines

調情

Would you like a drink?
你想飲啲乜嘢呢？
láy séung yám dì màt·yé lè

You look like someone I know.
你好似我識得
嗰個人。
láy hó·chí ngáw sìk·dàk
gáw gaw yàn

You're a fantastic dancer.
你跳得真係好。
láy tiu dàk jàn·hai hó

Can I ...?
我可唔可以
……呀？
ngáw háw·ǹg·háw·yí
... aa

dance with you 同你跳個舞 tùng láy tiu gaw mó
sit here 陪你坐下 pęui láy chǎw hǎa
take you home 送你返屋企 sung láy fàan ngùk·káy

local talk		
He/She is (a) ...	佢真係個……	kéui jàn·hai gaw ...
bastard	野仔	yé·jái
bitch	姣婆	hàau·pò
cute	可愛	háw·ngoy
hot	熱情	yit·chìng

What a babe.
真係可愛！ jàn·hai háw·ngoy

He/She gets around.
佢周圍鬼混。 kéui jàu·wài gwái·wan

rejections

俾人拒絕

No, thank you.
唔好啦，下次先啦。 ǹg hó laa haa·chi sìn làa

I'd rather not.
我唔想。 ngáw ǹg séung

I'm here with my girlfriend/boyfriend.
我同男(女) ngáw tùng làam (léui)
朋友一起嚟嘅。 pàng·yáu yàt·chài lài ge

Excuse me, I have to go now.
對唔住，我而家 deui·ǹg·jew ngáw yì·gàa
要走啦。 yiu jáu laa

Sorry, I am not interested in talking to you.
對唔住，我冇興趣 deui·ǹg·jew ngáw mó hing·cheui
同你傾偈。 tùng láy kìng·gái

Leave me alone!
唔好煩我！ ǹg hó fàan ngáw

Go away!
走開！ jáu·hòy

Piss off!
仆街啦去！ pùk·gàai laa heui

getting closer

I like you very much.
我好鍾意你。 ngáw hó jùng·yi láy

You're great.
你真係勁。 láy jàn·hai ging

Let's kiss!
錫啖先! sek daam sìn

Do you want to come inside for a while?
想唔想入嚟 séung·ǹg·séung yap lài
坐下啊? cháw háa aa

Do you want a massage?
你鍾唔鍾意俾 láy jùng·ǹg· jùng·yi báy
人按摩啊? yàn ngawn·mò aa

sex

Kiss me!
錫我啦! sek ngáw làa

I want you.
我要你。 ngáw yiu láy

I want to make love to you.
我要同你上床。 ngáw yiu tung láy séung·chàwng

Let's go to bed.
我地上床 ngáw·day séung·chàwng
好唔好啊。 hó·ǹg·hó aa

Touch me here.
摸我呢度。 máw ngáw lày·do

Do you like this?
敢樣鍾唔鍾意啊? gám·yéung jùng·ǹg· jùng·yi aa

Whisper these endearments into the ear of your 'treasure':

heart and liver	心肝	sàm·gàwn
root-of-my-life	命根	meng·gàn
treasure	寶貝	bó·bui

I (don't) like that.
(唔)鍾意敢樣。　　(ǹg·)jùng·yi gám·yéung

I think we should stop now.
夠啦。　　gàu laa

Do you have a (condom)?
你帶咗 (避孕套)　　láy daai·jáw (bay·yan·to)
未啊？　　may aa

Let's use a (condom).
用 (避孕套) 啦。　　yung (bay·yan·to) làa

I won't do it without protection.
冇保護，我唔做。　　mó bó·wu ngáw ǹg jo

What's this?
呢個係乜嘢嚟㗎？　　lày·gaw hai màt·yé lày gaa

It's my first time.
係我嘅第一次。　　hai ngáw ge dai yàt chi

Oh yeah!	好嘢！	hó yé
That's great.	真係勁。	jàn hai ging
Easy tiger!	慢啲嚟！	maan dì lài

faster	快點	faai dì
harder	出力	chèut·lik
slower	慢點	maan·dì
softer	輕點	hèng·dì

Don't worry, I'll do it myself.
無嘢，我自己嚟。　　mó yé ngáw ji·gáy lài

It helps to have a sense of humour.
笑下輕鬆下，幾好啊。　　siu háa hìng·sùng háa gáy hó àa

Do you know what they say about people with big feet?

你知唔知佢地點講　　　　láy jì·n̄g·jì kéui·day dím gáwng
啲大腳的人啊？　　　　　dì daai geuk ge yàn aa

Big shoes.

大鞋。　　　　　　　　　daai hàai

That was …	頭先真係……	tàu·sìn jàn hai …
amazing	不可思議	bàt háw sì·yí
weird	有啲怪	yáu dì gwaai
wild	好玩	hó wáan

Can I …?	我可唔可以……呀？	ngáw háw·n̄g·háw·yí … aa
call you	打電話俾你	dáa din·wáa báy láy
see you	見你	gin láy
stay over	喺呢度過夜	hái lày·do gaw·ye

love

愛情

Will you go out with me?

你想唔想同　　　　　　　láy séung·n̄g· séung tùng
我拍拖啊？　　　　　　　ngáw paak·tàw aa

I think we're good together.

我覺得我地　　　　　　　ngáw gwak·dàk ngáw·day
幾配。　　　　　　　　　gáy pui

I love you.

我愛你。　　　　　　　　ngáw ngoy láy

---

it's not you, it's them

Faced with a cheating lover? Console yourself with this proverb. It implies that 'a leopard never changes its spots'.

When a dog climbs the roof it takes its usual path.
狗上瓦坑有條路。　　gáu séung ngáak hàang yáu tìu lo

problems

Are you seeing someone else?
你係唔係另外
有咗朋友啊？

láy hai·ǹg·hai ling·ngoy
yáu·jáw pàng·yáu aa

She/He is just a friend.
佢祇係普通朋友。

kéui jí·hai pó·tùng pàng·yáu

You're just using me for sex.
你祇係用我嚟滿足
自己嘅情慾。

láy jí·hai yung ngáw lài mún·zùk
ji·gái ge chìng·yuk

I never want to see you again.
我唔想再見到你。

ngáw ǹg·séung joy gin dó láy

I don't think it's working out.
我地話不投機。

ngáw·day waa·bàt·tàu·gày

We'll work it out.
我地有辦法
搞掂。

ngáw·day yáu baan·faat
gáau·dim

leaving

I'm leaving soon.
我就走啦。

ngáw jàu jáu laa

I have to leave tomorrow.
我听日就走。

ngáw tìng·yat jau jáu

I'll never forget you.
我會永遠記得你。

ngáw wuí wíng·yéwn gay·dàk láy

I'll ...   我會⋯⋯   ngáw wuí ...
  come and visit you   嚟搵你   làv wán láy
  keep in touch   保持聯系   bó·chì lèwn·hai
  miss you   想你   séung láy

religion

信仰

Are you religious?
你信教㗎？　　　　láy seun gaau gàa

I'm not religious.
我唔信教。　　　　ngáw ǹg seun gaau

I (don't) believe in ... 我(唔)信…… ngáw (ǹg) seun ...

astrology	星相	sìng·seung
fate	命	meng
feng shui	風水	fùng·séui
fortune telling	算命	sewn·meng
God	上帝	seung·dai

I'm ... 我信…… ngáw seun ...

agnostic	不可知論	bàt·háw·ji·leun
atheist	冇神論	mò·sàn·leun
Buddhist	佛教	fat·gaau
Catholic	天主教	tìn·jéw·gaau
Christian	基督教	gày·dùk·gaau
Hindu	印度教	yan·do·gaau
Jewish	猶太教	yàu·taai·gaau
Muslim	伊斯蘭教	yì·sì·làan·gaau

Confucianism	儒教	yèw·gaau
Taoism	道教	do·gaau

Can I ... here?	我可唔可以 喺呢度……啊？	ngáw háw·ǹg·háw·yí hái lày·do ... aa
Where can I ...?	我喺邊度 可以……？	ngáw hái bìn·do háw·yí ...
attend a service	做禮拜	jo lái·baai
pray	祈禱	kày·tó
meditate	靜坐	jing·jaw

cultural differences

文化差异

Is this a local or national custom?
呢啲係唔係本地或者　　lày·di hai·ǹg·hai bún·day waak·jé
係呢個國家嘅風俗　　　　lày·gaw gawk·gàa ge fùng·zuk
嚟㗎？　　　　　　　　　lài gaa

I don't want to offend you.
我唔想得罪你。　　　　　ngáw ǹg séung dàk·jeui láy

I'm not used to this.
我冇呢個習慣。　　　　　ngáw mó lày gaw jaap·gwaan

I'd rather not join in.
我最好唔參加。　　　　　ngáw jeui hó ǹg chàam·gaa

I'll try it.
我會試下。　　　　　　　ngáw wuí si háa

I didn't mean to do anything wrong.
我唔想搞錯。　　　　　　ngáw ǹg·séung gáau·chaw

I'm sorry, it's against my ...	對唔住，敢 樣做違背 我嘅……	deui·ǹg·jew gám· yéung jo wài·bui ngáw ge ...
beliefs	信仰	seun·yéung
religion	宗教	jùng·gaau

This is ...	有啲……	yáu dì ...
different	與眾不同	yéw jung bàt tùng
fun	好玩	hó·wáan
interesting	得意	dàk·yi

When's the museum open?
博物館幾點開門？ bawk·màt·gún gáy·dím hòy·mùn

What kind of art are you interested in?
你鍾意邊類型嘅 láy jùng·yi bìn leui·yìng ge
藝術？ ngai·seut

What's in the collection?
呢度收藏咗啲乜嘢？ lày·do sàu·chàwng·jáw dì màt·yé

What do you think of …?
你覺得……點樣？ láy gawk·dàk … dím·yéung

It's a/an … exhibition.
係個……展覽。 hai gaw …. jín·láam

I'm interested in …
我對……有興趣。 ngáw deui … yáu hing·cheui

I like the works of …
我鍾意……嘅作品。 ngáw jùng·yi … ge jawk·bán

It reminds me of …
令我棯起…… ling ngáw lám·háy …

contemporary Chinese art	當代中國藝術	dàwng·doy jùng·gawk ngai·seut
contemporary Hong Kong art	當代香港藝術	dàwng·doy hèung·gáwng ngai·seut
cultural revolution	文化大革命	màn·faa·daai·gaap·ming
traditional Chinese art	傳統中國藝術	chewn·túng jùng·gawk ngai·seut
traditional Chinese painting	傳統國畫	chewn·túng gawk·wáa

... art	……藝術	... ngai·seut
comic	漫畫	maan·wáa
graphic	版畫	báan·wáa
impressionist	印象派	yan·jeung·paai
modern	現代派	yin·doy·paai
performance	表演	biú·yín
postmodern	後現代	hau·yin·doy
realist	現實主義	yin·sat·jéw·yi
Renaissance	文藝復興	man·ngai fuk·hìng
Western	西方	sài·fàwng

architecture	建築	gin·jùk
artwork	藝術品	ngai·seut·bán
bronze	青銅器	chìng·tùng·hày
calligraphy	書法	sèw·faat
ceramics	陶瓷	tò·chì
curator	館長	gún·jéung
design n	設計	chit·gai
dynasty	朝代	chiù·doy
etching	刻板	hàak·báan
exhibit	展出	jín·chèut
exhibition hall	展覽館	jín·láam·gún
installation	裝置	jàwng·ji
jade	玉器	yuk·hay
opening	開幕	hòy·mawk
painter	畫家	wáa·gàa
painting (the art)	畫畫	wáa·wáa
period	時期	si·kày
permanent collection	永久藏品	wíng·gáu chàwng·bán
print n	印刷	yan·chaat
scroll	書畫	sèw·wáa
sculptor	雕塑家	diù·sawk·gàa
sculpture	雕塑	diù·sawk
statue	塑像	sawk·jeung
studio	工作室	gùng·jawk·sàt
style n	風格	fùng·gaak
technique	方法	fàwng·faat
woodblock print	木版畫	muk·báan·wáa

sporting interests

體育活動

In Cantonese you can say you 'play' a sport by using the verb wáan 玩, which suggests that you simply have a playful interest in it. If you want to say you play a particular sport seriously, use a specific verb such as dáa 打 (hit), tek 踢 (kick), lin 練 (rigorously train) etc.

What sport do you play?
你鍾意玩邊種　　　　　　láy jùng·yi wáan bìn·júng
體育活動？　　　　　　　tái·yuk wut·dung

I play/do …
我鍾意玩⋯⋯　　　　　　ngáw jùng·yi wáan …

I follow …
我鍾意睇⋯⋯　　　　　　ngáw jùng·yi tái …

sports that take dáa 打 (hit)

I play/do …	我打⋯⋯	ngáw dáa …
badminton	羽毛球	yéw·mò·kàu
basketball	籃球	làam·kàu
handball	手球	sáu·kàu
hockey	曲棍球	kùk·gun·kàu
t'ai chi	太極拳	taai·gik·kèwn
tennis	網球	máwng·kàu
water polo	水球	séui·kàu

sports that take tek 踢 (kick)

I play/do …	我踢……	ngáw tek …
football (soccer)	足球	zùk·kàu
American Football	美式足球	máy·sìk zùk·kàu
Australian Rules Football	澳式足球	ngo·sìk zùk·kàu
rugby	橄欖球	gaam·láam·kàu

sports that take lin 練 (train)

I …	我練……	ngáw lin …
row	划船	wàa·sèwn
sail	帆船	fàan·sèwn
swim	游泳	yàu·wing

I play/do …	我練……	ngáw lin …
archery	射箭	se·jin
athletics (track & field)	田徑	tìn·ging
fencing	劍擊	gim·gìk
karate	空手道	hùng·sáu·do
martial arts	武術	mó·seut
long distance running	長跑	chèung·páau

I …	我……	ngáw …
cycle	踩單車	cháai dàan·chè
do gymnastics	做體操	jo tái·chò
play (beach) volleyball	(沙灘)排球	(sàa·tàan) pàai·kàu
run	跑步	páau·bo
walk	散步	saan·bo

Do you like (table tennis)?
你鍾唔鍾意打
(乒乓波)啊？

láy jùng·ǹg·jùng·yi dáa
(bìng·bàm·bàw) aa

Yes, very much.	好鍾意。	hó jùng·yi
Not really.	唔係好鍾意。	ǹg·hai hó jùng·yi
I like watching it.	我鍾意睇。	ngáw jùng·yi tái

Who's your favourite ...?	你最鍾意嘅…… 係邊個？	láy jeui jùng·yi ge ... hai bìn·gaw
sportsperson	球星	kàu·sìng
team	球隊	kàu·déui

going to a game

睇波

Would you like to go to a game?
你想唔想跟
我去睇波啊？

láy séung·ǹg·séung gàn
ngáw heui tái·bàw aa

Who are you supporting?
你捧邊隊？

láy púng bìn deui

Who's ...?	邊個……？	bìn·gaw ...
playing	喺度打緊	hái·do dáa·gán
winning	贏緊	yèng·gán

That was a ... game!	呢場賽打 得真係……！	làv chèung choy dáa dàk jàn·hai ...
bad	喳	jáa
boring	冇癮	mò·yán
great	精彩	jìng·chóy

scoring		
What's the score?	幾比幾？	gáy báy gáy
draw/even	平手	pìng·sáu
love (zero)	零	lìng
match-point	賽點	choy·dím

sports talk		
Come on!	加油！	gàa·yáu
What a hit!	好波！	hó bàw
What a …!	……得好！	… dàk·hó
goal	射	se
kick	踢得好	tek
pass	傳得好	chèwn
performance	打得好	dáa

playing sport

打波

Do you want to play?
你想唔想玩啊？

láy séung·n̄g·séung wáan aa

Can I join in?
可唔可以侵埋
我玩？

háw·n̄g·háw·yí chàm·màai
ngáw wáan

That would be great.
好。

hó

I can't.
唔得。

n̄g·dàk

I have an injury.
我傷咗。

ngáw sèung·jáw

Your point.
你得分。

láy dàk fàn

My point.
我得分。

ngáw dàk fàn

Kick it to me!
踢俾我！

tek báy ngáw

Pass it to me!
傳俾我！

chèwn báy ngáw

You're a good player.
你打得好好。

láy dáa dàk hó·hó

Where's a good place to …?	有乜好地方可以…… ?	yáu màt hó day·fàwng háw·yí …
fish	釣魚	diu·yéw
go horse riding	騎馬	kè·máa
run	跑步	páau·bo
ski	滑雪	waat·sewt
snorkel	潛水	chìm·séui
surf	滑浪	waat·lawng
Where's the nearest …?	附近邊度有…… ?	fu·gan bìn·do yáu …
golf course	高爾夫球場	gò·yí·fù·kàu·chèung
gym	健美中心	gin·máy jùng·sàm
swimming pool	游泳池	yàu·wìng·chì
tennis court	網球場	máwng·kàu·chèung

Do I have to be a member to attend?
淨係對會員
開放㗎？　　　　jing·hai deui wuí·yèwn
　　　　　　　　hòy·fawng gàa

Is there a women-only session?
有冇全女班㗎？　yáu·mó chèwn·léui·bàan gaa

Where are the changing rooms?
更衣室喺邊度？　gàng·yì·sàt hái bìn·do

Thanks for the game.
多謝，打得好。　dàw·je dáa dàk hó

What's the charge per …?	每……幾多錢？	múi … gáy·dàw chín
day	日	yat
game	場	chèung
hour	個鐘	gaw jùng
visit	次	chi
Can I hire a …?	我可唔可以租……啊？	ngáw háw·ǹg·háw·yí jò … aa
ball	個波	gaw bàw
bicycle	部單車	bo dàan·chè
court	個場	gaw chèung
racquet	副球拍	fu kàu·páak

badminton, squash, table tennis & tennis

羽毛球、壁球、乒乓球與網球

I'd like to play ...	我想打……	ngáw séung dáa ...
badminton	羽毛球	yéw·mò·kàu
squash	壁球	bìk·kàu
table tennis	乒乓波	bìng·bàm·bàw
tennis	網球	máwng·kàu

Can I book a ...?	我想租……。	ngáw séung jò ...
badminton	個	gaw
court	羽毛球場	yéw·mò·kàu·chèung
squash court	個	gaw
	壁球場	bìk·kàu·chèung
table	張台	jèung tóy

Can we play at night?
今晚打唔打啊？ gàm·máan dáa·ǹg·dáa aa

I need my racquet restrung.
我個球拍要換綫。 ngáw gaw kàu·páak yiu wǔn·sin

badminton racquet	羽毛球球拍	yéw·mò·kàu kàu·páak
bat	球拍	kàu·páak
net	網	máwng
serve v	發球	faat·kàu
shuttlecock	羽毛球	yéw·mò·kàu
squash racquet	壁球球拍	bik·kàu kàu·páak
table tennis ball	乒乓波	bìng·bàm·bàw
tennis court	網球場	máwng·kàu·chèung
tennis racquet	網球球拍	máwng·kàu kàu·páak

cycling

單車

Where does the race …?	比賽……？	báy·choy …
finish	喺邊度結束	hái bìn·do git·chùk
pass through	路線經過	lo·sin gìng·gaw
	邊度	bìn·do

Who's winning?
邊個領先？　　　　bìn·gaw líng·sìn

How many kilometres is today's leg?
今日嘅中途站　　　gàm·yat ge jùng·to·jaam
有幾遠？　　　　　yáu gáy yéwn

How many kilometres is today's race?
今日嘅比賽有幾遠？　gàm·yat ge báy·choy yáu gáy yéwn

My favourite cyclist is …
我最鍾意嘅　　　　ngáw jeui jùng·yi ge
單車手係……　　　dàan·chè sáu hai …

(yellow) jersey	(黃色)衫	(wàwng·sìk)·sàam
leg (in race)	中途站	jùng·to·jaam
stage winner	分段第一名	fàn·dewn dai·yàt mìng
time trial	計時	gai·sì
winner	第一名	dai·yàt mìng

For cycling terminology, see **transport**, page 47.

extreme sports

刺激運動

I'd like to go …	我想去……	ngáw séung heui …
do something exciting	搵刺激	wán chi·gìk
rock climbing	攀岩	pàan·ngàam
skydiving	跳傘	tiu·saan
snowboarding	滑雪	waat·sewt

The rope will hold, won't it?
條繩頂頂唔頂得順喋？　　　tiu síng díng·ǹg·díng·dàk·sẹun gaa

This is insane!
癲嘅！　　　　　　　　　dìn ge

golf

高爾夫球

How much …?	打……幾多錢？	dáa … gáy·dàw chín
for a round	一場	yàt chèung
to play 9 holes	九球洞	gáu kàu·dụng
to play 18 holes	十八球洞	sạp·baat kàu·dụng

Can I hire golf clubs?
有冇球棒租啊？　　　　　yáu·mó kàu·páang jò aa

What's the dress code?
要著乜嘢衫啊？　　　　　yiu jewk màt·yé sàam aa

Do I need golf shoes?
需唔需要　　　　　　　　sẹui·ǹg·sẹui·yiu
高爾夫球鞋啊？　　　　　gò·yí·fù·kàu·hàai aa

Do I need to hire a golf caddie?
需唔需要請個　　　　　　sẹui·ǹg·sẹui·yiu chéng gaw
球童啊？　　　　　　　　kàu·tùng aa

bunker	沙坑	sàa·hàang
flag	旗	kày
golf cart	球車	kàu·chè
golf course	高爾夫球場	gò·yí·fù·kàu·chèung
golf ball	高爾夫球	gò·yí·fù·kàu
green	草地	chó·dạy
hole	球洞	kàu·dụng
hole in one	一棒入洞	yàt páang yạp dụng
iron n	鐵杆	tit·gàwn
putter	推杆	tèui·gàwn
tee	球座	kàu·jaw
wood	木杆	mụk·gàwn

soccer/football

足球

Who plays for (làam-wáa)?
(南華)有邊啲
球星？

(làam·wáa) yáu bìn dì
kàu·sìng

He plays well.
佢踢得好勁。

kéui tek dàk hó gìng

He played brilliantly in the match against (Italy).
佢對(意大利)
嗰場踢得好
精彩。

kéui deui (yi·dàai·lày)
gáw chèung tek dàk hó
jìng·chóy

Which team is at the top of the league?
邊隊排名第一？

bìn deui pàai·mìng dai·yàt

What a great team!
呢隊真勁！

lày deui jàn gìng

What a terrible team!
呢隊真嗱！

lày deui jàn jáa

ball	波	bàw
coach n	教練	gaau·lìn
corner	角球	gawk·kàu
expulsion	罰出場	fat chèut·chèung
fan	球迷	kàu·mài
foul n	犯規	faan·kwài
free kick	任意球	yam·yi·kàu
goal	入門	yap·mùn
goalkeeper	守門	sáu·mùn
manager	經理	gìng·láy
offside	越位	yewt·wai
penalty	點球	dím·kàu
player	球員	kàu·yèwn
red card	紅牌	hùng·páai
referee	裁判	chòy·pun
striker	前鋒	chìn·fùng
throw in n	邊球	bìn·kàu
yellow card	黃牌	wàwng·páai

水上運動

Can I book a lesson?
我可唔可以　　　　　ngáw háw·ṇg·háw·yí
報名上堂？　　　　　bo·méng séung·tàwng

Are there any water hazards?
水底有冇危險？　　　séui·dái yáu·mó ngài·hím

Are there any …?	有冇……㗎？	yáu·mó … gaa
reefs	礁石	jiù·sek
rips	激流	gìk·làu

Can I hire (a) …?	我可唔可以 租……	ngáw háw·ṇg·háw·yí jò …
boat	隻船	jek sèwn
canoe	隻獨木舟	jek duk·muk·jàu
life jacket	件救生衣	gin gàu·sàng·yì
snorkelling gear	套潛水 裝備	to chìm·séui jàwng·bay
water-skis	塊 滑水板	faai waat·séui·báan
wetsuit	件潛水衣	gin chìm·séui·yì
sailboard	隻 滑浪風帆	jek waat·lawng·fùng·fàan

guide	導遊	do·yáu
motorboat	摩托艇	màw·tawk·téng
oars	船槳	sèwn·jéung
sailboarding	滑浪風帆	waat·lawng·fùng·fàan
sailing boat	帆船	fàan·sèwn
surfboard	滑浪板	waat·lawng·báan
surfing	滑浪	waat·lawng
wave n	浪	lawng

hiking

遠足

Where can I ...?	邊度可以……?	bìn·do háw·yí ...
buy supplies	買到預備品	máai·dó yew·bay·bún
find someone who knows this area	揾到識路嘅人	wan·dó sìk·lo ge yàn
get a map	買地圖	máai day·tò
hire hiking gear	租遠足旅行裝備	jò yéwn·jùk léui·hàng jàwng·bay

How ...?	有幾	yáu gáy
high is the climb	爬山……高?	pàa·sàan ... gò
long is the trail	步行……遠?	bo·hàng ... yéwn

Is it safe?
安唔安全㗎？
ngàwn·ǹg·ngàwn·chèwn gaa

Do we need a guide?
需唔需要嚮導啊？
sèui·ǹg·sèui·yiu héung·do aa

Are there guided treks?
有冇嚮導帶嘅
遠足旅行團啊？
yáu·mó héung·do daai ge
yéwn·jùk léui·hàng tèwn aa

Is there a hut?
有冇屋住㗎？
yáu·mó ngùk jew gaa

When does it get dark?
幾時天黑？
gáy·sì tìn·hàak

According to Chinese astrology, you can get traits from the animal sign under which you were born. For example, people born under the sign of the ox are believed to be as strong and resilient as this beast of burden.

The year 2000 was the year of the dragon and each successive year is assigned a new animal according to the order shown below:

dragon	龍	lùng
snake	蛇	sè
horse	馬	máa
sheep	羊	yèung
monkey	猴	hàu
rooster	雞	gài
dog	狗	gáu
pig	豬	jèw
rat	鼠	shéw
ox	牛	ngau4
tiger	虎	fú
rabbit	兔	to

Do we need to take ...?	需唔需要帶……啊？	sèui·ǹg·sèui·yiu daai ... aa
bedding	被	páy
food	食嘢	sik·yé
water	飲用水	yám·yung·séui

Is the track ...?	路……㗎？	lo ... gaa
long	長	chèung
open	通唔通	tùng·ǹg·tùng
scenic	風景好唔好	fùng·gíng hó·ǹg·hó
well-marked	好唔好揾	hó·ǹg·hó wán

Which is the ... route?	邊條路最……？	bìn tiù lo jeui ...
easiest	易行	yi hàang
most interesting	過癮	gaw yán
shortest	短	déwn

Where can I find the …?	喺邊度可以 搵倒……？	hái bìn·do háw·yí wán dó …
camping ground	露營地點	lo·ying day·dím
nearest village	條村	tiù chèvn
showers	地方沖涼	day·fàwng chùng·lèung
toilets	廁所	chi·sáw

Where have you come from?
你喺邊度過嚟？　　　láy hái bìn·do gaw lài

How long did it take?
走咗幾耐？　　　jáu·jáw gáy loy

Does this path go to …?
呢條路去……㗎？　　lày tiù lo heui … gaa

Can I go through here?
我可唔可以喺呢度
穿過去㗎？　　ngáw háw·ng·háw·yí hái
　　　lày·do chèvn·gaw·heui gaa

Is the water OK to drink?
呢度啲水
可唔可以飲㗎？　　lày·do dì séui
　　　háw·ng·háw·yí yúm gaa

I'm lost.
我蕩失路。　　　ngáw dawng·sàt lo

lookout	觀景臺	gùn·gíng·tòy
track (path)	山路	sàan·lo
sign n	招牌	jiù·pàai

---

listen for …

小心暗流。　　　**Be careful of the undertow!**
　siú·sàm ngam·làu

危險。　　　**It's dangerous!**
　ngai·hím

outdoors

157

beach

沙灘

Where's the ...	......沙灘	... sàa·tàan
beach?	點樣去？	dím·yéung heui
best	最好嘅	jeui·hó ge
nearest	最近嘅	jeui·kán ge
public	公共嘅	gùng·gung ge

Is it safe to swim here?
呢度游水
安唔安全㗎？
lày·do yàu·séui
ngàwn·ǹg·ngàwn·chèwn gaa

Is the water polluted?
啲水有冇污染？
dì séui yáu·mó wù·yím

What time is high tide?
幾點鐘漲潮？
gáy dím·jùng jeung chiù

What time is low tide?
幾點鐘退潮？
gáy dím·jùng teui chiù

Do we have to pay?
駛唔駛俾錢㗎？
sái·ǹg·sái báy·chín gaa

hat	帽	mó
towel	毛巾	mò·gàn
sand	沙	sàa
swimsuit	游泳衣	yàu·wìng·yì
umbrella	雨遮	yéw·jè

signs

不准跳水	bàt·jéun tiu·séui	**No Diving**
不准游泳	bàt·jéun yàu·wìng	**No Swimming**

weather

天氣

What's the weather like?
天氣點樣？   tìn·hay dím·yéung

What will the weather be like tomorrow?
听日天氣會點？   tìng·yat tìn·hay wuí dím

It's ...	天氣……	tìn·hay ...
cloudy	多雲	dàw·wan
cold	凍	dung
fine	好	hó
freezing	好凍	hó dung
hot	熱	yit
raining	落雨	lawk yéw
snowing	落雪	lawk sewt
sunny	晴朗	ching·láwng
warm	暖	léwn
windy	翻風	fàan·fùng

Where can I buy ...?	喺邊度可以 買到……？	hái bìn·do háw·yí máai·dó ...
a rain jacket	雨衣	yéw·yì
an umbrella	雨遮	yéw·jè

dry season	旱季	háwn·gwai
monsoon season	颱風季節	toy·fùng gwai·jit
wet season	雨季	yéw·gwai

local plants & animals

The *bauhinia blakeana* flower was adopted as the emblem of Hong Kong in 1965. It has featured in the flag for the Special Administrative Region of China (SAR) since 1997.

bauhinia blakeana	洋紫荊	yèung·jí·gìng
crane	鶴	háwk
narcissus	水仙	séui·sìn
panda	熊貓	hùng·màau
peony (flower)	牡丹	máau·dàan
scarlet kafirlily	君子蘭	gùn·jí·làan

outdoors

159

flora & fauna

動物與植物

What … is that?	嗰種係乜嘢……？	gáw júng hai màt·yé …
animal	動物	dung·mat
flower	花	fàa
plant	植物	jik·mat
tree	樹	sew

Is it …?	係唔係……嘅？	hai·ng·hai … ge
dangerous	危險	ngài·hím
endangered	瀕臨滅絕	pàn·làm mit·jewt
poisonous	有毒	yáu·duk
protected	受保護	sau bó·wu

What's it used for?
用嚟做乜嘢？ | yung lài jo màt·yé

Can you eat the fruit?
佢嘅果實 | kéui ge gwáw·sat
可唔可以食啊？ | háw·ng·háw·yí sik aa

---

star-crossed lovers

A Chinese legend tells the starry romance of ngàu long 牛郎 (literally 'the Cowboy', known to us as Altair, the 11th brightest star in the night sky), and jìk néui 織女 ('the Spinster's Maid', our star Vega). The two were permitted to be together only on the 7th evening of the 7th lunar month when joyful birds fly across the ngàn hò 銀河 (Milky Way) and form a bridge so that the lovers can meet.

Here are some other stellar bodies you can appreciate:

comet	so báa sìng	掃把星
Earth	dei kàu	地球
Moon	yuet	月
planet	hàng sìng	行星
star	sìng	星
Sun	taai yèung	太陽
universe	yéw jau	宇宙

basics

開頭

breakfast	早餐	jó·chàan
lunch	午餐	ńg·chàan
dinner	晚飯	máan·faan
snack	零食	lìng·sik
afternoon tea	下午茶	haa·ńg·chaa
late night snack	宵夜	siù·yé
eat v	食	sik
drink v	飲	yám
I'd like …	我想要……	ngáw séung yiu …
I'm starving!	餓死我囉！	ngaw sái ngáw law

out to eat

When you're at the table, wait until your host picks up his or her chopsticks before you begin eating. Always choose the dish closest to you – never reach over the table – or ask people to pass your dish of choice to you. If you're at a more casual gathering, the host may just tell everyone to help themselves, which is an indication to begin eating.

Help yourselves!

自己嚟，唔好客氣！ jì·gáy lài ǹg·sái haak·hay

Could you please pass me that dish?

唔該你遞個碟俾我。 ǹg·gòy láy dai gaw díp báy ngáw

breakfast

What's a typical breakfast?

早餐一般食嘢？ jó·chàan yàt bùn sik màt·yé

dim sum	點心	dím·sàm
fried bread stick	油炸鬼	yáu·jàa·gwái
fried rice	炒飯	cháw·faan
rice noodles	米粉	mái·fán
rice noodles with shrimp	蝦腸	hàa·chéung
rice noodles with beef	牛腸	ngàu·chéung
rice porridge	粥	jùk
rice porridge with beef	牛肉粥	ngàu·yuk·jùk
sesame seed pancake	薄餅	bawk·béng
steamed bun	蒸包	jìng bàau
soybean milk	豆漿	dau·jèung

For other breakfast items, see **self-catering**, page 175, and the **culinary reader**, page 181.

finding a place to eat

揾嘢食

Where would you go for (a) …?	你會去邊度……？	láy wuí heui bìn·do …
afternoon tea	飲下午茶	yám haa·ńg·chàa
banquet	食大餐	sik daai chàan
business lunch	食晏	sik ngaan
celebration	慶功宴	hing·gùng·yin
cheap meal	食平嘢	sik pèng·yé
local specialities	地方小食	day·fàwng siú·sik
yum cha	飲茶	yám·chàa

Can you recommend a ...?	有乜好…… 介紹？	yáu màt hó … gaai·xiu
bar	酒吧	jáu·bàa
café	咖啡屋	gaa·fè·ngùk
canteen	快餐廳	faai·chàan·tèng
cooked food stall	熟食檔	suk·sìk·dawng
floating restaurant	海鮮舫	hóy·sìn·fáwng
food court	美食 廣場	máy·sìk gwáwng·chèung
restaurant	茶樓	chàa·làu
street vendor	街頭小食	gàai·tàu siú·sìk
snack shop	零食店	lìng·sìk·dim
speakeasy (café with booths)	地下酒吧	day·haa jáu·bàa
seafood restaurant	海鮮酒家	hóy·sìn jáu·gàa
tea house	茶館	chàa·gún
Western-style restaurant	西餐廳	sài chàan·tèng

listen for ...

我地滿哂座啦。 ngáw·day mún·saai·jaw laa	We're full.
我地收咗鋪啦。 ngáw·day sàu·jáw po laa	We're closed.
等陣。 dáng·jan	One moment.
你想坐邊度？ láy séung cháw bìn·do	Where would you like to sit?
你想要乜嘢？ láy séung yiu màt·yé	What can I get for you?
上菜啦。 séung·choy laa	Here you go.
慢慢食。 máan·máan·sìk	Enjoy your meal.

eating out

I'd like to reserve a table for ...	我想訂張檯，……嘅。	ngáw séung deng jèung tóy ... ge
(two) people	(兩)位	(léung) wái
(eight) o'clock	(八)點鐘	(bàat) dím·jùng

I'd like a/the..., please.	唔該我要……	ǹg·gòy ngáw yiu ...
children's menu	個小童菜單	gaw siú·tung choy·dàan
drink list	酒料單	jáu·liú·dàan
half portion	半份	bun fan
menu (in English)	(英文)菜單	(yìng·màn) choy·dàan
table for (five)	(五位)嘅檯	(ńg wái) ge tóy
nonsmoking table	不吸煙嘅檯	bàt·kàp·yìn ge tóy
smoking table	吸煙嘅檯	kàp·yìn ge tóy
some toothpicks	啲牙簽	dì ngàa·chìm
set lunch	套餐	to·chàan

Are you still serving food?
仲有冇嘢食？ — jung yáu·mó yé·sik

How long is the wait?
要等幾耐？ — yiu dáng gáy·loy

restaurant

餐廳

What would you recommend?
有乜嘢好介紹？ — yáu màt·yé hó gaai·siu

What's in that dish?
呢道菜有啲乜嘢？ — lày do choy yáu dì màt·yé

I'll have that.
我點呢味。 — ngáw dím lày máy

Does it take long to prepare?
要等好耐㗎？ — yiu dáng hó loy gaa

Is it self-serve?
呢度係自助㗎？   lày do hai ji·jaw gaa

Is service included in the bill?
張單包唔包
服務費㗎？   jèung dàan bàau·ǹg·bàau
fuk·mo·fai gaa

Are these complimentary?
呢啲係唔係送嘅？   lày·dì hai·ǹg·hai sung ge

I'd like the menu.
我想要菜單。   ngáw séung yiu choy·dàan

I'd like …	我想食……	ngáw séung sik …
a local speciality	地方風味菜	day·fàwng fùng·may choy
a meal fit for a king	御菜	yew·choy
a sandwich	三文治	sàam·màn·ji
that dish	嗰個菜	gáw gaw choy
the chicken	雞	gài
the prawn dumpling	蝦餃	hàa·gáau

I'd like it with …	放多啲……	fawng dàw dì …
I'd like it without …	唔好放……	ǹg·hó fawng …
cheese	芝士	jì·sí
chilli (sauce)	辣椒(醬)	laat·jiù(·jeung)
dipping sauce	醬	jeung
garlic	蒜	sewn
MSG	味精	may·jìng
nuts	果仁	gwáw·yàn
oil	油	yàu
pepper	胡椒粉	wù·jiù·fán
salt	鹽	yìm
soy sauce	豉油	si·yàu
tomato sauce	茄汁	ké·jàp
vinegar	醋	cho

For additional items, see the **culinary reader**, page 181. For other specific meal requests, see **vegetarian & special meals**, page 179.

How do you eat with chopsticks?
你點樣用筷子食嘢?   láy dím·yéung yung faai·jí sik yé

I'd like a/the…, please.	唔該我要……	ǹg·gòy ngáw yiu …
bill	埋單	màai·dàan
cloth	抹布	maat·bo
(wine)glass	(酒)杯	(jáu) buì
serviette	餐巾	chàan·gàn

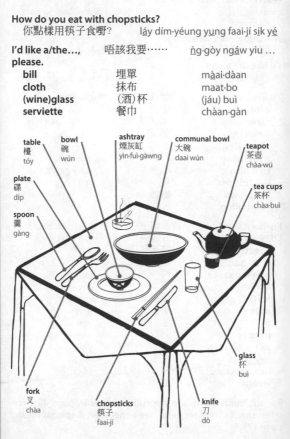

table
檯
tóy

bowl
碗
wún

ashtray
煙灰缸
yin·fui·gàwng

communal bowl
大碗
daai wún

teapot
茶壺
chàa·wú

plate
碟
díp

tea cups
茶杯
chàa·buì

spoon
羹
gàng

glass
杯
buì

fork
叉
chàa

chopsticks
筷子
faai·jí

knife
刀
dò

talking food

I love this dish.
我鐘意呢味菜。　　　　　　　ngáw jùng·yi lày·may choy

I love the local cuisine.
呢度嘅菜真係好食。　　　　　lày·do ge choy jàn·hai hó sik

That was delicious.
真好味。　　　　　　　　　　jàn hó·may

My compliments to the chef.
唔該幫我讚　　　　　　　　　ǹg·gòy bàwng ngáw jaan
下個廚師。　　　　　　　　　háa gaw chèw·sì

look for ...

涼盤	lèung·pún	**Appetisers**
點心	dím·sàm	**Dim Sum**
湯類	tàwng·leui	**Soups**
頭盤	tàu·pún	**Entrées**
主菜	jéw·choy	**Main Courses**
甜品	tìm·bán	**Desserts**
蔬菜	sàw·choy	**Vegetable Dishes**
海鮮	hóy·sìn	**Seafood**
沙律	sàa·léut	**Salads**
汽水	hay·séui	**Soft Drinks**
果汁	gwáw·jàp	**Fruit Juice**
烈酒	lit·jáu	**Spirits**
啤酒	bè·jáu	**Beers**
香檳	hèung·bàn	**Sparkling Wines**
加飯酒	gàa·faan·jáu	**Digestifs**
開胃酒	hòy·wai·jáu	**Apéritifs**
白葡萄酒	baak·pò·tò·jáu	**White Wines**
紅葡萄酒	hùng·pò·tò·jáu	**Red Wines**
甜葡萄酒	tìm·pò·tò·jáu	**Dessert Wines**

For more items you might see on a menu, see the **culinary reader**, page 181.

I'm full.	食飽啦。	sik·báau laa
This dish is ...	呢道菜……	lày do choy ...
(too) cold	（太）凍	(taai) dung
(too) spicy	（太）辣	(taai) laat
superb	真好味	jàn hó·may

methods of preparation

菜嘅做法

I'd like it ...	我要……嘅。	ngáw yiu ... ge
I don't want it ...	我唔要……嘅。	ngáw ǹg yiu ... ge
barbecued	燒烤	siu·hàau
boiled	煮	jéw
deep-fried	油炸	yàu·jàa
stir-fried	炒	cháau
grilled	鐵板燒	tit·báan·siu
medium	半生熟	bun·sàang·suk
rare	半生	bun·sàang
re-heated	熱番嘅	yit·fàan ge
steamed	蒸	jìng
well-done	熟	suk
with the dressing on the side	調料放一邊	tiù·liú fawng yàt bin
without ...	唔加……	ǹg·gàa ...

For more ways to prepare food, see the **dictionary**.

FOOD

168

Don't forget to check out what the suk·sik siú·fáan 熟食小販 (street vendors) have on offer.

What's this?

呢個係乜野嚟㗎？ lày·gaw hai màt·yé lày gaa

cow's organs	牛雜	ngàu·zaap
fish balls	魚蛋	yèw·dáan
rice noodles	豬腸粉	jèw·chèung·fán
roasted chestnuts	炒風栗	cháau fùng·léut

For more street food items, see the **culinary reader**.

in the bar

酒吧

Excuse me!	
唔該！	ǹg·gòy
I'm next.	
輪到我啦。	lèun·do ngáw laa
I'll have …	
我要……	ngáw yiu …
Same again, please.	
唔該再嚟一個。	ǹg·gòy joy lài yàt gaw
No ice, thanks.	
唔加冰。	ǹg gàa bìng
I'll buy you a drink.	
飲乜野我請。	yám màt·yé ngáw chéng

It's my round.
呢次我嚟請。
làytorch·chi ngáw lài chéng

What would you like?
你想飲乜嘢？
láy séung yám màt·yé

I don't drink alcohol.
我唔飲酒。
ngáw ǹg yám·jáu

How much is that?
幾多錢？
gáy·dàw chín

Do you serve meals here?
你地有啲乜嘢菜啊？
láy·day yáu dì màt·yé choy aa

nonalcoholic drinks

飲料

almond milk	杏仁奶露	hang·yàn láai·lo
fresh drinking yogurt	酸奶	sèwn·láai
lychee-flavoured soft drink	荔枝汁	lai·jì·jàp
orange juice	橙汁	cháang·jàp
soy milk	豆漿	dau·jèung
sour plum drink	酸梅湯	sèwn·mùi·tàwng
sugar cane juice	蔗汁	je·jàp
soft drink	汽水	hay·séui
... water	……水	...séui
boiled	滾	gún
sparkling mineral	礦泉氣	kawng·chèwn·hay
still mineral	礦泉	kawng·chèwn
cold	凍滾	dung·gún

(cup of) tea	（一杯）茶	(yàt buì) chàa
(cup of) coffee	（一杯）咖啡	(yàt buì) gaa·fè
... with (milk)	……加（牛奶）	... gàa (ngàu·láai)
... without (sugar)	……唔加（糖）	... ǹg gàa (tàwng)
black tea	紅茶	hùng·chàa
Chinese herbal tea	中國草藥茶	jùng·gawk chó·yewk·chàa
chrysanthemum tea	菊花茶	gùk·fàa·chàa
green tea	綠茶	luk·chàa
jasmine tea	花茶	fàa·chàa
oolong tea	烏龍茶	wù·lúng·chàa
... coffee	……咖啡	... gaa·fè
black	黑	hàak
decaffeinated	低咖啡因	dài·gaa·fè·yàn
iced	冰	bìng
strong	特濃	dak·lùng
weak	淡	táam
white	奶	láai
espresso	濃縮	lùng·sùk

food stores

If you're looking for a tasty treat, check out some of these places:

convenience store	便利店	bin·lay·dim
café	咖啡屋	gaa·fè·ngùk
fresh food market	街市	gàai·sí
greengrocer	果菜攤	gwáw·choy·tàan
noodle house	麵店	min·dim
snack shop	小食店	siú·sik·dim
street vendor	熟食小販	suk·sik siú·fáan
wonton stall	餛吞麵檔	wàn·tàn·min dawng
fish shop	檔	yéw·dim
butcher's shop	店	yuk·dim

alcoholic drinks

酒類

beer	啤酒	bè·jáu
brandy	白蘭地	baak·làan·dáy
champagne	香檳	hèung·bàn
Chinese-style vodka	白酒	baak·jáu
cocktail	雞尾酒	gài·máy·jáu
cognac	白蘭地	baak·làan·dáy
double distilled vodka	雙蒸	sèung·jìng
maotai (strong spirit)	茅臺	màau·tòy
rice wine	米酒	mái·jáu

a shot of ...	一杯……	yàt bùi ...
gin	氈酒	jìn·jáu
rum	冧酒	làm·jáu
tequila	特吉拉酒	dàk·gàt·làai·jáu
vodka	伏特加	fuk·dàk·gàa
whisky	威士忌	wài·si·gáy

a bottle of	一樽……	yàt jèun ...
... wine	葡萄酒	pò·tò·jáu
a glass of	一杯……	yàt bùi ...
... wine	葡萄酒	pò·tò·jáu
dessert	甜	tìm
red	紅	hung
rosé	粉紅	fán·hung
sparkling	香檳	hèung·bàn
white	白	baak

你食緊乜嘢？
láy sik·gán màt·yé — What are you having?

我杵你夠啦。
ngáw lám láy gau laa — I think you've had enough.

要刪門啦。
yiu sàan·mùn laa — Last orders.

a ... of beer	……啤酒	yàt ... bè·jáu
glass	杯	buì
pint	裝	jàwng
small bottle	細樽	sai jèun
large bottle	樽	jèun
jug	查	jàa

drinking up

飲酒

Cheers!
乾杯！
gàwn·buì

Down the hatch!
勝嘅！
sing ge

Dry your cup!
飲勝！
yúm·sing

This is hitting the spot.
好順喉。
hó seun·hàu

I feel fantastic!
好極！
hó gik

I think I've had one too many.
我係唔係飲多咗。
ngáw hai·ǹg·hai yám dàw jáw

I'm feeling drunk.
我有啲醉。
ngáw yáu dì jeui

I'm pissed.
我醉啦。
ngáw jeui laa

I feel ill.
我唔舒服。

ngáw ǹg sèw·fuk

Where's the toilet?
廁所喺邊度？

chi·sáw hái·bìn·do

I'm tired, I'd better go home.
我攰啦, 要返
屋企啦。

ngáw gui laa yiu fàan
ngùk·káy laa

Can you call a taxi for me?
你可唔可以幫我叫
架的士啊？

láy háw·ǹg·háw·yí bàwng
ngáw giu gaa dìk·sí a

I don't think you should drive.
你唔好開車啦。

láy ǹg hó hòy·chè laa

---

doctor's orders

You'll need a good reason for not drinking at a bar with your friends in China. If you don't want to join in, turn your glass upside down and explain to your companions that your doctor won't allow you to drink!

Sorry, my doctor won't let me drink.
對唔住, 醫生
唔准我飲酒。

deui·ǹg·jew yì·sàng
ǹg·jéun ngáw yám·jáu

buying food

買餸

What's the local speciality?
有乜嘢地方
特產？

yáu màt·yé day·fàwng
dak·cháan

What's that?
嗰啲係乜嘢？

gáw·dì hai màt·yé

Can I taste it?
可唔可以試下啊？

háw·ǹg·háw·yí si háa aa

Can I have a bag, please?
我買一包，
唔該。

ngáw máai yàt bàau
ǹg·gòy

How much is (a kilo of apples)?
一斤 (蘋果)
幾多錢？

yàt gàn (pìng·gwáw)
gáy·dàw chín

How much? (quantity)
幾多？

gáy·dàw

food stuff		
cooked	熟	suk
cured	咸	hàam
dried	乾	gàwn
fresh	鮮	sìn
frozen	急凍	gàp·dung
salted	鹽腌	yìm·yip
smoked	熏	fàn
pickled	酸	sèwn
raw	生	sàang

我有乜可以幫你啊？ ngáw yáu màt háw∙yí bàwng láy aa	**Can I help you?**
你想要乜嘢？ láy séung yiu màt∙yé	**What would you like?**
仲要啲乜嘢？ jung yiu dì màt∙yé	**Would you like anything else?**
一共（五）蚊。 yàt∙gung (ńg) màn	**That's (five) dollars.**

I'd like ...	我要……	ngáw yiu ...
(50) grams	（50）克	(ńg∙sap) hàak
half a dozen	半打	bun dàa
a dozen	一打	yàt dàa
half a kilo	一斤	yàt gàn
a kilo	一公斤	yàt gùng∙gàn
(two) kilos	（兩）公斤	(léung) gùng∙gàn
a bottle	一樽	yàt jèun
a jar (tin)	一罐	yàt gun
a litre	一公升	yàt gùng∙sìng
a packet	一盒	yàt hap
a piece	一塊	yàt faai
(three) pieces	（三）塊	(sàam) faai
a slice	一份	yàt fan
(six) slices	（六）份	(luk) fan
(just) a little	（少）一啲	(siú) yàt dì
more	多啲	dàw dì
some ...	一啲	yàt dì
that one	嗰個	gáw gaw
this one	呢個	lày gaw

Less.	少啲。	siú dì
A bit more.	多啲。	dàw dì
Enough.	夠啦。	gau laa

FOOD

176

Do you have ...?	你有冇……㗎？	láy yáu·móu ... gaa
anything cheaper	平啲	pèng dì
other kinds	第樣	dai·yéung
Where can I find the ... section?	邊度有……？	bìn·do yáu ...
dairy	奶製品	láai·jai·bán
frozen goods	冷藏 食品	láng·chàwng sik·bán
fruit and vegetable	生果 疏菜	sàang·gwáw sàw·choy
meat	肉	yuk
poultry	雞鴨鵝	gài ngaap ngàw
seafood	海鮮	hóy·sìn

cooking utensils

Could I please borrow (a/an) …?	我可唔可以借個……啊？	ngáw háw·ṉg·háw·yí je gaw … aa
I need (a/an) …	我想要個……	ngáw séung yiu gaw …
bottle opener	開瓶器	hòy·pìng·hay
bowl	碗	wún
can opener	開罐器	hòy·gun·hay
chopping board	鉆板	jàm·báan
chopsticks	筷子	faai·jí
corkscrew	螺旋開瓶器	làw·sèwn hòy·pìng·hay
cup	杯	buì
fork	叉	chàa
fridge	雪柜	sewt·gwai
frying pan	煎鑊	jin·wawk
glass	玻璃杯	bàw·lày·buì
knife	刀	dò
meat cleaver	菜刀	choy·dò
microwave	微波爐	mày·bàw·lò
oven	烘爐	hung·lò
plate	碟	díp
rice cooker	電飯煲	di̱n·f̱aan·bò
saucepan	煲	bò
spoon	匙羹	chì·gàng
steamer	蒸籠	jìng·lùng
toaster	烘麵包機	hawng mi̱n·bàau·gày
wok	鑊	wawk

vegetarian & special meals

齋與特殊食品

ordering food

Is there a ...	呢度附近有冇	làу·do fu·gan yáu·mó
restaurant nearby?	……餐館？	... chàan·gún
Do you have	有冇……食品？	yáu·mó ... sik·bán
... food?		
halal	清真	chìng·jàn
kosher	猶太	yàu·tàai
vegetarian	齋	jàai

I don't eat ...
我唔吃……   ngáw ng̀ sik ...

Is it cooked in/with ...?
你係唔係用……煮㗎？   láy hai·ng̀·hai yung ... jéw gaa

Could you prepare a meal without ...?
可唔可以煮味餸   háw·ng̀·háw·yí jéw may
唔落……㗎？   sung ng̀ lawk ... gaa

butter	牛油	ngàu·yàu
eggs	雞蛋	gài·dáan
fish	魚	yéw
fish stock	魚湯	yéw·tàwng
meat stock	肉湯	yuk·tàwng
MSG	味精	may·jìng
nuts	果仁	gwáw·yàn
pork	豬肉	jèw·yuk
poultry	雞鴨鵝	gài ngaap ngàw
peanuts	花生	fàa·sàng
red meat	牛羊肉	ngàu yèung yuk
seafood	海鮮	hóy·sìn
shellfish	貝殼類	bui·hawk·<u>l</u>eui

Is this ...?	呢樣係唔係 ……㗎?	lày·yèung hai·ǹg·hai ... gaa
free of animal produce	冇動物 材料	mó dung·mat chòy·líu
free-range	新鮮	sàn·sìn
genetically modified	基因改良	gày·yàn góy·lèung
gluten-free	冇麵筋麵粉	mó mìn·gàn mìn·fán
low fat	低脂肪	dài jì·fàwng
low sugar	低糖	dài tàwng
organic	有機	yáu·gày
salt-free	唔加鹽	ǹg gàa yìm

special diets & allergies

特殊膳食與過敏症

I'm on a special diet.	我節食。	ngáw jit·sik
I'm (a) ...	我係……	ngáw hai ...
Buddhist	佛教徒	fat·gaau·tò
Hindu	印度教徒	yan·do·gaau·tò
Jewish	猶太教徒	yàu·taai·gaau·tò
Muslim	回教徒	wuì·gaau·tò
vegan	食齋嘅	sik jàai ge
vegetarian	食齋嘅	sik jàai ge
I'm allergic to ...	我對…… 過敏。	ngáw deui ... gaw·mán
chilli	辣椒	laat·jiù
shellfish	蝦蟹類	hàa·háai·leui
dairy produce	奶製品	láai·jai·bán
gelatine	明膠	mìng·gàau
gluten	麵筋	mìn·gàn
honey	蜜糖	mat·tàwng
nuts	果仁	gáw·yàn
peanuts	花生	fàa·sàng

culinary reader

烹飪

This miniguide to Cantonese cuisine lists dishes and ingredients according to their pronunciation. It's designed to help you get the most out of your gastronomic experience by providing you with food terms that you may hear in restaurants and tea houses. For certain dishes we've marked the region or city where they're most popular.

B

baak·cheuk·hàa 白灼蝦 *fresh whole prawns, poached then simmered & served with a peanut oil & soy sauce dip*

baak·cho 白醋 *white rice vinegar*

baak·choy 白菜 *cabbage*

baak·faan 白飯 *rice*

baak·gaai·laat 白芥辣 *white mustard*

baak·jáu 白酒 *spirits • Chinese-style vodka*

baak·làan·dáy 白蘭地 *brandy*

baak·pò·tò·jáu 白葡萄酒 *white wine*

baak·wù·jiù 白胡椒 *white pepper*

baat·bó·faan 八寶飯 *'eight-treasure rice' – the celebrated rice dish is eaten at Chinese New Year*

baat·bó·laat·jeung 八寶辣醬 *'eight-treasure' – hot sauce made from pressed tofu & chilli*

baat·gawk 八角 *star anise*

baat·gawk·fán 八角粉 *powder made from ground star anise*

baau 爆 *'exploded' – stir-fried in super-hot oil*

bàau 包 *(steamed) dumpling*

bàau·choy·jái 包菜仔 *Brussels sprout*

bàau·yew 鮑魚 *abalone*

bàk·gìng hàau·ngáap 北京烤鴨 *Peking duck*

bat·sì pìng·gwáw 拔絲蘋果 *small apple pieces dipped in batter, deep fried & coated in toffee mix*

bàw·choy 菠菜 *spinach*

bàw·làw 菠蘿 *pineapple*

bawk·béng 薄餅 *egg & spring onion pancake*

bawk·hàw 薄荷 *mint*

bè·jáu 啤酒 *beer*

béng·dim 餅店 *cake shop*

béng·gàwn 餅乾 *cracker • biscuit*

bín·dau 扁荳 *green beans*

bing 冰 *ice cubes*

bo·dìng 布丁 *pudding*

bun·bun·gài 拌拌雞 *'bang bang chicken' – cooked shredded chicken, cucumber & cellophane noodles, served cold*

bun·sàang 半生 *rare*

bun·sàang·suk 半生熟 *medium*

C

chàa 茶 *tea*

chàa·gún 茶館 *tea house (also called chàa·sàt)*

chàa·làu 樓 *restaurant (also called jáu·làu and chàan·tèng)*

chàa·sàt 茶室 *tea house (also called chàa·gún)*

chàa·yip dáan 葉蛋 *tea-boiled eggs*

chàa·siù 叉燒 *barbecued sweet roast pork*

culinary reader

chàa·sìu·bàau 叉燒包 barbecued
    pork buns (steamed)
chàa·yip·dáan 茶葉蛋 'tea egg' –
    tea-flavoured hard-boiled egg
chàan·tèng 餐廳 restaurant (also called
    chàa·làu and jáu·làu)
cháang 橙 orange
cháang·jàp 汁 orange juice
cháang·jeung 醬 marmalade
chaat yèung·yuk 涮羊肉 Mongolian lamb
    hotpot – do-it-yourself meal cooked
    at the table in a flame-heated hotpot
    with broth
cháau 炒 stir-fried
cháau·faan 飯 fried rice
cháau·fán 粉 fried rice noodles
cháau·mìn 炒麵 hot-wok noodles
cháau sęung·so 炒上素 vegetarian stir-fry
    dish of mushrooms, lotus root, ginkgo
    nuts & fresh vegetables
chàn·cho 陳醋 dark vinegar
chan·pày 陳皮 mandarin or tangerine peel
    used as flavouring
chau dạu·fu 臭豆腐 'stinky tofu' – tofu
    fermented in cabbage juice
chèng·choy 青菜 leafy vegetables
chèng·gwàa 青瓜 cucumber
chèng·jiù 青椒 bell pepper • capsicum
cheui·pày 皮 pork crackling
chèun·géwn 春卷 spring roll –
    deep-fried pastry stuffed with a mixture
    that can include vegetables, chicken,
    pork, prawns, mushrooms, sprouts &
    noodles
chéung·fán 腸粉 rice noodle roll –
    shrimp, pork or beef filling encased by
    rice noodles to form a soft roll, then
    steamed & served with soy sauce &
    sesame oil
chęwn mạk mịn·bàau 全麥麵包
    wholemeal bread
chèwn·choy 川菜 Western (Sichuan)
    cuisine

chèwn·gàa·fuk 全家富 'family happiness
    seafood spectacular' – seafood braised
    with mushrooms & pig tendon
chí 柿 persimmon
chìm·béng 簽餅 fortune cookies
chìng·jàn 清真 halal
chìng·jìng dạai·jaap·háai 清蒸大閘蟹
    hairy crab stir-fried with ginger &
    shallots
chìng·tàwng 清湯 light broth
chiù·jàu ló·séui·ngáap 潮州鹵水鵝
    'Chui Chow soyed goose' – goose stewed
    in rich sauce, served with garlic & vinegar
    dip (Shantou)
chiù·jàu yéw·tàwng 潮州魚湯
    aromatic fish soup – sliced fish (usually
    pomfret), squid, celery, mushrooms &
    rice cooked in chicken stock & sprinkled
    with dried fish pieces (Shantou)
chiù·jàu yi·mịn 潮州伊麵 thin egg noodles
    pan-fried until crunchy, served with
    chives, sugar & vinegar (Shantou)
chiù·jàu·choy 潮州菜 Chuzhou cuisine
cho 醋 vinegar
chó·múi 草莓 strawberry
choy·dàan 菜單 menu
choy·sàm 菜心 Chinese flowering cabbage
choy·yàu 菜油 vegetable oil
chùng 蔥 shallots • spring onions
chùng·baau yèung·yuk 爆羊肉
    hot-wok lamb with shallots
chùng·hing fó·gwàw 重慶火鍋
    Chongqing hotpot
chùng·jí 松子 pine nuts
chùng·yàu·béng 蔥油餅 onion cakes –
    fried pastries filled with spring onion

D

dạai·bạak·choy 大白菜 Chinese white
    cabbage
dạai·chùng 大蔥 oversized spring
    onions
dạai·jaap·háai 大閘蟹 hairy crab

dáan 蛋 *egg(s)*

dáan·báak 白 *egg white*

daan·gòu 蛋糕 *cake*

daan·mjn 蛋面 *dried or fresh egg noodles*

daan·tàat 蛋撻 *egg tart – baked puff pastry with egg custard filling*

dáan·tàwng 蛋湯 *egg drop soup – chicken broth with egg mixed throughout*

dáan·wáwng 蛋黃 *egg yolk*

daan·wáwng·jeung 蛋黃醬 *mayonnaise*

dang 燉 *stewed*

dáu 豆 *beans*

dau·fán 豆粉 *bean noodles*

dau·fu 豆腐 *tofu*

dau·fu·ló 豆腐腦 *salty beancurd soup*

dau·fu·tàwng 豆腐湯 *bean curd casserole*

dau·gawk 豆角 *chopped green beans*

dau·jèung 豆漿 *fresh soy milk*

dau·jèung·fán 豆漿粉 *powdered soy milk*

dau·mjù 豆苗 *pea shoots*

dau·ngàa 豆芽 *beansprouts*

dau·sàa·bàau 豆沙包 *steamed sweet red bean bun*

dàw·sí 多士 *toast*

day·gwàa 地瓜 *sweet potato*

dím·sàm 點心 *dim sum – bite-sized portions of meat or vegetables wrapped in pastry then steamed or fried • originally referred to snacks but now refers to everything offered in* yám·chàa

dìng 丁 *cubed meat (chicken, pork, beef)*

dìng·hèung 丁香 *clove*

dùng·choy 冬菜 *pickled cabbage (Tianjin)*

dung·gún·séui 凍滾水 *chilled boiled water*

dùng·gwàa 冬瓜 *honeydew melon • winter melon*

F

fàa·chàa 花茶 *jasmine tea*

fàa·sàng 花生 *peanuts*

fàa·sàng·jeung 花生醬 *peanut butter*

fàa·sàng·yàu 花生油 *peanut oil*

fàan·ké 番茄 *tomato*

fàan·ké cháau·dáan 番茄炒蛋 *stir-fried tomato & egg*

faat·sìk mjn·bàau 法式麵包 *pastry (French bread)*

fai 肺 *lung*

fàn 燻 *smoked*

fán·sì 粉絲 *vermicelli*

fàn·yuk 燻肉 *bacon*

fat·sáu 佛手 *'Buddha's hand' – yellow citrus fruit*

fày·chéung 肥腸 *large intestines (pig)*

fày·yuk 肥肉 *fatty meat*

fó·gài 火雞 *turkey*

fó·téui 火腿 *ham • sausage made from pig offcuts*

fú·gwàa 苦瓜 *bitter melon (for the brave-hearted)*

fu·jùk 腐竹 *dried yellow sticks made from soy milk*

fu·pày 腐皮 *bean shoots*

fu·yéw 腐乳 *fermented tofu cubes, dried, steamed, then bottled with wine – has a Camembert-like taste & texture*

fuk·dak·gàa 伏特加 *vodka*

fung·jáau (gài·geuk) 鳳爪 (雞腳) *'phoenix claws' – chicken feet*

fùng·léut 風栗 *hot roasted chestnuts*

G

gaa·fè 咖啡 *coffee*

gaam·láam 橄欖 *olive*

gaam·láam·yàu 橄欖油 *olive oil*

gaap 鴿 *pigeon*

gàau·baak 茭白 *wild rice root*

gáau·jí 餃子 *boiled dumpling*

gài·báy 雞髀 *chicken drumsticks*

gài·dáan 雞蛋 *chicken eggs*

gài·máy·jáu 雞尾酒 *cocktail*

gài·tàwng 雞湯 *chicken stock*

gài·yjk 雞翼 *chicken wings*

gài·yuk 雞肉 chicken

gàm 柑 mandarin

gàm·jàm·gù 金針菇 golden needle
    mushrooms

gàm·je 甘蔗 sugar cane

gàp·dung 急凍 frozen

gáu·choy 韭菜 chinese chives

gáu·géy 枸杞 box thorn – green leafy
    vegetable similar in texture & nutritional
    value to spinach

gáu·yuk 狗肉 dog

gàwn 乾 dried

gàwn·siù 燒 'dry-fried' – chillies fried until
    there's not much left but a pile of dried
    remains

gàwn·siù ngàu·yuk 燒牛肉
    shredded beef deep-fried then tossed
    with chillies

gàwn·siù say·gwai·dáu 燒四季豆
    deep-fried snake beans stir-fried with
    garlic, ginger & shrimps

gèung 薑 ginger

gùk·fàa·chàa 菊花茶 chrysanthemum tea

gùng baau gài·dìng 宮爆雞丁
    marinated chicken cubes stir-fried with
    chillies & peanuts & seasoned with sweet
    bean sauce

gùng·fù·chàa 工夫茶 congou – variety of
    Chinese black tea

gwàa 瓜 melon • vegetable marrow

gwàa·jí 子 watermelon seed(s)

gwai·pày 桂皮 cinnamon bark

gwàt·séui 骨髓 bone marrow

gwáw·gàwn 果乾 dried fruit

gwáw·jàp 果汁 juice

gwáw·yàn 果仁 nuts

H

hàa 蝦 prawn

hàa·gáau 餃 translucent bonnet-shaped
    prawn dumpling

hàa·mái 餃米 dried shrimps

hàa·mat·gwàa 哈密瓜 cantaloupe

hàa·yàn gwàw·bàa 蝦仁鍋巴
    crisped rice with shrimp

hàak·jiù·jeung 黑椒醬
    blackbean dipping sauce

hàam 咸 savoury

hàam 咸 cured • sweet

hàam·béng 餡餅 small pork pie (Beijing)

hàam·choy 鹹菜 pickles • pickled
    vegetables

hàam·ngaap dáan 咸鴨蛋 pickled
    duck eggs

hàau 烤 roasted

hàau·mó 酵母 yeast

hang 杏 apricot

hang·yàn 杏仁 almonds

hap·faan 盒飯 rice & vegetable
    takeaway box

hap·tò 合桃 walnuts

hàt·yì·gài 乞依雞 'beggar's chicken' –
    marinated chicken stuffed with shiitake
    mushroom, cabbage & pork

háw·fán 河粉 slippery rice noodles –
    thin, round or flat noodles

hàw·làan·dáu 荷蘭豆 snow pea

hawn·bó·bàau 漢堡包 hamburger

hay·séui 汽水 soft drink

hèung·bàn 香檳 champagne

hèung·chéung 香腸 pork sausage

hèung·jiù 香蕉 banana

hèung·liú 香料 herbs • spices

hò 蠔 oyster

hò·yàu 油 oyster sauce

hò·yàu gaai·láan 油芥蘭 vegetables with
    oyster sauce (Southern China)

hóy·daai 海帶 kelp

hóy·jit 海蜇 jellyfish sold in sheets &
    packed in salt, served shredded

hóy·sàm 海參 sea cucumber

hóy·sàm·gwáw 開心果 pistachio

hóy·sìn 海鮮 seafood

hùng·chàa 紅茶 black tea

hùng·cho 紅醋 red rice vinegar

hùng·dáu 紅豆 red mung beans

hùng·làw·baak 紅蘿蔔 carrot
hùng·pò·tò·jáu 紅葡萄酒 red wine
hung·siù 紅燒 'red-fried' – braised in sweet
  star anise sauce
hung·siù pàai·gwàt 紅燒排骨
  red-fried spareribs

J

jàn·jí 榛子 hazelnuts
jáu·bàa 酒吧 bar
jáu·làuu 酒樓 restaurant (also called 茶樓
  chàa·làuu and 餐廳 chàan·tèng)
jáu·leuí 酒類 alcoholic drinks
jèm jam jam
jeung 醬 dipping sauce
jeung jek pàai·gwàt 醬炙排骨
  barbecued pork ribs (Wuxi)
jéw 煮 boiled
jéw·choy 主菜 main course(s)
jèw·gù·lìk 朱古力 chocolate
jèw·hung 豬紅 blood curd (pig)
jèw·jàang 豬蹄 hock (fatty pork elbow)
jèw·sìk 主食 staples
jèw·yàu 豬油 pork lard
jèw·yuk 豬肉 pork
jí·choy 紫菜 thin seaweed
ji·jàw·chàan 自助餐 buffet
ji·màa·jeung 芝麻醬 sesame paste
ji·sí 芝士 cheese
jìk·sìk·mìn 即食麵 instant noodles
jìn 煎 braised
jìn·béng 煎餅 egg pancake
jìng 蒸 steamed
jit·choy 浙菜 Zhejiang (Shanghai) cuisine
jó·báat 棗 date (fruit)
jó·chàan 早餐 breakfast
joy yit 再熱 re-heated
jùk 粥 porridge
jùk sùk·mái 粥粟米 corn
jùk siú·mái 粥小米 millet
jùk baak·mái 粥白米 plain rice
júng 粽 sticky rice wrapped in
  bamboo leaves

K

kàn·choy 芹菜 celery
kawng·chèwn·séui 礦泉水 mineral water
ké·gwàa 茄瓜 aubergine • eggplant
ké·jàp 茄汁 tomato sauce • ketchup
kùk·kày 曲奇 cookie • biscuit

L

láai·jai·bán 奶製品 dairy
làam·gwàa 南瓜 pumpkin
laat 辣 spicy
laat·jí gài·dìng 子雞丁 braised chilli
  chicken
laat·jiù 椒 chilli • hot pepper
laat·jiù·jeung 椒醬 chilli sauce
lai·jì·jàp 荔枝汁 lychee-flavoured soft
  drink
làu·lìn 榴蓮 durian
làw·baak 蘿蔔 radish
làw·baak·gò 蘿蔔糕 fried radish cakes
làw·hawn·jàai 羅漢齋 vegetarian stew in
  a claypot
law·mái 糯米 glutinous rice • sticky rice •
  sweet rice
láy 梨 pear
láy·yéw 鯉魚 carp
lèung·fán 涼粉 cold clear noodles
lèung·pún 涼盤 appetisers • cold dishes
leut·jí 栗子 chestnuts
lìm·gò 黏糕 rice cake
lìn·gò 年糕 Chinese New Year sweets
lìn·ngáu 蓮藕 lotus root – tuber stem
  of the water lily stuffed with rice &
  steamed, stir-fried, or used in soups &
  stews
lìng·mùng 檸檬 lemon
lìng·mùng·gài 檸檬雞 lemon chicken
lìng·sìk 零食 snack
lò·séun 蘆筍 asparagus
lò·yuk 驢肉 donkey

luk·chàa 綠茶 *green tea*
luk·dáu 綠豆 *green mung beans*
lùng·hàa 龍蝦 *rock lobster*

M

màa·fàa 麻花 *bread twists (Tianjin)*
máa·ngái séung·sew 螞蟻上樹
   *'ants climbing a tree' – cellophane
   noodles braised with minced pork,
   seasoned with a liberal amount of soy
   sauce & sprinkled with chopped spring
   onions*
màa·pàw dau·fu 麻婆豆腐 *a spicy bean
   curd dish (Sichuan)*
máan·faan 晚飯 *dinner*
maan·tàu 饅頭 *steamed bun(s)*
maan·yew 鱔魚 *river eel*
màau·tòy 茅臺 *maotai – a very strong
   good quality spirit (alcoholic drink)*
mái·fán 米粉 *rice noodles*
mak·pày 麥皮 *oats*
mán·choy 閩菜 *Hokkien cuisine*
mat·tàwng 蜜糖 *honey*
màw·gù 蘑菇 *mushroom*
màwng·gwáw 芒果 *mango*
may·do 味道 *flavour • taste*
mày·hàu·tò 獼猴桃 *kiwifruit*
may·jing 味精 *MSG (monosodium
   glutimate)*
min 麵 *noodles*
min·bàau 麵包 *bread*
min·fán 麵粉 *flour*
min·gàn·kàu 面筋球 *gluten made into balls
   & deep-fried – has a meaty texture & is
   used mostly in vegetarian cooking*
mò·dáu 毛豆 *fresh soy beans*
mò·fàa·gwáw 無花果 *fig*
mui 梅 *plum*
mui·choy kau·yuk 梅菜扣肉
   *double-cooked steamed pork with
   pickled salted cabbage*
muk·gwàa 木瓜 *papaya • pawpaw*

muk·sèui·yuk 木須肉
   stir-fried pork with wood ear fungus
mut·láy·fàa·chàa 茉莉花茶 *jasmine tea*

N

ńg·chàan 午餐 *lunch*
ngaap 鴨 *duck*
ngaap·béng 餅 *salted, boned &
   pressed duck immersed in peanut oil
   then steamed*
ngàu·luk sìk jó·chàan 歐陸式早餐
   continental breakfast
ngàu·yàu 牛油 *butter*
ngàu·yàu·gwáw 牛油果 *avocado*
ngàu·yuk 牛肉 *beef*
ngàu·yuk·tàwng 牛肉湯 *beef stock*
ngàw 鵝 *goose*

P

pàai·gwàt 排骨 *spareribs*
páwng 蚌 *clams • mussels*
pày dáan 皮蛋 *hard-boiled eggs*
pày·dáan sau·yuk juk 皮蛋瘦肉粥
   preserved duck egg & pork congee
pín 片 *slices*
ping·gwáw 蘋果 *apple*
pó·láy·chàa 普洱茶 *black jasmine tea*
pò·tài·jí 葡提子 *raisin(s)*
pò·tài·jí 葡提子 *grapes*
pò·tò·jáu 葡萄酒 *wine*

S

saa·dè 沙嗲 *satay*
sàa·ding·yéw 沙丁魚 *sardine*
sàa·gwàw dau·fu 砂鍋豆腐
   *beancurd claypot containing dried
   bamboo & vermicelli*
sàa·léut 沙律 *salad*
sàa·tàwng 砂糖 *sugar*
sàam·màn·ji 三文治 *sandwich*

sàam·màn·yéw 三文魚 *salmon*

saam·múi 山梅 *raspberry*

sàang 生 *raw*

sàang·choy 生菜 *lettuce*

sài·gwàa 西瓜 *watermelon*

sài·làan·fàa 西蘭花 *broccoli*

sài·ngàwn wu·lò·gài 西安葫蘆雞 *chicken casserole (Xi'an)*

sài·wú·lò 西葫蘆 *courgette • zuchinni*

sài·yáu 西柚 *grapefruit*

sau·yuk 瘦肉 *lean meat*

sàw·choy 蔬菜 *vegetable • vegetable dishes (not vegetarian, but usually 'featuring a vegetable')*

say·chèwn·gài 四川雞 *pepper chicken (Sichuan)*

say·gwai pàai·gwàt 四季排骨 *braised spareribs*

sè·yuk 蛇肉 *snake*

séui·gwáw 水果 *fruit*

séui·hàu·séui 水喉水 *tap water*

séui·jìng ngàau·yuk 水晶肴肉 *pig trotter jelly*

séui·yéw 水魚 *turtoise*

séun 筍 *bamboo shoots*

sèung·choy 湘菜 *Hunan cuisine*

sèw·jái 薯仔 *potato*

sewn 蒜 *garlic*

sèwn 酸 *sour*

sèwn·làai 奶 *yogurt*

sèwn·laat 辣 *'hot & sour' – usually a style of cooking soup, with plenty of Chinese vinegar & chilli oil*

sèwn·laat·tàwng 辣湯 *hot & sour soup with pepper, chillies & vinegar – a warming winter dish traditionally including solidified chicken blood (Sichuan, northern China)*

sèwn·mui 梅 *dried sour plums*

sèwn·mui·tàwng 酸梅湯 *sour plum drink*

sewn·miù 蒜苗 *garlic chives*

sewn·tàuh 蒜頭 *garlic*

sewn·yùng 蒜蓉 *'garlic-fried' – cooked with a liberal dose of crushed garlic & oil*

sewt·gò 雪糕 *ice cream*

si·yàu 豉油 *soy sauce*

sìn 鮮 *fresh*

siù 燒 *roasted with sweet sauce*

siù·hàau 烤 *barbecued*

siù·baak·choy 小白菜 *bok choy (leafy vegetable)*

siù·béng 燒餅 *flat bread topped with sesame seeds (northern China)*

siù·máai 燒賣 *steamed dumplings – won ton wrappers filled with pork, prawns, water chestnuts & bamboo shoots then steamed*

siù·yé 宵夜 *evening snack*

siù·yuk 燒肉 *red-fried pork*

sò·choy 蘇菜 *Jiangsu cuisine*

suk 熟 *cooked • well-done*

sùk·mái 粟米 *corn • corn cob*

T

tàn·làa·yéw 吞拿魚 *tuna*

tàwng·cho 糖醋 *sweet & sour*

tàwng·cho láy·yéw 糖醋鯉魚 *sweet & sour fish*

tàwng·cho pàai·gwàt 糖醋排骨 *sweet & sour pork ribs*

tàwng·gwáw 糖果 *candy • lollies*

tàwng·hap·tò 糖合桃 *candied walnuts*

tàwng·lèui 湯類 *soups*

tàwng·wu·lò 糖葫蘆 *toffee crab apple on sticks*

tìm 甜 *sweet (taste)*

tìm·bán 品 *desserts*

tìm·choy 甜菜 *beetroot*

tìn·gài 田雞 *'field chicken' – frog*

tit·báan·siù 鐵板燒 *grilled on a hot plate*

tiu·may·bán 調味品 *flavour enhancers*

tó 桃 *peach*

to·yuk 兔肉 *rabbit*

W

wài·si·gáy 威士忌 *whisky*

wan·lày·láa 雲呢那 *vanilla*

wàn·tàn 餛吞 *wonton soup*

wàw·tip 鍋貼 *fried dumpling*

wàwng·dáu 黃豆 *soy beans*

wàwng·jàu 黃酒 *yellow wine*

wàwng·sín 黃鱔 *paddy eel*

wù·jiù·fán 胡椒粉 *pepper*

wù·lúng·chàa 烏龍茶 *oolong tea*

wų·táu 芋頭 *yam*

wui·wàw·yuk 回鍋肉 *sweet & sour pork*

wún·dąu 豌豆 *pea*

Y

yám·liụ 飲料 *cold drink*

yàn·sàm 人參 *ginseng, prized as a tonic & aphrodisiac*

yáu 柚 *grapefruit*

yàu·cháau·min 油炒麵 *oily fried noodles*

yàu·choy 油菜 *mustard greens*

yàu·jaa 油炸 *deep-fried*

yáu·jaa·gwái 油炸鬼 *fried bread sticks*

yàu·yéw 魷魚 *calamari • squid*

yè·choy·fàa 椰菜花 *cauliflower*

yè·jí 椰子 *coconut*

yéun 潤 *liver*

yèung·chùng 洋蔥 *onion(s)*

yèung·jàu cháau·faan 揚州炒飯 *Yangzhou fried rice – a classic rice dish made with chicken, pork sausage and marinated mushrooms*

yèung·jàu jeui hàa 揚州醉蝦 *Yangzhou drunken prawns – a stir-fry of prawns marinated in a mixture of soy & oyster sauce*

yèung·jàu si·jí·tàu 揚州獅子頭 *'lion's head meatballs' – oversized pork meatballs and vegetables cooked in a claypot*

yèung·yuk 羊肉 *lamb*

yéw 魚 *fish*

yéw·gàwn 乾 *dried fish*

yéw·hèung 香 *'fish-fragrant' – braised with either fish sauce or small dried fish*

yèw·hèung ké·jí 魚香茄子 *shredded eggplant in a fish-flavoured sauce of vinegar, wine, garlic, ginger, pepper, spring onions & bean paste (no fish)*

yew·choy 粵菜 *southern cuisine • Cantonese cuisine*

yéwn·choy 皖菜 *Anhui cuisine*

yèwn·liú 原料 *ingredient*

yi·fán 意粉 *pasta*

yì·min 伊面 *deep-fried egg noodles*

yìm 鹽 *salt*

yìm·guk·gài 焗雞 *salt-baked chicken*

ying·tò 櫻桃 *cherry*

yit jèw·gú·lik 熱朱古力 *hot chocolate*

yit gàa (ngàu·láai) 熱加 (牛奶) *hot chocolate (with milk)*

yit ņg gàa (tàwng) 熱唔加 (糖) *hot chocolate (without sugar)*

yiu 腰 *kidneys*

yiù·gwáw 腰果 *cashew nuts*

yuk 肉 *meat (usually refers to pork)*

yuk·béng 餅 *large pork pie*

yuk·gaap·máw 夾饃 *finely chopped braised pork & coriander stuffed into a pocket of flat bread*

yuk·háam 餡 *mince*

yuk·pàai 排 *steak (beef)*

yám·chàa 飲茶 *'drink tea' – varieties of dim sum served as a meal, usually accompanied with tea*

emergencies

緊急意外

Help!	救命！	gau·meng
Stop!	企喺度！	káy hái·do
Go away!	走開！	jáu·hòy
Thief!	有賊啊！	yáu cháat aa
Fire!	火燭啊！	fó·jùk aa
Watch out!	小心！	siú·sàm

Call the police!
快啲叫警察！ faai·dì giu gíng·chaat

Call a doctor!
快啲叫醫生！ faai·dì giu yì·sàng

Call an ambulance!
快啲叫救傷車！ faai·dì giu gau·sèung·chè

It's an emergency.
有緊急意外。 yáu gán·gàp yi·ngoy

There's been an accident.
有意外。 yáu yi·ngoy

Could you please help?
唔該幫幫 ǹg·gòy bàwng bàwng
忙。 màwng

Can I use your phone?
唔該借個電話 ǹg·gòy je gaw din·wáa
用下。 yung háa

I'm lost.
我蕩失路。 ngáw dawng·sàk·lo

Where are the toilets?
廁所喺邊度？ chi·sáw hái bìn·do

Is it safe …?	……安唔安全㗎？	… ngàwn·ǹg·ngàwn·chèwn gaa
at night	晚黑	máan·hàak
for gay people	對同性戀嘅人	deui tùng·sing·léwn ge yàn
for travellers	對旅客	deui léui·haak
for women	對女人	deui léui·yán
on your own	自己一個人	ji·gáy yàt gaw yàn

police

Where's the police station?
警察局喺邊度？　　　gíng·chaat·gúk hái·bìn·do

Please phone the Tourist Police.
唔該打電話俾
旅遊區警局。　　　ǹg·gòy dáa dịn·wáa báy
léui·yàu·kèui gíng·gúk

I want to report an offence.
我要報案。　　　ngáw yiu bo·ngawn

It was him/her.
係佢做嘅。　　　hai kéui jo ge

My … was/were stolen.	我……俾人偷咗。	ngáw … báy·yàn tàu·jáw
I've lost my …	我……唔見咗。	ngáw … ǹg·gin·jáw
backpack	個背囊	gaw bui·làwng
bags	啲行李	dì hang·láy
credit card	張信用卡	jèung seun·yung·kàat
handbag	個手袋	gaw sáu·dóy
jewellery	啲首飾	dì sáu·sìk
money	啲錢	dì chín
papers	啲文件	dì màn·gín
passport	個護照	gaw wu·jiu
travellers cheques	啲旅行支票	dì léui·hang jì·piu
wallet	個銀包	gaw ngàn·bàau

190

I've been ...	有人……我。	yáu·yàn ... ngáw
He/She has been ...	有人……佢。	yáu·yàn ... kéui
assaulted	打	dáa
raped	強奸	kèung·gàan
robbed	打劫	dáa·gip

I have insurance.
我買咗保險。　　　ngáw máai·jáw bó·hím

I need a loss report.
我要開個遺失證明。　ngáw yiu hòy gaw wài·sàk jing·ming

What am I accused of?
我犯咗乜嘢罪？　　ngáw faan·jáw màt·yé jeui

I'm sorry.
我道歉。　　　　ngáw do·hip

I didn't realise I was doing anything wrong.
我唔知自己　　　ngáw ǹg·jì ji·gáy
做錯咗啲乜嘢。　jo·chaw·jáw dì màt·yé

---

the police may say ...

而家告	yì·gàa go	You're charged
你……	láy ...	with ...
而家告	yì·gàa go	He's/She's
佢……	kéui ...	charged with ...
人身侵犯	yàn·sàn chàm·faan	assault
破壞秩序	paw·waai dit·jeui	disturbing the peace
非法入境	fày·faat yap·gíng	not having a visa
簽證	chìm·jing	overstaying
過期	gaw·kay	your visa
攜帶違禁	kwài·daai wài·gàm	possession (of
物品	mat·bán	illegal substances)
高買	gò·máai	shoplifting
盜竊	do·sit	theft
呢張係……	lày·jèung hai ...	It's a ... fine.
罰款。	fat·fún	
違規泊車	wài·kwài paak·chè	parking
超速	chiu·chùk	speeding

醫院	yì·yéwn	**Hospital**
警察	gíng·chaat	**Police**
派出所	paai·chèut·sáw	**Police Station**
急症室	gàp·jing·sàt	**Emergency Department**

I didn't do it.
唔係我做嘅。　　　　　　ǹg hai ngáw jo ge

Can I pay an on-the-spot fine?
我可唔可以俾　　　　　　ngáw háw·ǹg·háw·yí báy
罰款呀？　　　　　　　　fat·fún aa

I want to contact my embassy.
我要聯繫我嘅　　　　　　ngáw yiu lèwn·hai ngáw ge
大使館。　　　　　　　　daai·si·gún

I want to contact my consulate.
我要聯繫我嘅　　　　　　ngáw yiu lèwn·hai ngáw ge
領事館。　　　　　　　　líng·si·gún

Can I make a phone call?
我可唔可以　　　　　　　ngáw háw·ǹg·háw·yí dáa
打個電話啊？　　　　　　gaw din·wáa aa

Can I have a lawyer who speaks English?
我想請個　　　　　　　　ngáw séung chéng gaw
會講英文嘅律師。　　　　wuí gáwng yìng·mán ge leut·sì

I want an English interpreter.
我要個英文翻譯。　　　　ngáw yiu gaw yìng·mán fàan·yik

This drug is for personal use.
呢啲藥係自己用嘅。　　　làу·dì yeuk hai ji·gáy yung ge

I have a prescription for this drug.
我有呢啲藥嘅　　　　　　ngáw yáu làу·dì yeuk ge
處方。　　　　　　　　　chéw·fàwng

I (don't) understand.
我(唔)明白。　　　　　　ngáw (ǹg) ming·baak

doctor

醫生

Where's the nearest ...?	最近嘅……喺 邊度？	jeui kán ge ... hái bìn·do
dentist	牙醫	ngàa·yì
doctor	醫生	yì·sàng
emergency department	急症室	gàp·jing·sàt
hospital	醫院	yì·yéwn
medical centre	醫療中心	yì·liù jùng·sàm
optometrist	配鏡師	pui·geng·sì
(night) pharmacist	(晝夜) 藥房	(jau·ye) yeuk·fàwng

I need a doctor (who speaks English).
我要睇(識講　　　ngáw yiu tái (sìk gáwng
英文嘅)醫生。　　　yìng·mán ge) yì·sàng

Could I see a female doctor?
最好睇個女醫生。　jèui·hó tái gaw léui yì·sàng

Could the doctor come here?
醫生可唔可以　　　yì·sàng háw·ǹg·háw·yí
出診啊？　　　　　chèut·chàn aa

Is there an after-hours emergency number?
有冇夜晚急診電話？　yáu·mó ye·máan gàp·chán dìn·wáa

I've run out of my medication.
我啲藥用完啦。　　ngáw dì yeuk yung yèwn laa

the doctor may say ...

有乜嘢問題？
yáu màt·yé man·tài

What's the problem?

邊度痛？
bìn·do tung

Where does it hurt?

你發燒啊？
láy faat·siù aa

Do you have a temperature?

呢種情況有咗幾耐？
làv júng chìng·fawng
yáu·jáw gáy·loy

How long have you been
like this?

以前有冇敢樣㗎？
yì·chìn yáu·mó
gám·yéung gaa

Have you had this before?

你有冇性生活啊？
láy yáu·mó sing·sàng·wut

Are you sexually active?

你有冇用避孕套啊？
láy yáu·mó yung
bay·yan·to aa

Have you had
unprotected sex?

你……啊？	láy ... aa	Do you ...?
飲唔飲酒	yám·ǹg·yám jáu	drink
食唔食煙	sik·ǹg·sik yìn	smoke
吸唔吸食	kàp·ǹg·kàp sik	take drugs
毒品	duk·bán	

你有冇……呀？	láy yáu·mó ... aa	Are you ...?
過敏	gaw·mán	allergic to anything
食醫生開 嘅藥	sik yì·sàng hòy ge yeuk	on medication

你需要住院。
láy sèui·yiu jew·yéwn

You need to be admitted
to hospital.

你最好返嚟養病。
láy fàan·lai ge si·hau
yiu jo gím·cha

You should have it checked
when you go home.

你返嚟嘅時候要做檢查。
láy jeⱼui·hó fàan·lⱼai
yéung·beng
You should return home for treatment.

你準備旅行幾耐？
láy jéun·bay léui·hàng
gáy·loy
How long are you travelling for?

你有憂鬱症。
láy yáu yàu·wàt·jing
You're a hypochondriac.

This is my usual medicine.
我平時食呢啲藥。
ngáw pìng·sì sik lày dì yeuk

My child weighs (20) kilos.
我個細路有
(二十) 公斤重。
ngáw gaw sai·lo yáu
(yiⱼsap) gùng·gàn chúng

What's the correct dosage?
劑量啱唔啱？
jài·leung ngàam·ǹg·ngàam

I don't want a blood transfusion.
我唔想輸血。
ngáw ǹg séung sèw·hewt

Please use a new syringe.
唔該用個新針頭。
ǹg·gòy yung gaw sàn jàm·táu

I have my own syringe.
我自己帶咗針頭。
ngáw ji·gáy daai·jáw jàm·táu

I've been vaccinated against ...	我打咗……嘅防疫針。	ngáw dáa·jáw ... ge fàwng·yik·jàm
He/She has been vaccinated against ...	佢打咗……嘅防疫針。	kéui dáa·jáw ... ge fàwng·yik·jàm
hepatitis A/B/C	肝炎 A/B/C	gàwn·yìm ày/bì/sì
rabies	狂犬病	kàwng·héwn·beng
tetanus	破傷風	paw·sèung·fùng
typhoid	傷寒	sèung·hàwn

I need new ...	我要買新……	ngáw yiu máai sàn ...
contact lenses	隱形	yán·yìng
	眼鏡	ngáan·géng
glasses	眼鏡	ngáan·géng

My prescription is ...
我雙眼係……度。 ngáw séung ngáan hai ... do

How much will it cost?
總共要幾多錢？ júng·gung yiu gáy·dàw chín

Can I have a receipt for my insurance?
我買嘅保險唔該 ngáw máai ge bó·hím ǹg·gòy
俾張收據。 báy jèung sàu·geui

symptoms & conditions

病症與病態

I'm sick.
我病咗。 ngáw beng·jáw

My friend is sick.
我個朋友病咗。 ngáw gaw pàng·yáu beng·jáw

My child is sick.
我個細路病咗。 ngáw gaw sai·lo beng·jáw

I've been ...	我……	ngáw ...
He/She has been ...	佢……	kéui ...
injured	受咗傷	sau·jáw sèung
vomiting	嘔咗一輪	ngáu·jaw yàt leun

I feel ...	我覺得……	ngáw gawk·dàk ...
anxious	精神緊張	jìng·sàn gán·jèung
better	好啲	hó dì
depressed	憂鬱	yàu·wàt
dizzy	頭暈	tàu·wùn
hot and cold	忽冷忽熱	fàt·láang fàt·yit
nauseous	反胃	fáan·wai
shivery	打冷震	dáa láang·jan
weak	冇力	mó·lìk
worse	仲衰咗	jung·sèui·jáw

It hurts here.
呢度痛。 làydo tung

I'm dehydrated.
我脫水。 ngáw tewt·séui

I can't sleep.
我失眠。 ngáw sàt·mìn

I think it's the medication I'm on.
可能同醫生開俾 háwlàng tung yìsàng hòy báy
我嘅藥有關。 ngáw ge yeuk yáugwàan

I'm on medication for …
我食緊醫生開 ngáw sikgán yìsàng hòy
嘅……藥。 ge … yeuk

He/She is on medication for …
佢食緊醫生開嘅 kéui sikgán yìsàng hòy ge
……藥。 … yeuk

I have (a/an) …
我有…… ngáw yáu …

He/She has (a/an) …
佢有…… kéui yáu …

chinese herbal medicine

Is this a traditional remedy?
係唔係傳統 hainghai chùntúng
療法嚟㗎？ liufaat làigaa?

Is this safe for people with …
對……嘅人安唔安 deui … ge yan ngònngngòn
全㗎？ chùn gaa?

I'd like some herbs for …
要啲醫……嘅 ngáw séung yiu dì yì … ge
草藥。 chóyeuk

freeze-dried powder	凍乾粉	dung gòn fán
herbs	草藥	chóyeuk
modern	現代	yindoi
traditional	傳統	chùntúng

asthma	哮喘	hàau·chéwn
cold n	發冷	faat·láang
cholera	霍亂	fàwk·lewn
constipation	便秘	bin·bay
cough n	咳嗽	kàt·sau
diabetes	糖尿病	tàwng·liu·beng
dengue fever	登革熱	dàng·gaap·yit
diarrhoea	肚痾	tó·ngàw
dysentery	痢疾	lay·jat
epilepsy	癲癇	dìn·gáan
fever	發燒	faat·sìu
giardiasis	賈第虫病	gáa·dik·chùng·beng
headache	頭痛	tàu·tung
influenza	感冒	gám·mo
malaria	瘧疾	yeuk·jat
nausea	作嘔	jawk·ngáu
SARS	沙斯	sà·sì
sore throat	喉嚨疼	hàu·lùng·tung

women's health

婦女衛生

(I think) I'm pregnant.
(我好似)懷咗孕。 (ngáw hó·chí) wàai·jáw·yan

I'm on the pill.
我用緊避孕藥。 ngáw yung·gán bay·yan·yeuk

I haven't had my period for (six) weeks.
我(六)個星期 ngáw (luk) gaw sìng·kày
冇嚟月經。 mó lày yewt·gìng

I've noticed a lump here.
我呢度生咗個瘤。 ngáw lày·do sàang·jáw gaw láu

I need …	我要買……	ngáw yiu máai …
a pregnancy test	驗孕用品	yim·yan yung·bán
contraception	避孕用品	bay·yan yung·bán
the morning-after pill	事後避孕藥	si·hau bay·yan·yeuk

SAFE TRAVEL

198

allergies

過敏症

I'm allergic to ...	我對······	ngáw deui ...
	過敏。	gaw·mán
He/She is	佢對······過敏。	kéui deui ... gaw·mán
allergic to ...		
antibiotics	抗菌素	kawng·kún·so
anti-	消炎藥	siù·yìm yeuk
inflammatories		
aspirin	阿斯匹林	àa·sì·pàt·làm
bees	蜜蜂	mat·fùng
codeine	可待因	háw·doy·yàn
penicillin	青黴素	chìng·mui·so
pollen	花粉	fàa·fán
sulphur-based	硫基藥物	làu·gày yeuk·mat
drugs		

I have a skin allergy.
我皮膚過敏。 　　　　ngáw pày·fù gaw·mán

antihistamines	抗組胺藥	kawng·jó·ngàwn·yeuk
inhaler	吸入器	kàp·yap·hay
injection	打針	dáa·jàm

For food-related allergies, see **vegetarian & special meals**, page 179.

alternative treatments

非主流醫療

I don't use (Western medicine).
我唔食(西藥)。 　　　ngáw ǹg sik (sài·yeuk)

I prefer ...	我寧願睇…… 醫師。	ngáw lìng·yéwn tái ... yì·sì
Can I see someone who practices ...?	我想睇…… 醫師。	ngáw séung tái ... yì·sì
acupuncture	識針灸嘅	sìk jàm·gau ge
Chinese herbal medicine	識中藥嘅	sìk jùng·yeuk ge
Chinese medicine	中	jùng
meridian massage	識經絡 按摩嘅嘅	sìk gìng·lawk ge ngawn·mò ge
naturopathy	識自然 療法嘅	sìk ji·yìn liu·faat ge
reflexology	識反射 療法嘅	sìk fáan·se liu·faat ge

SAFE TRAVEL

200

parts of the body

身體部位

My ... hurts.
我嘅……好痛。

ngáw ge ... hó·tung

I can't move my ...
我嘅……唔郁得。

ngáw ge ... ńg yùk·dàk

I have a cramp in my ...
我嘅……抽筋。

ngáw ge ... chàu·gàn

My ... is swollen.
我嘅……腫咗。

ngáw ge ... júng·jáw

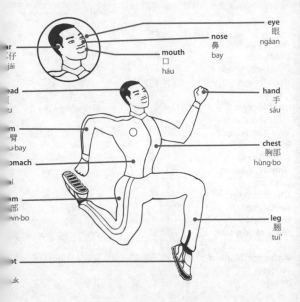

eye
眼
ngáan

nose
鼻
bay

mouth
口
háu

ear
仔
jái

hand
手
sáu

** head**

u

arm
臂
u·bay

chest
胸部
hùng·bo

stomach

ai

arm
部
wn·bo

leg
腿
tuí

foot

uk

pharmacist

I need something for …
我要……嘅藥。 ngáw yiu … ge yeuk

Do I need a prescription for …?
……需唔需要 … sèui·ǹg·sèui·yiu yì·sàng
開處方呀？ hòy chéw·fàwng aa

I have a prescription.
我有處方。 ngáw yáu chéw·fàwng

How many times a day?
每日食幾次？ muí·yat sik gáy chi

Will it make me drowsy?
食咗會唔會 sik·jáw wuí·ǹg·wuí
治眼瞓㗎？ hàp·ngáan·fan gaa

antiseptic n	消毒	siù·duk
band-aid	瘡口貼	chàwng·háu
contraceptives	避孕藥	bay·yan·yeuk
dental floss	潔牙綫	git·ngàa·sin
gauze	紗布	sàa·bo
gut blockers (for diarrhoea)	止痾藥	jí·ngàw·yeuk
insect repellent	防蟲劑	fàwng·chùng·jài
iodine	碘酒	dìn·jáu
painkillers	止痛藥	jí·tung·yeuk
sanitary napkin	衛生巾	wai·sàng·gàn
tampon	棉塞	mìn·sàk
thermometer	探熱器	taam·yit·hay
toothbrush	牙刷	ngàa·cháat
toothpaste	牙膏	ngàa·gò
rehydration salts	補充水份 沖劑	bó·chùng séui·fan chùng·jài
water purification tablets	食水淨化劑	sik·séui jing·faa·jài
needle	針	jàm

每日（飯後）食兩次。
muí·yat (faan·haau)
sik léung chi

Twice a day (with food).

以前食過未啊？
yí·chìn sik·gaw mày aa

Have you taken this before?

啲藥一定要食晒。
dì yeuk yàt·ding yiu
sik saai

You must complete the course.

dentist

牙科

Could I see a dentist who speaks English?
我想睇個（識
講英文嘅）牙醫。
ngáw séung tái gaw (sik
gáwng yìng·mán ge) ngàa·yì

I've lost a filling.
我崩咗牙。
ngáw bàng·jáw ngàa

My dentures are broken.
我啲假牙崩咗。
ngáw dì gáa·ngàa bàng·jáw

I have a ...	我有……	ngáw yáu ...
broken tooth	崩牙	bàng·ngàa
cavity	牙窿	ngàa·lùng
toothache	牙痛	ngàa·tung

I need (a/an) ...	我要……	ngáw yiu ...
anaesthetic	麻醉藥	maa·jeui·yeuk
filling	補牙	bó·ngàa

health

203

My gums hurt.
我牙齦好痛。   ngáw ngàa·gàn hó tung

I don't want it extracted.
唔好萌我隻牙。   ǹg·hó màng ngáw jek ngàa

Ouch!
哎唷！   ài·yaw

the dentist may say ...	
擘開口。 maak·hòy háu	Open wide.
唔會痛。 ǹg·wuí tung	This won't hurt a bit.
咬一下。 gáau yàt háa	Bite down on this.
唔好郁。 ǹg·hó yùk	Don't move.
浪口！ láwng·háu	Rinse!
返嚟，仲未完！ fàan lài jung·may yèwn	Come back, I haven't finished.

Some words are marked either **HK** or **China** to show that they are used solely in Hong Kong or in Cantonese-speaking regions of China. They symbols ⓝ, ⓐ and ⓥ stand for noun, adjective and verb and have been added for clarity

A

aboard 上咗 séung·jáw
abortion 墮胎 daw·tòy
about 關于 gwàan·yew
above 以上 yí·seung
abroad 國外 gawk·ngoy
accident 意外 yi·ngoy
accommodation 住宿 jew·sùk
account (bank) 賬單 jeung·dàan
across 對面 deui·min
activist 積極份子 jìk·gik·fan·jí
actor 演員 yín·yewn
acupuncture 針灸 jàm·gau
adaptor 轉換插頭 jéwn·wun chaap·tàu
addiction 毒癮 duk·yán
address 地址 day·jí
administration 行政部門 hàng·jing bo·mùn
admission (price) 票價 piu·gaa
admit 准 jéun
adult ⓝ 大人 daai·yàn
advertisement 廣告 gáwng·go
advice 建議 gin·yí
aerobics 體操 tái·chò
aeroplane 飛機 fày·gày
Africa 非洲 fày·jàu
after 以後 yí·hau
(this) afternoon (今日) 下晝 (gàm·yat) haa·jau
afternoon tea 下午茶 haa·ńg·chàa
aftershave 鬚後水 sò·hau·séui
again 再次 joy·chi
age ⓝ 年齡 lìn·lìng
(three days) ago (三日) 前 (sàam yat) chìn
agree 同意 tùng·yi
agriculture 農業 lùng·yip
ahead 前面 chìn·min

AIDS 愛滋病 ngoy·jì·beng
air 空氣 hùng·hay
air-conditioned 有空調嘅／有冷氣嘅 yáu hùng·tiu ge/yáu láang·hay ge **HK/China**
air conditioning 空調／冷氣 hùng·tiu/láang·hay **HK/China**
airline 航空公司 hàwng·hùng gùng·sì
airmail 空郵 hùng·yàu
airplane 飛機 fày·gày
airport 飛機場 fày·gày·chèung
airport tax 機場稅 gày·chèung·seui
aisle (on plane) 走廊 jáu·láwng
alarm clock 鬧鐘 law·jùng
alcohol 酒精 jáu·jing
all 所有嘅 sáw·yáu·ge
allergic 過敏 gaw·mán
alleyway 巷仔 hawng·jái
almond 杏仁 hang·yàn
almost 差唔多 chàa·dì
alone 一個人 yàt gaw yàn
already 已經 yí·gìng
also 都 dò
altar 祭壇 jai·tàan
altitude 海拔 hóy·bat
always 每次 muí·chi
ambassador 大使 daai·si
ambulance 急傷車 gau·sèung·chè
American football 美式橄欖球 máy·sìk gaam·láam·kàu
anaemia 貧血 pàn·hewt
anarchist 無政府主義者 mò·jing·fú·jéw·yi·jé
ancestors 祖先 jó·sìn
ancestral home 祖屋 jó·ngùk
ancient 古代 gú·doy
and 同埋 tùng·mài
angry 嬲 nàu
animal 動物 dung·mat
ankle 腳踝 geui·jàang

another 另一個 ling yàt gaw
answer ⓥ 答復 daap·fùk
ant 螞蟻 máa·ngái
antibiotics 抗菌素 kawng·kún·so
antinuclear 反核 fáan hat
antique ⓐ 古董 gú·dúng
antique market 古董市場
　gú·dúng sí·chèung
antique shop 古董鋪 gú·túng·pó
antiseptic ⓐ 消毒劑 siu·duk·jai
any 任何 yum·hàw
apartment (up-market) 公寓 gùng·yew
appendix (body) 盲腸 màng·chéung
apple 蘋果 ping·gwáw
appointment (to meet someone)
　有約 yáu yeuk
apricot 杏 hang
April 四月 say·yewt
archaeology 考古學 háw·gú·hawk
architect 建築師 gin·jùk·sì
architecture 建築 gin·jùk
argue 鬧交 naau·gàau
arm 胳膊 sáu·bey
aromatherapy 香氣療法
　hèung·hay liù·faat
arrest ⓥ 逮捕 dai·bo
arrivals 抵達 dái·daa
arrive 到達 do·daat
art 藝術 ngai·seut
art gallery 藝術館 ngai·seut·gún
artist 藝術家 ngai·seut·gàa
ashtray 煙灰缸 yìn·fèui·gàwng
Asia 亞洲 ngaa·jàu
ask (a question) 問 man
ask (for something) 請求 chéng·kàu
asparagus 蘆筍 lò·séun
aspirin 阿斯匹靈 à·sì·pàt·lìng
asthma 哮喘 hàau·chéwn
at 喺 hái
athletics 田徑 tìn·ging
atmosphere (ambience) 氣氛 hay·fàn
aubergine 茄子 ké·jí
August 八月 baat·yewt
aunt (mother's sister) 阿姨 a·yì
aunt (father's sister) 姑姐 gù·jè
Australia 澳大利亞 ngo·daai·lay·a
Australian Rules Football
　澳式橄欖球 ngo·sik gaam·láam·kàu
automated teller machine (ATM)
　自動提款機 ji·dung tài·fún·gày
autumn 秋天 chàu·tìn

avenue 大道 daai·do
avocado 牛油果 ngàu·yáu·gwáw
awful 可怕 háw·paa

B

B&W (film) 黑白 (片) hàak·baak(·pín)
baby BB仔 bì·bì·jái
baby food 嬰兒食品 yìng·yi sik·bán
baby powder 爽身粉 sáwng·sàn·fán
babysitter 臨時保姆 làm·si bó·mó
back (body) 背脊 bui·jek
back (position) 後邊 hau·bìn
backpack 背囊 bui·làwng
bacon 煙肉 yìn·yuk
bad 壞 waai
badminton 羽毛球 yéw·mò·kau
bag 包 bàau
baggage 行李 hàng·láy
baggage allowance 免費行李
　mín·fai hàng·láy
baggage claim 行李認領處
　hàng·láy ying·líng·chew
bakery 麵包店 mìn·bàau·dim
balance (account) 找續 jáau·juk
balcony 騎樓 kè·láu
ball (sport) 波 bàw
ballet 芭蕾舞 bàa·leui·mó
bamboo 竹 jùk
banana 香蕉 hèung·jiù
band (music) 樂隊 ngawk·déui
bandage 繃帶 bàng·dáai
Band-Aid 瘡口貼 chòng·háu·tip
bank ⓝ 銀行 ngàn·hàwng
bank account 銀行賬戶
　ngàn·hàwng jeung·wu
banknote 紙幣 jí·bai
baptism 洗禮 sái·lái
bar 酒吧 jáu·bàa
bar work 酒吧工作 jáu·bàa gùng·jawk
barber 飛髮鋪 fày·faat·pó
baseball 棒球 páang·kàu
basin 盆 pun
basket 籃 láam
basketball 籃球 làam·kàu
bath ⓝ 沖涼 chùng·lèung
bathing suit 游水衣 yàu·séui·yì
bathroom 廁所 chi·sáw
battery 電池 dìn·chì
be 做 jo
beach 沙灘 sàa·tàan

beach volleyball 沙灘排球
  sàa·tàan pàai·kàu
bean 荳 dáu
beansprout 芽菜 ngàa·choy
beautiful 美麗 máy·lai
beauty salon 美容店 máy·yùng·dim
because 因為 yàn·wai
bed 床 chàwng
bed linen 床單 chàwng·dàan
bedding 被褥 páy·yúk
bedroom 睡房 seui·fáwng
bee 蜜蜂 mat·fùng
beef 牛肉 ngàu·yuk
beer 啤酒 bè·jáu
beetroot 甜菜 tìm·choy
before 以前 yí·chìn
beggar 乞依 hàt·yì
behind 後面 hau·min
Beijing 北京 bàk·gìng
Belgium 比利時 báy·lay·sì
below 下面 haa·min
beside 旁邊 pàwng·bìn
best 最好嘅 jeui·hó·ge
bet ⓝ 賭 dó
better 更好 gang·hó
between 中間 jùng·gàan
Bible 聖經 sing·gìng
bicycle 單車 dàan·chè
big 大 daai
bigger 更大 gang daai
biggest 最大 jeui daai
bike 單車 dàan·chè
bike chain 車鏈 chè·lín
bike lock 車鎖 chè·sáw
bike path 自行車道 dàan·chè ging
bike shop 修車店 sàu·chè·dim
bill (restaurant etc) 單 dàan
binoculars 望遠鏡 mawng·yéwn·geng
bird 雀 jéuk
birth certificate 出世紙 chèut·sai·jí
birthday 生日 sàang·yat
biscuit 餅乾 béng·gàwn
bite (dog/insect) ⓝ 咬 ngáau
bitter 苦 fú
black 黑色 hàak·sìk
bladder 膀胱 pàwng·gwàwng
blanket 氈 jìn
blind ⓐ 盲眼 màang·ngáan
blister 起泡 háy·pàwk
blocked (toilet) 塞咗 sàt·jáw
blood 血液 hewt·yìk

blood group 血型 hewt·yìng
blood pressure 血壓 hewt·ngaat
blood test 驗血 yìm·hewt
blow dry ⓥ 吹乾 chèui gàwn
blue 藍色 làam·sìk
board (a plane, ship etc) ⓥ 上 séung
boarding house 招待所 jiù·doy·sáw
boarding pass 登機卡 dàng·gày·kàat
boat 船 sèwn
body 身體 sàn·tái
boiled 煮熟 jéw
bone 骨頭 gwàt·tàu
book ⓝ 書 sèw
book ⓥ 訂 deng
book shop 書店 sèw·dim
booked out 訂滿 deng mún
boots (footwear) 靴 hèu
border 邊界 bìn·gaai
bored 悶 mun
boring 冇聊 mò·liù
borrow 借 je
botanic garden 植物公園
  jik·mat gùng·yéwn
both 兩個都 léung gaw dò
bottle 樽 jèun
bottle opener 開瓶器 hòy·pìng·hay
bottle shop 酒舖 jáu pó
bottom (body) 屁股 pay·gú
bottom (position) 底 dái
bowl 碗 wún
box ⓝ 箱 sèung
boxer shorts 短褲 déwn·fu
boxing 拳擊 kèwn·gìk
boy 男仔 làam·jái
boyfriend 男朋友 làam·pàng·yáu
bra 胸罩 yéw·jaau
braise 燜 màn
brakes 逼力 bìk·lik
brandy 白蘭地 baak·làan·dáy
brave ⓐ 勇敢 yúng·gám
bread 麵包 min·bàau
break ⓥ 斷 téw
break down ⓥ 崩潰 bàng·kuí
breakfast 早餐 jó·chàan
breast (body) 乳房 yéw·fàwng
breast-feed 用母乳直接喂奶
  yung mó·yéw jik·jip wai·láai
breathe 呼吸 fù·kàp
bribe ⓝ 賄賂 kuí·lo
bridge 橋 kiù
briefcase 手袋 sáu·dóy

brilliant (clever) 聰明 chùng·mìng
bring 帶 daai
broccoli 西蘭花 sài·làan·fàa
brochure 說明書 sewt·mìng·sèw
broken 壞咗 waai·jáw
broken down (vehicle) 拋錨 pàau·làau
bronchitis 肺炎 fai·yìm
bronze 青銅 ching·tùng
brother 兄弟 hìng·dai
brother (elder) 哥哥 gàw·gàw
brother (younger) 細佬 sai·ló
brown 咖啡色 gaa·fè·sìk
bruise ⓝ 青腫 chèng·júng
brush ⓝ 毛筆 mò·bàt
Brussels sprout 包菜仔 bàau·choy·jái
bucket 水桶 séui·túng
Buddha 佛祖 fàt
Buddhism 佛教 fàt·gaau
Buddhist 佛教徒 fàt·gaau·tò
budget ⓝ 開支 hòy·jì
buffet ⓝ 自助餐 jì·jawk·chàan
bug 蟲 chung
build 起 háy
builder 建築公司 gin·jùk·gùng·sì
building 樓 láu
humbag 腰攣 yiù·dóy
burn ⓥ 燒傷 siu·séung
burnt 燒燶 siu·lùng
bus 巴士／公共汽車
　bàa·sí/gùng·gung hay·chè HK/China
bus (intercity) 巴士／長途汽車
　bàa·sí/chèung·tò hay·chè HK/China
business 生意 sàang·yi
business class 頭等艙 tàu·dáng·chàwng
business person 生意人 sàang·yi·yàn
business trip 出差 chèut·chàai
busker 街頭藝人 gàai·tàu ngai·yàn
bus stop (intercity) 巴士站 bàa·sí·jaam
busy 忙 màwng
but 但係 daan·hai
butcher 豬肉佬 jèw·yuk·ló
butcher's shop 肉店 yuk·dim
butter 牛油 ngàu·yàu
butterfly 蝴蝶 wù·díp
button 紐 náu
buy 買 màai

C

cabbage 白菜 baak·choy
cable car 纜車 laam·chè
café 咖啡屋 gaa·fè·ngùk

cake 蛋糕 daan·gò
cake shop 餅店 béng·dim
calculator 計算機 gai·sewn·gày
calendar 日曆 yat·lik
call ⓥ 叫 giu
camera 相機 séung·gày
camera shop 相機鋪 séung·gày·pó
camp ⓥ 露營 lo·yìng
camping ground 營地 yìng·day
camping store 露營用品店
　lo·yìng yung·bán·dim
campsite 露營地點 lo·yìng day·dím
can (be able) 可唔可以 háw·ǹg háw·yí
can (have permission) 可以 háw·yí
can (tin) 罐頭 gun·táu
can opener 開罐器 hòy·gun·hay
Canada 加拿大 gàa·làa·daai
cancel 取消 chéui·siù
cancer 癌症 ngàam·jing
candle 蠟燭 laap·jùk
candy 糖果 tàwng·gwáw
cantaloupe 哈密瓜 hàa·mat·gwàa
canteen 快餐廳 faai·chàan·tèng
Cantonese (language)
　廣東話 gwáwng·dùng·wáa
Cantopop (music style) 粵語流行曲
　yewt·yéw làu·hàng·kùk
capitalism 資本主義 jì·bún·jéw·yi
capsicum 青椒 chèng·jiù
car 車 chè
car hire 汽車出租 hay·chè chèut·jò
car owner's title 車主所有權
　chè·jéw sáw·yáu·kèwn
car park 停車場 ting·chè·cheung
car registration 車牌號碼
　chè·pàai ho·máa
caravan 流動屋 làu·dung·ngùk
cardiac arrest 心臟病 sàm·jawng·beng
cards (playing) 啤牌 pè·páai
care (for someone) ⓥ 關心 gwàan·sàm
carp 鯉魚 láy·yéw
carpark 停車場 ting·chè·cheung
carpet 地氈 day·jin
carpenter 木匠 muk·jeung
carrot 紅蘿蔔 hùng·làw·baak
carry 揹 mè
carton 箱 sèung
cash ⓝ 現金 yin·gàm
cash (a cheque) ⓥ 兌現 deui·yin
cash register 收銀機 sàu·ngán·chew
cashew 腰果 yiù·gwáw

cashier 出納 chèut·laap
casino 賭場 dó·chèung
cassette 錄音帶 luk·yàm·dáai
castle 城堡 sìng·bó
casual work 臨時工 làm·sì·gùng
cat 貓 màau
cathedral 天主教教堂
  tìn·jéw·gaau gaau·tàwng
Catholic 天主教 tìn·jéw·gaau
cauliflower 椰菜花 yè·choy·fàa
cave 山窿 sàan·lùng
CD CD sì·dì
celebration 慶祝 hing·jùk
cell phone 手機 sáu·gày
cemetery 墳場 fàn·chèung
cent 分 fàn
centimetre 厘米 lày·mái
centre 中心 jùng·sàm
ceramics 陶瓷 tò·cì
cereal 麥片粥 mat·pín·jùk
certificate 證明 jing·mìng
chain 鍊 lín
chair 凳 dang
chairlift (skiing) 纜車 laam·chè
champagne 香檳 hèung·bàn
championships 錦標賽 gám·biù·choy
chance 機會 gày·wui
change (coins) 找錢 jáau·chín
change (money) 換錢 wun chín
changing room (in shop)
  更衣室 gàng·yì·sàt
charming 有魅力 yáu mui·lik
chat ⊙ 傾偈 king·gái
chat up 調情 tiu·chìng
cheap 平 pèng
cheat 騙局 pin·guk
check ⊙ 查 chàa
check (banking) 支票 jì·piu
check (bill) 賬單 jeung·dàan
check-in (desk) 登記 (台)
  dàng·gay·(tóy)
checkpoint 監察點 gàam·chaat·jaam
cheese 芝士 jì·sí
cheese shop 芝士店 jì·sí·dim
chef 廚師 chèw·sì
chemist (pharmacy) 藥房 yeuk·fàwng
chemist (pharmacist) 藥劑師 yeuk·jài·sì
cheque (banking) 支票 jì·piu
cheque (bill) 賬單 jeung·dàan
cherry 櫻桃 ying·tò

chess (Chinese) 象棋 jeung·káy
chess (Western) 國際象棋
  gawk·jai jeung·káy
chessboard 棋盤 káy·pún
chest (body) 胸 hùng
chestnut 栗子 leut·jí
chewing gum 香口膠
  hèung·háu·gàau
chi (energy) 氣 hay
chicken 雞 gài
chicken pox 水痘 súi·dáu
chickpea 鷹嘴豆 yìng·jéui·dáu
child 細路仔 sai·lo·jái
child seat 小童座 siú·tùng·jaw
childminding 幼稚園 yau·jì·yéwn
children 細路仔 sai·lo·jái
chilli 辣椒 laat·jiù
chilli sauce 辣椒醬 laat·jiù·jeung
China 中國 jùng·gawk
chinaware 瓷器 chì·hay
Chinese 中國人 jùng·gawk·yàn
Chinese herbal medicine
  中草藥 jùng·chó·yeuk
Chinese medicine doctor 中醫 jùng·yì
chiropractor 脊椎按摩治法醫師
  jek·jèui lagwn·mò liù·faat yì·sì
chocolate 朱古力 jèw·gù·lik
cholera 霍亂 fàwk·lewn
choose 選擇 séwn·jaak
chopping board 砧板 jàm·báan
chopsticks 筷子 faai·jí
Christian 基督徒 gày·dùk·tò
Christian name 名 méng
Christmas 聖誕節 sing·daan·jit
Christmas Day 聖誕日 sing·daan·yat
Christmas Eve 平安夜 pìng·ngàwn·ye
church 教堂 gaau·tàwng
cider 蘋果酒 pìng·gwáw·jáu
cigar 雪茄 seut·kàa
cigarette 香煙 hèung·yìn
cigarette lighter 打火機 dáa·fó·gày
cigarette paper 捲煙紙 géwn·yìn·jí
cinema 戲院 hay·yéwn
circus 雜技 jaap·gay
citizenship 公民 gùng·màn
city 城市 sìng·sí
city centre 市中心 sí·jùng·sàm
civil rights 公民權 gùng·màn·kèwn
class (category) 類 leui
class system 階級制度 gàai·kùp jai·do

classical 古典 gú-dín
classical Chinese art 傳統藝術
  chèwn-túng ngai-seut
classical Western art
  古典藝術 gú-dín ngai-seut
classical Beijing opera 京劇 gìng-kek
clean ⓐ 乾淨 gàwn-jeng
clean ⓥ 打掃 dáa-so
cleaning 清潔 chìng-git
client 客戶 haak-wu
cliff 懸崖 yèwn-ngàai
climb (mountain) ⓥ 爬山 pàa-sàan
cloakroom 寄存處 gai-chèwn-chew
clock 鐘 jùng
close ⓥ 關 gwàan
close ⓐ 附近 fu-gan
closed 關門 gwàan-mùn
clothesline 晾衫繩 lawng-sàam-síng
clothing 衣服 yì-fuk
clothing store 服裝店 fuk-jàwng-dim
cloud 雲 wùn
cloudy 天陰 tìn-yàm
clutch (car) ⓝ 極離子 gik-lik-jí
coach (bus) 旅遊巴 léui-yàu-bàa
coast 海邊 hóy-bìn
coat 大衣 daai-yì
cocaine 白粉 baak-fán
cockroach 甲由 gaat-jáat
cocktail 雞尾酒 gài-máy-jáu
cocoa 可可 háw-háw
coconut 椰子 yè-jí
coffee 咖啡 gaa-fè
coffee house 咖啡屋 gaa-fè-ngùk
cognac 白蘭地 baak-làan-dáy
coins 硬幣 ngaan-bai
colleague 同事 tùng-si
collect call 對方付款 deui-fàwng fu-fún
college (university) 大學 daai-hawk
colour ⓝ 顏色 ngàan-sìk
comb ⓝ 梳 sàw
come 嚟 lài
comedy 喜劇片 háy-kek-pín
comfortable 舒服 sèw-fuk
commission 佣金 yúng-gàm
common people 百姓 baak-sing
communal bowl 公碗 gùng-wún
communications (profession)
  交通 gàau-tùng
communion 教會 gaau-wui

communism 共產主義
  gung-cháan-jéw-yi
communist (party member)
  黨員 dáwng-yèwn
communist party official 幹部 gawn-bo
companion 同伴 tung-bun
company (firm) 公司 gùng-sì
compass 指南針 jí-làam-jàm
complain 抱怨 pó-yewn
complaint 投訴 tàu-so
complimentary (free) 贈券 jang-gewn
computer 電腦 dìn-ló
computer game 電子游戲 dìn-jí yàu-hay
comrade 同志 tùng-ji
concert 音樂會 yàm-ngawk-wúi
concussion 昏迷 fàn-mài
conditioner (hair) 護髮素 wu-faat-so
condom 避孕套 bay-yan-to
conference 會議 wúi-yí
confession 坦白 táan-baak
confirm (a booking) 確定 kawk-dìng
congratulations 恭喜 gùng-háy
conjunctivitis 結膜炎 git-màwk-yìm
connection 連接 lìn-jip
conservative ⓝ 保守 bó-sáu
constipation 便秘 bin-bay
consulate 領事館 lìng-si-gún
contact lens 隱形眼鏡
  yán-yìng ngáan-géng
contact lens solution 隱形眼鏡水
  yán-yìng ngáan-géng séui
contraceptives 避孕用品
  bay-yan yung-bán
contract ⓝ 合同 hap-tung
convenience store 便利店 bin-lay-dim
convent 女修道院 léui sàu-do-yéwn
cook ⓝ 廚師 chèw-sì
cook ⓥ 煮飯 jéw-faan
cooked food stall 熟食檔 suk-sik-dawng
cookie 曲奇 kùk-kày
cooking 煮飯 jéw-faan
cool (temperature) 涼 lèung
corkscrew 螺絲開瓶器
  làw-sì hòy-pìng-hay
corn 粟米 sùk-mái
corner 角 gawk
cornflakes 粟米片 sùk-mái-pín
corrupt 貪污 tàam-wù
cost (price) ⓝ 價錢 gaa-chìn
cost ⓥ 駛 … 錢 sái … chìn
cotton 棉花 mìn-fàa

cotton balls 棉球 mìn-kàu
cotton buds 棉棒 mìn-páang
cough ⓥ 咳嗽 kàt-sau
cough medicine 咳藥 kàt-yeuk
count ⓥ 計 gai
counter (at hotel) 櫃臺 gwai-tóy
country 國家 gawk-gàa
countryside 鄉下 hèung-háa
coupon 票 piu
courgette 西葫蘆 sài-wù-ló
court (legal) 法庭 faat-tìng
court (tennis) (網球) 場 (máwng-kàu) chèung
couscous 粉蒸羊肉 fán-jìng yéung-yuk
cover charge 入場費 yap-chèung-fai
cow 牛 ngàu
cracker (biscuit) 餅乾 béng-gàwn
crafts 手工藝 sáu-gùng-ngai
crash ⓝ 撞車 jawng-chè
crazy 癲㖞 dìn-ge
cream 忌廉 gay-lìm
crèche 幼稚園 yau-ji-yéwn
credit 信用 seun-yung
credit card 信用卡 seun-yung-kàat
cricket (sport) 板球 báan-kàu
cross (religious) 十字架 sap-ji-gáa
crowded 好逼 hó-bìk
cucumber 黃瓜 wàwng-gwàa
cup 杯 bùi
cupboard 櫃 gwai
cupping (traditional therapy)
  拔火罐 bat-fó-gun
currency exchange
  外幣兌換 ngoy-bai deui-wun
current (electricity) 電流 dìn-làu
current affairs 時事 sì-sí
curry 咖喱 gaa-làry
custom 風俗 fùng-juk
customs (immigration) 海關 hóy-gwàan
cut ⓥ 切 chit
cutlery 刀叉 dò-chàa
CV 簡歷 gáan-lìk
cycle ⓥ 踩單車 cháai dàan-chè
cycling 單車賽 dàan-chè-choy
cyclist 單車手 dàan-chè-sáu
cystitis 膀胱炎 pàwng-gwàwng-yìm

D

dad 爸爸 bàa-bàa
daily 日常 yàt-sèung
dance ⓥ 跳舞 tiu-mó

dancing 舞蹈 mó-do
dangerous 危險 ngài-hím
date (appointment) ⓝ 約會 yeuk-wui
date (calendar) ⓝ 日期 yat-kày
date (fruit) 棗 jó
dark (night) 黑暗 hàak-ngam
dark (of colour) 深色 sàm-sìk
date (go out with) 拍拖 paak-tàw
date of birth 出生日期
  chèut-sàng yat-kày
daughter 女 léui
dawn 日出 yat-chèut
day 日頭 yat-táu
day after tomorrow (the) 後日 hau-yat
day before yesterday (the)
  前日 chìn-yat
dead 死咗 séi-jáw
deaf 耳聾 yí-lùng
deal (cards) 發牌 faat páai
December 十二月 sap-yi-yewt
decide 決定 kewt-dìng
deep 深 sàm
deep-fried 炸 jaa
deforestation 斬伐森林
  jáam-fat sèw-làm
degrees (temperature) 度 do
delay ⓝ 推遲 tùi-chì
delicatessen 熟食店 suk-sik-dim
deliver 送 sung
democracy 民主制 màn-jéw-jai
democratic 民主 màn-jéw
dengue fever 登革熱 dàng-gaap-yit
Denmark 丹麥 dàan-mak
dental floss 潔牙線 git-ngàa-sin
dentist 牙科 ngàa-fò
deodorant 香水 hèung-séui
depart 離開 lày-hoy
department store 百貨公司
  baak-fo gùng-sì
departure 出發 chèut-faat
departure gate 登機閘口
  dàng-gày jaap-háu
deposit (bank) 存錢 chewn-chín
derailleur 換波裝置 wun-bàw jàwng-ji
descendent 後人 hau-yàn
desert 沙漠 sàa-mawk
design 設計 chit-gai
dessert 甜品 tìm-bán
destination 目的地 muk-dìk-day
details 細節 sai-jit
diabetes 糖尿病 tàwng-liu-beng

dial tone 撥號音 but·ho·yàm
diaper 尿片 liu·pín
diaphragm (contraceptive)
子宮帽 jí·gùng·mó
diarrhoea 肚痾 tó·ngàw
diary 日記 yat·gay
dice 色仔 sìk·jái
dictionary 詞典 chì·dín
die ⊙ 去世 heui·sai
diet ⓝ 減肥 gáam·fày
different 唔同 n̄g·tùng
difficult 難 làam
dim sum 點心 dím·sàm
dining car 餐卡 chàan·kàa
dinner 晚飯 máan·faan
dipping sauce 醬 jeung
direct 直接 jik·jip
direct-dial 直撥 jik·but
direction 方向 fàwng·heung
director (film) 導演 do·yín
dirty 污穢 wù·jò
disabled 傷殘 sèung·chàan
disco 的士高 dìk·sì·gò
discount 折扣 jit·kau
discrimination 歧視 kày·si
disease 疾病 jat·beng
dish (of food) 碟 díp
disk (CD-ROM) CD sì·dì
disk (floppy) 軟盤 yéwn·pún
diving (sport) 潛水 chìm·séui
diving equipment 潛水裝備
chìm·séui jàwng·bay
divorced 離婚 lày·fàn
dizzy 頭暈 tàu·wàn
do ⊙ 做 jo
doctor 醫生 yì·sàng
documentary 記錄片 gay·luk·pín
dog 狗 gáu
dole 救濟 gau·jai
doll 公仔 gùng·jái
dollar 美金 máy·gàm
doona 被 páy
door 門 mun
dope (drugs) 大麻 daai·màa
dormitory 宿舍 sùk·se
double 雙人 sèung·yàn
double bed 雙人床 sèung·yàn·chàwng
double room 雙人房 sèung·yàn·fàwng
down (location) 下面 haa·min
downhill 落山 lawk·sàan
dozen 打 dàa

drama 戲劇 hay·kek
dream ⓝ 夢 mung
dress ⓝ 衫 sàam
dried 乾 gàwn
dried fruit 果乾 gwáw·gàwn
drink (alcoholic) ⓝ 酒料 jáu·líu
drink ⓝ 飲料 yám·líu
drink ⊙ 飲 yám
drive ⊙ 開車 hòy·chè
drivers licence 駕駛執照 gaa·sái jàp·jiu
drug(s) 毒品 duk·bán
drug addiction 毒品上癮
duk·bán séung·yán
drug dealer 毒販 duk·fáan
drug trafficking 販毒 fáan·duk
drug user 癮君子 yán·gùn·jí
drum ⓝ 鼓 gú
drunk 醉 jeui
dry ⓐ 乾 gàwn
dry (clothes) ⊙ 晾乾 lawng·gàwn
duck 鴨 ngaap
dummy (pacifier) 奶嘴 láai·jéui
dumpling 餃 gáau
dumpling (boiled) 煮餃 jéw gáau
dumpling (fried) 煎餃 jìn gáau
dumpling (steamed) 蒸餃 jìng gáau
DVD DVD dì·wì·dì
dynasty 朝代 chìu·doy
dysentery 痢疾 lay·jat

E

each 每個 muí·gaw
ear 耳仔 yí·jái
early 早 jó
earn (money) ⊙ 掙 (錢) jaan·(chín)
earplugs 耳機 yí·gày
earrings 耳鑲 yí·wáan
Earth 地球 day·kàu
earthquake 地震 day·jan
east 東方 dùng·fàwng
Easter 復活節 fuk·wut·ji
easy 易 yung·yi
eat 食 sik
economy class 經濟艙 gìng·jai·chàwng
ecstasy (drug) 迷幻劑 mài·waan·yeuk
eczema 濕疹 sàp·chán
editor 編輯 pìn·chàp
education 教育 gaau·yuk
egg (chicken) 雞蛋 gài·dáan
eggplant 茄瓜 ké·gwàa

election 選舉 séwn·géui
electrical store 電子用品店 dīn·jí yūng·bán·dim
electricity 電 dīn
elevator 電梯 dīn·tài
email ⑩ 電子郵件 dīn·jí yàu·gín
embarrassed 唔好意思 ṅg·hó yi·sì
embarrassed (very) 尷尬 gaam·gaai
embassy 大使館 daai·sí·gún
embroidery 刺繡 chi·sau
emergency 緊急意外 ṅ gán·gàp yi·ngoy
emotional 動情 dùng·chíng
emperor 皇帝 wàwng·dai
employee 僱員 gu·yèwn
employer 僱主 gu·jéw
empress 皇后 wàwng·hau
empty 空 hùng
end ⑩ 結束 git·chùk
endangered species 瀕臨滅絕物種 pàn·làm mit·jewt mat·júng
engaged (marriage) 訂婚 dīng·fàn
engagement (marriage) 訂婚儀式 dīng·fàn yì·sìk
engine 發動機 faat·dùng·gày
engineer 工程師 gùng·chìng·sì
engineering 工程學 gùng·chìng·hawk
England 英國 yìng·gawk
English 英文 yìng·man
English teacher 英文教師 yìng·man gaau·sì
enjoy oneself 玩 wáan
enough 夠 gau
enter 入 yap
entertainment guide 娛樂指南 yèw·lawk jí·làam
entry 入口 yàn·háu
envelope 信封 seun·fùng
environment 環境 wàan·ging
epilepsy 癲癇 dìn·gáan
equal opportunity 平等待遇 pìng·dáng doy·yew
equality 平等 pìng·dáng
equipment 設備 chit·bay
escalator 電梯 dīn·tài
estate agency 房地產代理 fàwng·day·cháan doy·láy
euro (currency) 歐元 ngàu·yèwn
Europe 歐洲 ngàu·jàu
euthanasia 安樂死 ngàwn·lawk·sáy
evening 夜晚 ye·máan
every 每次 múi·chi

everyone 每個人 múi·gaw·yàn
everything 一切 yàt·chai
exactly 確切 kawk·chit
example 例子 lai
excellent 好極 hó·gik
excess (baggage) 過重(行李) gaw·chúng (hàng·láy)
exchange ⑩ 交換 gàau·wun
exchange ⑩ 換 wun
exchange rate 兌換率 deui·wun·léut
excluded 排除 pàai·chèui
exhaust (car) 廢氣 fai·hay
exhibition 展覽 jín·láam
exit ⑩ 出口 chèut·háu
expensive 貴 gwai
experience 經驗 gìng·yim
exploitation 剝削 màwk·seuk
express ⑧ 速遞 chùk·dai
(by) express mail (寄)速遞信 (gay) chùk·dai seun
extension (visa) (簽證)延期 (chìm·jing) yìn·kày
eye 眼睛 ngáan·jīng
eye drops 眼樂水 ngáan·yeuk·séui
eyes 眼睛 ngáan·jīng

F

fabric 布料 bo·líu
face (body) ⑩ 面 mīn
face (social standing) 面子 mīn·jí
face cloth 毛巾 mò·gàn
factory 工廠 gùng·cháwng
factory worker 工人 gùng·yàn
fall (autumn) 秋天 chàu·tin
fall (down) ⑩ 跌 dit
family 家庭 gàa·tìng
family name 姓 sing
famine 饑荒 gày·fàwng
famous 出名 chèut·méng
fan (machine) 電風扇 dīn·fùng·sin
fan (sport etc) (球)迷 (kàu) mài
fanbelt 風扇帶 fùng·sin·dáai
far 遠 yéwn
fare 票價 piu·gaa
farm ⑩ 農地 lùng·day
farmer 農民 lùng·màn
fashion 時髦 sì·mò
fast ⑧ 快 faai
fat ⑧ 肥 fày
father 父親 fu·chàn

father-in-law 岳父 ngawk·fú
faucet 水喉 séui·hàu
fault (someone's) 責任 jàak·yam
faulty 唔妥 ǹg·táw
fax machine 傳真 chèwn·jàn
February 二月 yi·yewt
feed ⓥ 喂 wai
feel (touch) 摸 mó
feeling (physical) 情感 chìng·gám
feelings 感情 gám·chìng
female 女性 léui·sing
fence 籬笆 lày·bàa
fencing (sport) 劍擊 gim·gìk
feng shui 風水 fùng·séui
ferry ⓝ 小輪 siú·lèun
festival 節日 jit·yat
fever 發燒 faat·sìu
few 一啲 yàt·dì
fiancé 未婚夫 may·fàn·fù
fiancée 未婚妻 may·fàn·chài
fiction (novel) 小說 siú·sewt
fig 無花果 mò·fàa·gwáw
fight ⓥ 打交 dáa·gàau
fill 入滿 yap·mún
fillet 柳 láu
film (cinema) 電影 dìn·yíng
film (for camera) 菲林 fày·lám
film speed 感光度 gám·gwàwng·do
filtered 過濾 gaw·leui
find ⓥ 搵到 wún·dó
fine (penalty) ⓝ 罰款 fat·fún
fine ⓐ 好 hó
finger 手指 sáu·jí
finish ⓝ 結束 git·chùk
Finland 芬蘭 fàn·làan
fire 火 fó
firewood 火柴 fó·chàai
first 第一 dai·yàt
first-aid kit 救傷用品
    gau·sèung yung·bán
first class 頭等艙 tàu·dáng·chàwng
first name 名 méng
fish ⓝ 魚 yéw
fish shop 魚攤 yéw·tàan
fishing 釣魚 diu·yéw
flag 國旗 gawk·kày
flannel 絨布 yúng·bo
flashlight 電筒 dìn·túng
flask 暖水壺 léwn·séui·wú
flat (apartment) 樓 láu
flat ⓐ 平 pìng

flea 跳虱 tiu·sàt
fleamarket 古董市場
    gú·dúng sí·chèung
flight 航班 hàwng·bàan
floating restaurant 海鮮舫
    hóy·sìn·fáwng
flood ⓝ 水浸 séui·jam
floor 地板 day·báan
floor (storey) 層 chàng
florist 花店 fàa·dim
flour 麵粉 min·fán
flower 花 fàa
flu 感冒 gám·mo
fly ⓥ 飛 fày
foggy 有霧 yáu mo
folk music 民謠 màn·yìu
follow 跟 gàn
food 食物 sik·mat
food court 美食廣場
    máy·sik gwáwng·chèung
food stall 熟食檔 suk·sik·dawng
food supplies 食品供應
    sik·bán gùng·ying
foot 腳 geui
football (soccer) 足球 jùk·kàu
footpath 路仔 lo·jái
foreign (goods) 外國 ngoy·gawk
forest 森林 sàm·làam
forever 永遠 wíng·yéwn
forget 忘記 màwng·gay
forgive 原諒 yèwn·leung
fork 叉 chàa
fortnight 雙周 sèung·jàu
fortune cookies 幸運曲奇
    hang·wun kùk·kày
fortune teller 算命佬 sewn·meng·ló
foul 犯規 faan·kwài
foyer 大堂 daai·tàwng
fragile 弱 yeuk
France 法蘭西 faat·làan·sài
free (available) 得閒 dàk·hàan
free (gratis) 免費 mín·fai
free (not bound) 自由 ji·yàu
freeze 冰凍 bìng·dung
fresh 新鮮 sàn·sìn
Friday 禮拜五 lái·baai·ńg
fridge 雪櫃 sewt·gwai
fried (deep-fried) 炸 jaa
friend 朋友 pàng·yáu
from 從 chùng
frost 霜 sèung

frozen 冰凍 bìng·dung
fruit 水果 séui·gwáw
fruit picking 摘水果 jaak séui·gwáw
fry (to stir-fry) 炒 cháau
frying pan (wok) 鍋 wawk
full 滿 mún
full-time 全職 chèwn·jìk
fun 好玩 hó·wáan
funeral 葬禮 jawng·láy
funny 搞笑 gáau·siu
furniture 傢俬 gàa·sì
future ⓝ 將來 jèung·lòy

G

gamble 賭錢 dó·chín
game 比賽 báy·choy
garage 車房 chè·fàwng
garbage 垃圾 laap·saap
garbage can 垃圾箱 laap·saap·sèung
garden 花園 fàa·yéwn
gardener 園丁 yéwn·dìng
gardening 種花 jung·fàa
garlic 蒜 sewn
gas (cooking) 煤氣 mui·hay
gas (petrol) 汽油 hay·yàu
gas cartridge 石油氣筒 sęk·yàu·hay·túng
gastroenteritis 腸胃炎 chèung·wài·yìm
gate (airport etc) 登機口 dàng·gày·háu
gauze 紗布 sàa·bo
gay 同志 tung·ji
gay bar 同志吧 tung·ji·bàa
geomancy 風水 fùng·séui
Germany 德國 dàk·gawk
get (fetch) 攞 láw
get off (train etc) 落 (車) lawk(·chè)
giardiasis 賈第虫病 gáa·dịk·chùng·bẹng
gift 禮物 lái·mạt
gig 節目 jit·mụk
gin 氈酒 jìn·jáu
ginger 薑 gèung
ginseng 人參 yàn·sàm
girl 女仔 léui·jái
girlfriend 女朋友 léui·pàng·yáu
give 送 sung
glandular fever 腺熱 sin·yit
glass (material) 玻璃 bàw·lày
glasses (spectacles) 眼鏡 ngáan·géng
glove(s) 手套 sáu·to
glue 膠水 gàau·séui
go 去 heui

go out 出去 chèut·heui
go out with 拍拖 paak·tàw
go shopping 行公司 hàang gùng·sì
goal (purpose) 目的 mụk·dịk
goal (score) 入門 yạp·mùn
goalkeeper 守門員 sáu·mùn·yèwn
goat 山羊 sàan·yèung
god (general) 神 sàn
goggles (skiing) 滑雪護眼鏡
    waat·sewt wụ·ngáan·geng
goggles (swimming) 游水護眼鏡
    yàu·séui wụ·ngáan·geng
gold 黃金 wàwng·gàm
golf ball 高爾夫球 gò·yí·fù·kàu
golf course 高爾夫球場
    gò·yí·fù·kàu·chèung
good 好 hó
goodbye 再見 joy·gin
goose 鵝 ngàw
government 政府 jing·fú
grade (advanced/upper) 高級 gò·kạp
grandchild 孫 sèwn
grandfather (maternal) 外公
    ngoy·gùng
grandfather (paternal) 阿爺 a·yè
grandmother (maternal) 外婆 ngoy·pò
grandmother (paternal) 阿嫲 a·màa
grapefruit 葡萄柚 pò·tò·yáu
grapes 葡萄 pò·tò
grass 草 chó
grasslands 草原 chó·yèwn
grateful 感激 gám·gìk
grave 墳墓 fàn·mọ
gray 灰色 fui·sìk
great (fantastic) 好極 hó·gịk
Great Wall 長城 chèung·sìng
green 綠色 lụk·sìk
green tea 綠茶 lụk·chàa
greengrocer 果菜販 gwáw·choy·fáan
grey 灰色 fui·sìk
grocery 雜貨 jaap·fo
groundnut (peanut) 花生 fàa·sàng
grow 長大 jéung·daai
g-string G字褲 jì·jị·dáai
Guangdong 廣東 gwáwng·dùng
guaranteed 有保證 yáu·bó·jing
guess ⓥ 估 gú
guesthouse 賓館 bàn·gún
guide (audio) 錄音導游 lụk·yàm dọ·yàu
guide (person) 導游 dọ·yàu
guidebook 指南 jí·làam

guide dog 盲公狗 màang·gùng·gáu
guided tour 旅行團 léui·hàng·tèwn
guilty 有罪 yáu jeui
guitar 結他 git·tàa
gum 香口膠 hèung·háu·gàau
gun 手槍 sáu·chèung
gym (place) 健美中心 gin·máy jùng·sàm
gymnastics 體操 tái·chò
gynaecologist 婦科醫生 fú·fàw yì·sàng

H

hair 頭髮 tàu·faat
hairbrush 頭刷 tàu·cháat
haircut 剪髮 jín·faa
hairdresser 髮型屋 faa·yìng·ngùk
halal 清真 chìng·jàn
half 半 bun
hallucination 幻想 waan·séung
ham 火腿 fáw·téui
hammer 鎚 chéui
hammock 吊床 diu·chàwng
hand ⓝ 手 sáu
handbag 手袋 sáu·dóy
handball 手球 sáu·kàu
handicrafts 手工藝 sáu·gùng·ngai
handkerchief 手巾 sáu·gàn
handlebars 把手 báa·sáu
handmade 手工 sáu·gùng
handsome 英俊 yìng·jeun
happy 快樂 faai·lawk
harassment 騷擾 sò·yíu
harbour 港口 gáwng·háu
hard (not soft) 硬 ngaan
hard-boiled (egg) 茶葉蛋 chàa·yìp·dáan
hard-sleeper (ticket) 硬臥 (飛)
    ngaan·ngaw·(fày)
hardware store 五金鋪 ńg·gàm·pó
hash 大雜燴 daai·jaap·wúi
hat 帽 mó
have 有 yáu
have a cold 傷風 sèung·fùng
have fun 玩得開心 wáan dàk hòy·sàm dì
hay fever 花粉熱 fàa·fán·yìt
hazelnut 榛果仁 jèut·gwáw·yàn
he 佢 kéui
head 頭 tàu
headache 頭疼 tàu·tung
headlights 車頭燈 chè·tàu·dàng
health 健康 gin·hàwng

hear 聽到 tèng·dó
hearing aid 助聽器 jawk·tìng·hay
heart 心臟 sàm·jawng
heart attack 心臟病突發
    sàm·jawng·beng tat·faat
heart condition 心臟病 sàm·jawng·beng
heat ⓝ 熱 yìt
heated 有暖氣 yáu léwn·hay
heater 暖爐 léwn·lò
heating 暖氣 léwn·hay
heavy 重 chúng
helmet 頭盔 tàu·kwài
help ⓥ 幫助 bàwng·jaw
hepatitis 肝炎 gàwn·yìm
her (ownership) 佢嘅 kéui·ge
herb (cooking) 調味料 tiu·may·liú
herb (medicine) 藥材 yeuk·chóy
herbalist 中草藥醫生
    jùng·chó·yeuk yì·sàng
here 呢度 làry·do
heroin 白粉 baak·fán
herring (salted in a can) 鹹魚罐頭
    hàam·yéw gun·tàu
high 高 gò
highchair 高凳 gò·dang
high school 中學 jùng·hawk
highway 高速公路 gò·chùk gùng·lo
hike 遠足 yéwn·jùk
hiking 遠足 yéwn·jùk
hiking boots 步行靴 yéwn·jùk·hèu
hiking route 步行路徑 yéwn·jùk lo·ging
hill 山丘 sàan·yàu
Hindu 印度 yan·do
hire ⓥ 租 jò
his 佢嘅 kéui ge
historical (site) 名勝古蹟
    mìng·sìng gú·jìk
history 歷史 lìk·sí
hitchhike 搭順風車 daap seun·fùng·chè
HIV 愛滋病毒 ngoy·jì·beng·dùk
hockey 曲棍球 kùk·gun·kàu
holiday(s) 假期 gaa·kày
home 屋企 ngùk·káy
homeless 冇家可歸 mò gàa háw gwài
homemaker 主婦 jéw·fú
homeopathy 順勢療法 seun·sai liù·faat
homosexual 同性戀 tung·sìng·léwn
honey 蜂蜜 fùng·mat
honeymoon 蜜月 mat·yewt
Hong Kong 香港 hèung·gáwng
horoscope 星座 sìng·jawk

horse 馬 máa
horse riding 騎馬 kèh·máa
hospital 醫院 yì·yéwn
hospitality 酒店業 jáu·dim·yip
hot 熱 yit
hot water 熱水 yit·séui
hotel 酒店 jáu·dim
hour 鐘頭 jùng·tàu
house 屋 ngùk
housework 家務 gàa·mo
hovercraft 氣墊船 hay·din·sèwn
how 點樣 dím·yéung
how much 幾多 gáy·dàw
hug ⓥ 抱 póuh
huge 巨大 geui·daai
humanities 文科 màn·fò
human resources 人事 yàn·si
human rights 人權 yàn·kèwn
hundred 百 baak
hungry 餓 ngaw
hunting 打獵 dáa·lip
hurt ⓥ 痛 tung
husband 老公 lóuh·gùng
hydrofoil 飛翔船 fày·chèung·sèwn

I

I 我 ngáw
ice 冰 bìng
ice axe 冰鎚 bìng
ice cream 雪糕 sewt·gò
ice hockey 冰球 bìng
identification 證件 jing·gín
identification card (ID) 身份證 sàn·fán·jing
idiot 白痴 baak·chì
if 如果 yèw·gwáw
ill 有病 yáu·beng
immigration 移民 yì·màn
important 重要 jung·yiu
impossible 冇可能 móh·háw·làng
in 喺……裡面 hái … léui·min
in a hurry 忙 mawng
in front of 喺……前面 hái … chìn·min
included 包括 bàau·kut
income tax 入息稅 yàp·sìk·seui
India 印度 yan·do
indicator 指標 jí·bìu
indigestion 肚痛 tó·tung
indoor 室內 sàt·loy
industry 行業 hàwng·yip

infection 感染 gám·yím
inflammation 發炎 faat·yìm
influenza 感冒 gám·mo
information 信息 seun·sìk
ingredient 原料 yèwn·líu
inject 注射 jew·se
injection 打針 dáa·jàm
injured 受傷 sauh·séung
injury 傷 séung
inn 旅店 léui·dim
inner tube 內肽 loy·tàai
innocent 無辜 mò·gù
inside 裡面 léui·min
instructor 教練 gaau·lin
insurance 保險 bó·hím
interesting 過癮 gaw·yán
intermission 休息 yàu·sìk
international 國際 gawk·jai
Internet 互聯網 wu·lèwn·máwng
Internet café 網吧 máwng·bàa
interpreter 翻譯 fàan·yik
interview ⓝ 採訪 chóy·fáwng
invite 請客 chéng·haak
Ireland 愛爾蘭 ngoy·yí·làan
iron (for clothes) ⓝ 燙斗 tawng·dáu
island 島 dó
Israel 以色列 yi·sìk·lit
it 佢 kéui
IT (information technology) 信息技術 seun·sìk·gay·seut
Italy 意大利 yi·daai·lay
itch ⓝ 痕 hàn
itemised 分項嘅 fàn·hawng ge
itinerary 行程表 hang·chìng·bíu
IUD (contraceptive) 宮内節育器 gùng·loy jit·yuk·hay

J

jacket 外套 ngoy·to
jade 玉 yuk
jail 監獄 gàam·yuk
jam 果醬 gwáw·jeung
January 一月 yàt·yewt
Japan 日本 yat·bún
jar 玻璃罐 bàw·lày·gun
jasmine 茉莉 mut·láy
jaw 下巴 haa·pàa
jealous 妒忌 do·gai
jeans 牛仔褲 ngàu·jái·fu
jeep 吉普車 gàt·pó·chè

jet lag 飛行時差反應
   fày·hàng sì·chàa fáan·ying
jetfoil 飛翼船 fày·yìk·sèwn
jewellery 首飾 sáu·sìk
Jewish 猶太 yàu·taai
job 工作 gùng·jawk
jogging 跑步 páau·bo
joke ⓝ 講笑 gáwng·síu
journalist 記者 gay·jé
journey 旅程 léui·chìng
judge ⓝ 法官 faat·gùn
juice 果汁 gwáw·jàp
July 七月 chàt·yewt
jump ⓥ 跳 tiu
jumper (sweater) 冷衫 làang·sàam
jumper leads 跳線 tiu·sin
June 六月 lùk·yewt

K

ketchup 茄汁 ké·jàp
key 鑰匙 sáw·sì
keyboard 鍵盤 gin·pún
kick ⓥ 踢 tek
kidney 腎 san
kilo 公斤 gùng·gàn
kilogram 公斤 gùng·gàn
kilometre 公里 gùng·láy
kind (nice) 乖 gwàai
kindergarten 幼稚園 yau·ji·yéwn
king 國王 gawk·wàwng
kiosk 小賣部 síu·maai·bo
kiss ⓝ 吻 mán
kiss ⓥ 錫 sek
kitchen 廚房 chèw·fáwng
kiwifruit 彌猴桃 mày·hàu·to
knee 膝頭 sàt·tàu
knife 刀 dò
know 知道 jì·do
kosher 猶太教食品
   yau·tàai·gaau sìk·bán

L

Labour Day 勞動節 lò·dung·jit
labourer 勞工 lò·gùng
labyrinth 迷宮 mài·gùng
lace 花邊 fàa·bìn
lacquerware 漆器 chàt·hay
lake 湖 wù
lamb 羊肉 yèung·yuk

land ⓝ 土地 tó·day
landlady/landlord 房東 fàwng·dùng
language 語言 yéw·yìn
laptop 手提電腦 sáu·tài dìn·ló
large 大 daai
last (previous) 上個 seung·gaw
late 遲到 chì·do
later 以後 yí·hau
laugh ⓥ 笑 siu
launderette 洗衣店 sái·yì·dim
laundry (clothes) 洗 sái
laundry (place) 洗衣店 sái·yì·dim
laundry (room) 洗衣房 sái·sàam·fàwng
law 法律 faat·leut
law (study, professsion) 法律 faat·leut
lawyer 律師 leut·sì
laxative 輕瀉劑 hìng·se·jài
lazy 懶惰 láan·daw
leader 領導 líng·do
leaf 葉 yip
learn 學 hawk
leather 皮 páy
lecturer 講師 gáwng·sì
ledge 邊 bìn
leek 韭葱 gáu·chùng
left (direction) 左邊 jáw·bìn
left luggage 行李寄存
   hàng·láy gay·chèwn
left luggage (office) 行李寄存處
   hàng·láy gay·chèwn chew
left-wing 左派 jáw·paai
leg 腿 téui
legal 法律 faat·leut
legislation 法規 faat·kwài
legume 豆 dáu
leisure 消遣 siu·hín
lemon 檸檬 lìng·mùng
lemonade 檸檬汁 lìng·mùng·jàp
lens 鏡片 geng·pín
lentil 小扁豆 síu·bín·dau
lesbian ⓝ 女同性戀 léui tung·sing·léwn
less 少 síu
letter (mail) 信 seun
lettuce 生菜 sàang·choy
liar 騙子 pin·jí
library 圖書館 tò·sèw·gún
lice 頭虱 tàu·sàt
licence 執照 jàp·jiu
licence plate number
   車牌號碼 chè·pàai ho·máa
lie (not stand) 瞓低 fan·dài

life 命 meng
life jacket 救生衣 gau·sàang·yì
lift (elevator) 電梯 dìn·tài
light ⑪ 光 gwàwng
light (not heavy) 輕 hèng
light (of colour) 淺色 chín·sìk
light bulb 燈膽 dàng·dáam
light meter 測光表 chàak·gwàwng·bìu
lighter (cigarette) 打火機 dáa·fó·gày
like ⊙ 同⋯一樣 tung ... yàt·yeung
lime (fruit) 檸檬 lìng·mùng
lime (flavour) 檸檬味 lìng·mùng·may
linen (material) 亞麻布 a·màa·bo
linen (sheets etc) 床單 chàwng·dàan
lip balm 唇膏 sèun·gò
lips 嘴唇 jéui·sèun
lipstick 唇膏 sèun·gò
liquor store 酒鋪 jáu·pó
listen (to) 聽 tèng
litre 公升 gùng·sìng
little (amount) 一啲 yàt dì
little (size) 小 síu
live (somewhere) ⊙ 住 jew
liver 肝 gàwn
lizard 壁虎 bìk·fú
local 地方 day·fàwng
lock ⑪ 鎖 sáw
lock ⊙ 鎖 sáw
locked (door) 鎖咗 sáw·jáw
lollies 糖果 tàwng·gwáw
long 長 chèung
look ⊙ 睇 tái
look after 照顧 jiu·gu
look for 搵 wán
lookout 觀景臺 gùn·gíng·tòy
loose 鬆 sùng
loose change 散紙 sáan·jí
lose 跌 dit
lost (one's way) 蕩失路 dawng·sàt·lo
lost property 失物 sàt·mat
(a) lot 好多 hó·dàw
lotus 蓮 lìn
loud 大聲 daai·sèng
love ⑪ 愛情 ngoy·chìng
love ⊙ 愛 ngoy
lover 愛人 ngoy·yàn
low 低 dài
lubricant 潤滑油 yeun·waat·yáu
luck 運氣 wan·hay
lucky 好運氣 hó·wan·hay

luggage 行李 hàng·láy
luggage lockers 行李洛卡
　　hàng·láy làwk·káa
luggage tag 行李標簽
　　hàng·láy bìu·chìm
lump 瘤 láu
lunch 午餐 ńg·chàan
lung 肺 fai
luxury 奢侈 chè·chí

M

machine 機器 gày·hay
magazine 雜紙 jaap·jí
mah jong 麻雀 màa·jéut
mail (letters) 信 seun
mail (postal system) 郵 yàu
mailbox 信箱 seun·sèung
main 主要 jéw·yiu
main road 幹道 gawn·do
make 製作 jai·jawk
make-up 扮扮 dáa·baan
malaria 瘧疾 yeuk·jat
mammogram 乳房X光照片
　　yéw·fàwng ìk·sì gwàwng jiu·pín
man (male person) 男人 làam·yán
manager 經理 gìng·láy
mandarin (fruit) 柑 gàm
Mandarin (language)
　　普通話 pó·tùng·wáa
mango 芒果 màwng·gwáw
manual worker 勞工 lò·gùng
many 好多 hó·dàw
maotai (alcoholic drink) 茅台 màau·tòy
map 地圖 day·tò
March 三月 sàam·yewt
margarine 人造牛油 yàn·jo ngàu·yàu
marijuana 大麻 daai·màa
marital status 婚姻狀況
　　fàn·yàn jawng·fàwng
market 街市／市場
　　gàai·sí/ sí·chèung HK/China
marmalade 橙醬 cháang·jeung
marriage 婚姻 fàn·yàn
married 已婚 yí·fàn
marry 結婚 git·fàn
martial arts 武術 mó·seut
mass (Catholic) 禮拜 lái·baai
massage 按摩 ngawn·mò
massage (foot) 腳按摩 geui ngawn·mò

massage (head) 頭按摩 tàu ngawn·mò
masseur/masseuse 按摩師傅
    ngawn·mò sì·fú
mat 地氈 day·jin
match (sports) 比賽 báy·choy
matches (for lighting) 火柴 fó·chàai
mattress 床墊 chàwng·din
May 五月 ńg·yewt
maybe 可能 háw·làng
mayonnaise 蛋黃醬 daan·wáwng·jeung
mayor 市長 sí·jéung
me 我 ngáw
meal 一餐飯 yàt chàan faan
measles 麻疹 mà·a·chán
meat 肉 yuk
mechanic 修車師傅 sàu·chè sì·fú
media 媒體 mui·tái
medicine (medication) 醫藥 yì·yeuk
medicine (study, profession)
    醫學 yì·hawk
meditation 靜坐 jing·jawk
meet 見 gin
melon 瓜 gwàa
member 成員 sìng·yèwn
menstruation 月經 yèwt·gìng
menu 菜單 choy·dàan
message 口信 háu·seun
metal 金屬 gàm·suk
metre 公尺 gùng·chek
metro (train) 地鐵 day·tit
metro station 地鐵站 day·tit·jaam
microwave (oven) 微波爐 may·bàw·lò
midday 中午 jùng·ńg
midnight 午夜 ńg·ye
migraine 偏頭疼 pìn·tàu·tung
military ⓐ 國防 gawk·fàwng
military service 兵役 bìng·yik
milk 牛奶 ngàu·láai
millimetre 毫米 hò·mái
million 百萬 baak·maan
mince (meat) 免治肉 mín·ji·yuk
mineral water 礦泉水 kawng·chewn·séui
minibus 小巴 síu·bàa
minute 分鐘 fàn·jùng
mirror 鏡 geng
miscarriage 流產 làu·cháan
miss (feel absence of) 想念 séung·lim
Miss (title) 小姐 síu·jé
mistake ⓝ 錯誤 chaw·ńg
mix ⓥ 攪拌 gáau·bun
mobile phone 手機 sáu·gày
modem 調解器 tìu·gáai·hay

modern 現代 yin·doy
moisturiser 護膚膏 wu·fù·gò
monastery (Buddhist) 佛寺 fat·jí
Monday 星期一 sìng·kay·yàt
money 錢 chín
Mongolia 蒙古 mùng·gú
monk (Buddhist) 和尚 wàw·séung
month 月 yewt
monument 紀念碑 gay·lim·hày
moon 月 yewt
more 多 dàw
morning 朝早 jiù·jó
morning sickness 孕婦晨吐
    yan·fú sàn·to
mosque 清真寺 chìng·jàn·jí
mosquito 蚊 màn
mosquito coil 蚊香 màn·hèung
mosquito net 蚊帳 màn·jeung
motel 汽車旅館 hay·chè léui·gún
mother 媽媽 mà·a·màa
mother-in-law 岳母 ngawk·mó
motorbike 電單車 din·dàan·chè
motorboat 電船 din·sèwn
motorcycle 電單車 din·dàan·chè
motorway (tollway) 收費公路
    sàu·fai gùng·lo
mountain 山 sàan
mountain bike 爬山單車
    pàa·sàan dàan·chè
mountain path 山路 sàan·lo
mountain range 山脈 sàan·mak
mountaineering 爬山 pàa·sàan
mouse 老鼠 ló·séw
mouth 口 háu
movie 電影 din·yíng
Mr 先生 sìn·sàang
Mrs 女士 léui·si
Ms 小姐 síu·jé
MSG (monosodium glutimate)
    味精 may·jìng
mud 泥 lài
muesli 穆茲利 muk·jì·lay
mum 阿媽 a·màa
mumps 麻疹 mà·a·chán
murder ⓝ 殺人犯 saat·yàn·fáan
murder ⓥ 殺人 saat·yàn
muscle 肌肉 gày·yuk
museum 博物館 bawk·mat·gún
mushroom 蘑菇 màw·gù
music 音樂 yàm·ngawk
music shop 音樂店 yàm·ngawk·dim
musician 音樂家 yàm·ngawk·gàa

220

Muslim 穆斯林 muk·sì·làm
mussel 青口 chèng·háu
mustard 芥辣 gaai·laat
mustard greens 油菜 yàu·choy
mute 啞巴 ngáa·bàa
my 我嘅 ngáw ge

N

nail clippers 指甲鉗 jí·gaap·kím
name 名 méng
napkin 餐巾 chàan·gàn
nappy 尿片 liu·pín
nappy rash 尿褲疹 liu·fu·chán
National Day 國慶節 gawk·hing·jit
national park 自然保護區
   ji·yìn bó·wu·kèui
nationality 國籍 gawk·jik
nature 大自然 daai·ji·yìn
naturopathy 自然療法 ji·yìn liù·faat
nausea 反胃 fáan·wai
near 近 kán
nearby 附近 fu·gan
nearest 最近 jeui·gan
necessary 必要 bìt·yiu
necklace 頸鏈 géng·lín
nectarine 蜜桃 mat·tò
need ⊙ 需要 sèui·yiu
needle (syringe) 針 jàm
needle and thread 針錢 jàm·sin
negative 消極 siù·gik
neither 兩個都唔… lèung gaw dò ng …
net 網 máwng
Netherlands 荷蘭 hàw·làan
never 從未 chùng·may
new 新 sàn
New Year (Chinese) 農曆年 lùng·lik·lìn
New Year's Day 元旦 yèwn·daan
New Year's Eve 除夕 cheut·jik
New Zealand 新西蘭 sàn·sài·làan
news 新聞 sàn·màn
newsagency 報攤 bo·tàan
newspaper 報紙 bo·jí
newsstand 報攤 bo·tàan
next (month) 下(個月)
   haa (gaw yewt)
next to 旁邊 pàwng·bìn
nice 得人鐘意 dàk yàn jùng·yi
nickname 花名 fàa·méng
night 夜晚 ye·máan
nightclub 夜總會 ye·júng·wúi
night out 夜晚活動 ye·máan wut·dung

no 唔得 ǹg·dàk
noisy 嘈 chò
none 一個都冇 yàt gaw dò mó
non-smoking 不吸煙 bàt·kàp·yìn
noodle house 麵店 min·dim
noodles 麵條 min·tiu
noon 中午 jùng·ńg
north 北邊 bàk·bìn
Norway 挪威 làw·wài
nose 鼻 bay
not 唔係 ǹg·hai
notebook 筆記簿 bàt·gay·bó
nothing 乜都冇 màt·dò·mó
no vacancy 滿 mún
November 十一月 sap·yàt·yewt
now 而家 yì·gàa
nuclear 核子 hat·jí
nuclear energy 核電 hat·din
nuclear testing 核試 hat·si
nuclear waste 核廢物 hat·fai·mat
number 號碼 ho·máa
numberplate 車牌 chè·pàai
nun 修女 sàu·léui
nurse 護士 wu·si
nut(s) 果仁 gwáw·yàn

O

oats 燕麥 yìn·mat
occupied/busy 有事 yáu·si
ocean 海洋 hóy·yèung
October 十月 sap·yewt
Octopus card 八達通 baat·daat·tùng
off (spoiled) 變質 bin·jàt
office 辦公室 baan·gùng·sàt
office worker 白領 baak·líng
often 經常 gìng·sèung
oil 石油 sek·yàu
old 老 ló
old man (derogatory) 老坑 ló·hàang
old man (respectful) 老伯 ló·baak
old woman (derogatory) 伯爺婆
   baak·yè·pó
old woman (respectful) 老太太
   ló·taai·táai
olive 橄欖 gaam·láam
olive oil 橄欖油 gaam·láam·yàu
Olympic Games 奧運會 au·wun·wúi
omelette 炒蛋 cháau·dáan
on 喺 hái
on time 準時 jéun·sì
once 一次 yàt·chi

one 一 yàt
one-way (ticket) 單程 dàan·chìng
onion 洋蔥 yèung·chùng
only 只有 jí·yàu
oolong tea 烏龍茶 wù·lúng·chàa
open ⓐ 開放 hòy·fawng
open ⓥ 開 hòy
opening hours 營業時間
　　yìng·yìp sì·gaan
opera (Chinese) 京劇 gìng·kek
opera (Western) 歌劇 gàw·kek
opera house 劇場 kek·chèung
operator 操作員 chò·jawk·yèwn
opinion 睇法 tái·faat
opposite 對面 deui·mìn
optometrist 驗眼師 yìm·ngáan·sì
or 或者 waak·jé
orange (colour) 橙色 cháang·sìk
orange (fruit) 橙 cháang
orange juice 橙汁 cháang·jàp
orchestra 交響樂隊
　　gàau·héung ngawk·déui
order ⓐ 落單 lawk·dàan
order ⓥ 點菜 dím·choy
ordinary 普通 pó·tùng
orgasm 高潮 gò·chìu
original 開創性 hòy·chawng·sing
other 其他 kày·tàa
our 我地嘅 ngáw·day ge
out of order 壞咗 waai·jáw
outside 外面 ngoy·mìn
ovarian cyst 卵巢膿包
　　léun·chàau lùng·bàau
ovary 卵巢 léun·chàau
oven 焗爐 guk·lò
overcoat 大衣 daai·yì
overdose 過量 gaw·leung
overnight 過夜 gaw·ye
overseas 海外 hóy·ngoy
owe 欠 him
owner 主人 jéw·yàn
oxygen 氧氣 yéung·hay
oyster 蠔 hò
ozone layer 臭氧層 chau·yéung·chàn

P

pacemaker 心律調節器
　　sàm·leut tiu·jit·hay
pacifier (dummy) 奶嘴 láai·jéui
package 包裹 bàau·gáw

packet 包 bàau
padlock 鎖 sáw
page 頁 yìp
pagoda 塔 taap
pain 痛 tung
painful 好痛 hó tung
painkiller 止痛藥 jí·tung·yeuk
painter 畫家 wáa·gàa
painting (a work) 畫 wáa
painting (the art) 畫畫 waa·wáa
pair (couple) 對 deui
Pakistan 巴基斯坦 bàa·gày·sì·táan
palace 宮殿 gùng·dìn
pan 煎鍋 gìn·wawk
panda 熊貓 hung·màau
pants (trousers) 長褲 chèung·fu
panty liners 底褲墊 dái·fu gin
pantyhose 連襪褲 lìn·mat·fu
pap smear 子宮頸癌預防檢查
　　jí·gùng·géng·ngàam yew·fàwng
　　gím·chàa
paper 紙 jí
paper cut 剪紙 jín·jí
paperwork 手續 sáu·juk
paraplegic 下身癱瘓 haa·sàn táan·wun
parcel 包裹 bàau·gáw
parents 父母 fu·mó
park ⓐ 公園 gùng·yéwn
park (a car) ⓥ 泊 (車) paak(·chè)
parliament 議會 yí·wúi
part (component) 部份 bo·fan
part-time 半職 bun·jìk
party (night out) 去蒲 heui pò
party (politics) 黨 dáwng
pass ⓥ 通過 tùng·gaw
passenger 乘客 sìng·haak
passionfruit 雞蛋果 gài·dáan·gwáw
passport 護照 wu·jiu
passport number 護照號碼
　　wu·jiu ho·máa
past ⓐ 過去 gaw·heui
pasta 意粉 yi·fán
pastry (French bread) 法式麵包
　　faat·sìk mìn·bàau
path 路仔 lo·jái
pavillion 亭 tíng
pay ⓥ 俾錢 báy·chín
payment 錢 chín
pea 豌豆 wún·dau
peace 和平 waw·pìng
peach 桃 tó

peak (mountain) 山頂 sàan·déng
peanut 花生 fàa·sàng
pear 梨 láy
pedal ⓝ 腳踏 geui·daap
pedestrian 行人 hàng·yàn
pedestrian overpass 行人天橋
    hàng·yàn tìn·kìu
pedicab 三輪車 sàam·lèun·chè
pen (ballpoint) 原子筆 yèwn·jí·bàt
pencil 鉛筆 yèwn·bàt
penis 陽具 yèung·geui
penknife 刀仔 dò·jái
pensioner 退休職工 teui·yàu·jik·gùng
people 人 yàn
pepper (bell) 青椒 chèng·jìu
per (day) 每 (日) muí·yat
per cent 百分比 baak·fan·báy
perfect ⓐ 完美 yèwn·máy
performance 演出 yín·chèut
perfume 香水 hèung·séui
period pain 經痛 gìng·tung
permission 許可 héui·háw
permit ⓝ 許可證 héui·háw·jing
person 人 yàn
personal seal 圖章 tò·jèung
petition 請願 chíng·yewn
petrol 汽油 hay·yàu
petrol station 汽油站 hay·yàu·jaam
pharmacy 藥房 yeuk·fàwng
phone 電話 dìn·wáa
phone book 電話簿 dìn·wáa·bó
phone box 公共電話
    gùng·gung dìn·wáa
phonecard 電話卡 dìn·wáa·kàat
photo 相 séung
photographer 攝影家 sip·yíng·gàa
photography 攝影 sip·yíng
phrasebook 常用語手冊
    sèung·yung·yéw sáu·chàak
pickaxe 鶴嘴鋤 hawk·jéui·chàwk
pickles 醃菜 yìp·choy
picnic 野餐 yé·chàan
pie 餡餅 háam·béng
piece 塊 faai
pig 豬 jèw
pill 藥片 yeuk·pín
(the) pill 避孕藥 bay·yan·yeuk
pillow 枕頭 jám·tàu
pillowcase 枕頭套 jám·tàu·to
pineapple 菠蘿 bàw·làw
pink 粉紅色 fán·hung·sìk

pistachio 開心果 hòy·sàm·gwáw
PLA (People's Liberation Army)
    解放軍 gáai·fawng·gùn
place ⓝ 地方 day·fàwng
place of birth 出生地 chèut·sàng·day
plane 飛機 fày·gày
planet 星球 sìng·kàu
plant ⓝ 植物 jik·mat
plastic 塑膠 sawk·gàau
plate 碟 díp
plateau 高原 gò·yèwn
platform 月台 yewt·tòy
play (cards) 打 dáa
play (guitar) 彈 tàan
play (theatre) ⓝ 劇 kek
plug (bath) 塞 sàk
plug (electricity) 插頭 chaap·táu
plum 梅 muí
poached 煮 jéw
pocket 袋 dóy
pocket knife 刀仔 dò·jái
poetry 詩歌 sì·gàw
point (objective) ⓝ 點 dím
point ⓥ 指 jí
poisonous 有毒 yáu·duk
police (officer) 警察 gíng·chaat
police station 警察局 gíng·chaat·gúk
policy 政策 jing·chaak
politician 政客 jing·haak
politics 政治 jing·ji
pollen 花粉 fàa·fán
pollution 污染 wù·yím
pool (game) 檯球 tóy·kàu
pool (swimming) 游泳池 yàu·wìng·chì
poor 窮 kùng
popular 流行 làu·hàng
porcelain 瓷器 chì·hay
pork 豬肉 jèw·yuk
pork sausage 香腸 hèung·chéung
porridge 粥 jùk
port (sea) 港口 gáwng·háu
portrait sketcher 人像速寫畫師
    yàn·jeung·chùk·sé wáa·sì
positive 正 jing
possible 有可能 yáu háw·làng
postage 郵費 yàu·fai
postcard 明信片 ming·seun·pín
postcode 郵政編碼 yàu·jing pìn·máa
poster 畫報 wáa·bo
post office 郵局 yàu·gúk
pot (ceramics) 罐 gun

pot (dope) 大麻 daai·màa
potato 薯仔 sèw·jái
pottery 陶器 tò·hay
pound (money, weight) 鎊 bawng
poverty 窮 kùng
powder 粉 fán
power 權力 kèwn·lik
prawn 蝦 hàa
prayer 祈禱 kày·tó
prayer book 祈禱書 kày·tó sèw
PRC (People's Republic of China)
  中華人民共和國
  jùng·wàa yàn·màn gung·wàw·gawk
prefer 寧願 lìng·yéwn
pregnancy test kit 妊娠檢測
  yam·san gím·chàak
pregnant 懷孕 wàai·yan
prehistoric art 原始藝術
  yèwn·chí ngai·seut
premenstrual tension 經前緊張
  gìng chìn gán·jèung
prepare 準備 jéun·bay
prescription 藥方 yeuk·fàwng
present (gift) 禮物 lái·mat
present (time) 而家 yì·gàa
president 總統 júng·túng
pressure 壓力 ngaat·lik
pressure point massage 經絡按摩
  gìng·lawk ngawn·mò
pretty 靚 leng
price 價錢 gaa·chìn
priest 牧師 muk·sì
prime minister 首相 sáu·seung
printer (computer) 打印機 dáa·yan·gày
prison 監獄 gàam·yuk
prisoner 罪犯 jeui·fáan
private 私人 sì·yàn
produce ⓥ 生產 sàng·cháan
profit ⓝ 利潤 lày·yeun
program 節目 jit·muk
projector 投影機 tàu·yíng·gày
promise ⓥ 發誓 faat·sai
prostitute 妓女 gay·léui
protect 保護 bó·wu
protest ⓝ 遊行 yàu·hàng
protest ⓥ 抗議 kawng·yí
provisions 糧食 lèung·sik
prune 梅乾 mùi·gàwn
PSB (Public Security Bureau)
  公安局 gùng·ngàwn·gúk
pub (bar) 酒吧 jáu·bàa

public 公共 gùng·gung
public gardens 公園 gùng·yéwn
public relations 公關 gùng·gwàan
public telephone 公共電話
  gùng·gùng din·wáa
public toilet 公廁 gùng·chi
publishing 出版 chèut·báan
pull 拉 làai
pump ⓝ 砵 bàm
pumpkin 南瓜 làam·gwàa
puncture 穿窿 chèwn·lùng
puppet theatre 木偶劇場
  muk·ngáu kek·chèung
pure 純 seun
purple 紫色 jí·sik
purse 銀包 ngàn·bàau
push ⓥ 推 tèui
put 放 fawng

quadriplegic 四肢癱瘓 sai·jì táan·wun
qualifications 學歷 hawk·lik
quality 質量 jàt·leung
quarantine 檢疫站 gím·yik·jàam
quarter 四分一 sai·fan·yàt
queen 女王 léui·wawng
question ⓝ 問題 màn·tài
queue ⓝ 排隊 pàai·déui
quick 快 faai
quiet 安靜 ngàwn·jing
quit 退出 teui·chèut

rabbit 兔仔 to·jái
race (sport) 比賽 báy·choy
racetrack 賽場 choy·chèung
racing bike 賽車 choy·chè
racism 種族歧視 júng·juk kày·si
racquet 球拍 kàu·páak
radiator 電暖爐 din·léwn·lò
radio 收音機 sàu·yàm·gày
radish 蘿蔔 làw·baak
railway station 火車站 fó·chè·jaam
rain 落雨 lawk·yéw
raincoat 雨衣 yéw·yì
raisin 葡提子 pò·tài·jí
rally ⓝ 集會 jaap·wúi
rape ⓝ 強奸 kèung·gàan
rare (food) 半熟生 bun·sàang·suk

rare (uncommon) 罕見 háwn·gin
rash 疹 chán
raspberry 山梅 sàan·múi
rat 老鼠 ló·séw
rave ⓝ 電子狂歡舞會
　　dín·jí kàwng·fùn mó·wúi
raw 生 sàang
razor 剃刀 tai·dò
razor blade 刀片 dò·pín
read 讀 duk
reading 睇書 tái·sèw
ready 準備好 jéun·bay·hó
real estate agent 房地產代理
　　fàwng·day·cháan doy·láy
realistic 現實 yin·sat
rear (seat etc) 後 hau
reason 原因 yèwn·yàn
receipt 收據 sàu·geui
recently 最近 jèui·gan
recommend 推薦 tèui·jin
record ⓥ 錄 luk
recording 錄音 luk·yàm
recyclable 可回收 háw wuì·sàu
recycle 回收 wuì·sàu
red 紅色 hung·sik
referee 裁判 chòy·pun
reference (letter) 推薦信 tèui·jin·seun
reflexology 反射療法 fáan·se liù·faat
refrigerator 雪櫃 sewt·gwai
refugee 難民 laan·màn
refund ⓝ 退錢 teui·chín
refuse ⓥ 拒絕 kéui·jewt
regional 地方性 day·fàwng·sing
(by) registered mail 掛號 gwaa·ho
rehydration salts 補液鹽 bó·yik·yìm
reiki 靈氣按摩 ling·hay ngawn·mò
relationship 關係 gwàan·hai
relax 放鬆 fawng·sùng
relic 遺跡 wài·jik
religion 宗教 jùng·gaau
religious 宗教嘅 jùng·gaau·ge
remote 偏僻 pin·pik
remote control 遙控 pìn·pik
rent ⓥ 租 jò
repair 修理 sàu·láy
republic 共和國 gung·waw·gawk
reservation (booking) 預定 yew·deng
rest ⓥ 休息 yàu·sik
restaurant 酒樓 jáu·làu
résumé (CV) 簡歷 gáan·lik
retired 退休 teui·yàu

return (come back) 返嚟 fàan·làvy
return (ticket) 雙程 (飛)
　　sèung·chìng (fày)
reverse-charge call ⓝ 對方付款
　　deui·fàwng fu·fún
review ⓝ 審核 sám·hat
rhythm 節奏 jit·jau
ribs (beef) 排骨 pàai·gwat
rice 米 mái
rice (cooked) 飯 faan
rice paddy 水稻田 séui·do·tìn
rice wine 米酒 mái·jáu
rich (wealthy) 有錢 yáu·chín
rickshaw 人力車 yàn·lik·chè
ride ⓥ 騎 kè
right (correct) 啱 ngàam
right (direction) 右邊 yau·bìn
right-wing 右派 yau·paai
ring (on finger) 戒指 gaai·jí
ring (phone) ⓥ 打 dáa
rip-off 揾笨 wán·ban
risk ⓝ 風險 fùng·hím
river 河 hàw
road 路 lo
road map 交通地圖 gàau·tùng day·to
rob 偷 tàu
rock (stone) ⓝ 石頭 sek·tàu
rock (music) 搖滾 yìu·gún
rock climbing 攀岩 pàan·ngàam
rock group 搖滾樂隊
　　yìu·gún ngàwk·déui
rockmelon 哈密瓜 hàa·mat·gwàa
roll (bread) 麵包 min·bàau
rollerblading 旱地滑冰
　　háwn·day waat·bìng
romantic 浪漫 lawng·maan
room 房 fáwng
room number 房號 fáwng·ho
rope 繩 síng
round ⓐ 圓 yèwn
roundabout 圓環交叉路口
　　yèwn·wàan gàau·chàa lo·háu
route 路綫 lo·sin
rowing 扒艇 pàa·téng
rubbish 垃圾 laap·saap
rubella 德國麻疹 dàk·gawk màa·chán
rug 地氈 day·jin
rugby 英式欖球
　　yìng·sik gaam·láam·kàu
ruins 廢墟 fai·hèui
rule ⓝ 規定 kwài·ding

rum 冧酒 làm·jáu
run ⓥ 走 jáu
running 跑步 páau·bo
runny nose 流鼻涕 làu bay·tai

S

sad 鬱悶 wàt·mun
saddle 馬鞍 máa·ngàwn
safe ⓝ 保險箱 bó·hím·sèung
safe ⓐ 安全 ngàwn·chèwn
safe sex 安全性交
　ngàwn·chèwn·sing·gàau
sailboarding 滑浪風帆
　waat·làwng fùng·fàan
saint 聖人 sing·yàn
salad 沙律 sàa·léut
salami 香腸 hèung·chéung
salary 薪水 sàn·séui
sale 大減價 daai·gáam·gaa
sales tax 銷售稅 siu·sau·seui
salmon 三文魚 sàam·màn·yéw
salt 鹽 yìm
same 一樣 yàt·yeung
sand 沙 sàa
sandal 涼鞋 lèung·hàai
sanitary napkin 衛生巾 wai·sàng·gàn
SAR (Special Administrative Region)
　特別行政區 dak·bit hàng·jing·kèui
sardine 鹹魚 hàam·yéw
SARS (virus) 沙斯 sàa·sì
Saturday 星期六 sìng·kày·luk
sauce 醬 jeung
saucepan 煲 bò
sauna 桑那 sàwng·làa
sausage 香腸 hèung·chéung
say 講 gáwng
scalp 頭皮 tàu·pày
scarf 頸巾 tàu·gàn
scenic area 風景區 fùng·gíng·kèui
school 學校 hawk·haau
science 科學 fò·hawk
scientist 科學家 fò·hawk·gàa
scissors 較剪 gaau·jín
score ⓥ 入球 yap·kau
scoreboard 積分牌 jik·fàn·páai
Scotland 蘇格蘭 sò·gaak·làan
scrambled 炒 cháau
scroll (paper) 字畫 ji·wáa
sculpture 塑像 sawk·jeung
sea 海 hóy

seafood 海鮮 hóy·sìn
seafood restaurant 海鮮酒家
　hóy·sìn·jáu·gàa
seasick 暈船 wùn·sèwn
seaside 海邊 hóy·bìn
season 季節 gwai·jit
seat (hard) 硬座 ngaang·jaw
seat (place) 座位 jawk·wái
seat (soft) 軟座 yéwn·jaw
seatbelt 安全帶 ngàwn·chèwn·dáai
second ⓝ 秒 miú
second ⓐ 第二 dai·yi
second class 二等 yi·dáng
second-hand 二手 yi·sáu
second-hand shop 舊貨鋪 gau·fo·pó
secretary 秘書 bay·sèw
see 睇 tái
self-employed 自己做老細
　ji·gáy jo ló·sai
selfish 自私 ji·sì
self service 自助 ji·jawk
sell 賣 maai
send 寄 gay
sensible 有理 yáu·láy
sensual 肉體上嘅 yuk·tái seung ge
separate 分開 fàn·hòy
September 九月 gáu·yeut
serious 嚴肅 yìm·sùk
serve ⓥ 服務 fuk·mo
service 服務 fuk·mo
service charge 服務費 fuk·mo·fai
service station 加油站 gàa·yàu·jàam
serviette 餐巾 chàan·gàn
several 好幾個 hó·gáy·gaw
sew (not mend) 縫紉 fùng·yan
sex 性 sing
sexism 性別歧視 sing·bit kày·si
sexy 性感 sing·gám
shade 樹蔭 sew·yam
shadow 影 yíng
shampoo ⓝ 洗頭水 sái·tàu·séui
Shanghai 上海 seung·hóy
shape ⓝ 形狀 yìng·jawng
share ⓥ 公用 gùng·yung
shave ⓥ 剃鬚 tai·sò
shaving cream 剃鬚膏 tai·sò·gò
she 佢 kéui
sheep 綿羊 mìn·yéung
sheet (bed) 床單 chàwng·dàan
shelf 架 gáa
shiatsu 推拿 tèui·làa

shingles (illness) 帶狀泡疹 dáai·jawng·bàau·chán

ship 船 sèwn

shirt 恤衫 sèut·sàam

shoe(s) 鞋 hàai

shoe shop 鞋店 hàai·dim

shoot 射 se

shop ⓝ 店 dim

shop ⓥ 買嘢 máai·yé

shopping 行公司 hàang·gùng·sì

shopping centre 商場 sèung·chèung

short (height) 矮 ngái

shortage 短缺 déwn·kewt

shorts 短褲 déwn·fu

shoulder 膊頭 bawk·tàu

shout ⓥ 嗌 ngaai

show ⓝ 表演 biú·yín

shower 沖涼室 chùng·lèung·fáwng

shrine 廟 miú

shut ⓐ 柵 sàan

shuttle bus 穿梭巴士 chèwn·sàw·bàa·sí

shuttlecock 羽毛球 yéw·mò·kàu

shy 怕醜 paa·cháu

sick 病 beng

side ⓝ 旁邊 pàwng·bìn

sign ⓝ 招牌 jiù·pàai

signature 簽名 chìm·méng

silk 絲綢 sì·chàu

silver 銀 ngàan

SIM card SIM卡 sím·kàat

similar 一樣 yàt·yeung

simple 簡單 gáan·dàan

since (May) 自從 (五月) ji·chùng (ńg·yewt)

sing 唱歌 cheung·gàw

Singapore 新加坡 sàn·gaa·bàw

singer 歌手 gàw·sáu

single (person) 單人 dàan·yàn

single room 單人房 dàan·yàn·fáwng

singlet 背心 bui·sàm

sister (elder) 家姐 gàa·jè

sister (younger) 妹妹 mui·múi

sister(s) 家姐 gàa·jè

sit 坐底 cháw·dài

size 尺碼 chek·máa

skate (ice) ⓥ 溜冰 làu·bìng

skateboarding 滑板 waat·báan

ski ⓥ 滑雪 waat·sewt

skiing 滑雪 waat·sewt

skim milk 低脂牛奶 dài·jì ngàu·láai

skin 皮膚 pày·fù

skirt 裙 kùn

skull 骷髏頭 fù·lò·tàu

sky 天 tìn

sleep ⓥ 瞓覺 fan·gaau

sleeping 瞓覺 fan·gaau

sleeping bag 睡袋 sheui·dóy

sleeping berth 臥鋪 ngaw·pò

sleeping car 臥鋪車廂 ngaw·pò·chè·sèung

sleeping pills 安眠藥 ngàwn·mìn·yeuk

sleepy 洽眼瞓 hàp·ngáan·fan

slice (cake) ⓝ 蛋糕 daan·gò

slide (film) 幻燈片 waan·dàng·pín

slippers 拖鞋 tàw·hàai

slow 慢 maan

slowly 慢慢 maan·máan

small 細 sai

smaller 細啲 sai·dì

smallest 最細 jeui·sai

smell ⓝ 味道 may·do

smile ⓥ 微笑 mày·siu

smoke ⓥ 食煙 sik·yìn

snack ⓝ 小食 siú·sik

snack shop 小食店 siú·sik·dim

snail 蝸牛 wàw·ngàu

snake 蛇 sè

snorkelling 潛水 chìm·séui

snow ⓝ 雪 sewt

snowboarding 滑雪板 waat·sewt·báan

snow pea 荷蘭豆 hàw·làan·dáu

soap 肥皂 fày·jo

soap opera 肥皂劇 fày·jo·kek

soccer 足球 jùk·kàu

socialism 社會主義 sé·wúi·jéw·yi

socialist 社會主義者 sé·wúi·jéw·yi·jé

social welfare 社會福利 sé·wúi·fùk·lay

sock(s) 襪 mat

soft drink 汽水 hay·séui

soft-boiled 半熟 (雞蛋) bun·suk (gài·dáan)

soft-sleeper (ticket) 軟臥 (飛) yéwn·ngaw (fày)

soldier 軍人 gun·yàn

some 一啲 yàt·dì

someone 某人 máu·yàn

something 有啲嘢 yáu dì yé

sometimes 偶然 ngáu·yìn

son 仔 jái

song 歌曲 gàw·kùk

soon 快 faai

sore ⓐ 痛 tung

soup 湯 tàwng
soup spoon 湯匙 tàwng·chì
sour cream 酸奶 sèwn·láai
sour plum drink
　　酸梅湯 sèwn·muì·tàwng
south 南 làam
souvenir 紀念品 gay·lìm·bán
souvenir shop 紀念品店
　　gay·lìm·bán·dim
soy 大豆 daai·dáu
soy bean 黃豆 wàwng·dáu
soy milk (fresh) 豆漿 dau·jèung
soy milk (powdered) 豆漿粉
　　dau·jèung·fán
soy sauce 豉油 si·yàu
space 空間 hùng·gàan
Spain 西班牙 sài·bàan·ngàa
sparkling wine 香檳 hèung·bàn
speak 講 gáwng
special 特別 dak·bit
specialist 專家 jèwn·gàa
speed (velocity) 速度 chùk·do
speed limit 最高車速 jeui·gò chè·chùk
speedboat 快艇 faai·téng
speedometer 速度表 chùk·do·bíu
spider 蜘蛛 ji·jèw
spinach 菠菜 bàw·choy
spirits (Chinese alcohol) 白酒 baak·jáu
spoiled (gone off) 爛咗 laan·jáw
spoke ⓝ 車輻 chè·fùk
spoon 羹 gàng
sport 體育 tái·yuk
sports shop 體育用品店
　　tái·yuk yung·bán·dim
sportsperson 運動員 wan·dung·yèwn
sprain ⓝ 扭傷 láu·sèung
spring (coil) 彈弓 daan·gùng
spring (season) 春天 chèun·tin
Spring Festival 春節 chèun·jit
square (town) 廣場 gwáwng·chèung
squash 壁球 bik·kàu
stadium 體育館 tái·yuk·gún
stairway 樓梯 làu·tài
stale 過氣 gaw·hay
stamp ⓝ 郵票 yàu·piu
stand-by ticket 月台票 yewt·tòy·piu
star 星 sìng
start 開頭 hòy·chí
station 車站 chè·jaam
stationer 文具店 màn·geui·dim
statue 彫像 diù·jeung

stay (at a hotel) ⓥ 住 jew
stay in (one place) ⓥ 留喺 làu·hái
steak (beef) 排骨 pàai·gwàt
steal 偷 tàu
steamed bun 饅頭 maan·tàu
steep ⓐ 斜 che
step ⓝ 梯級 tài·kùp
stereo 立體聲 lap·tái·sìng
still water 死水 sái·séui
stir-fried 蛋 dáan
stock (food) 原汁 yèwn·jàp
stockings 長襪 chèung·mat
stolen 偷咗 tàu·jáw
stomach 肚 tó
stomachache 肚痛 tó·tung
stone 石頭 sek·tàu
stoned (drugged) 吸咗毒 kàp·jáw duk
stop (bus, tram, etc) 停 tìng
stop (cease) 停止 tìng·jí
stop (prevent) 防止 fàwng·jí
storm 打風 dáa·fùng
story 故仔 gú·jái
stove 爐 ló
straight 直 jik
strange 古怪 gú·gwaai
stranger 生薄人 sàang·bó·jàn
strawberry 草莓 chó·muí
stream 泉 chèwn
street 街 gàai
street market 街市 gàai·sí
street vendor 小販 síu·fáan
strike ⓝ 罷工 baa·gùng
string 繩 síng
stroke (health) 中風 jung·fùng
stroll ⓝ 散步 saan·bo
stroller 手推車 sáu·tèui·chè
strong 強勁 kèung·ging
stubborn 固執 gu·jàp
student 學生 hawk·sàang
studio 工作室 gùng·jawk·sàt
stupid 蠢 chéun
style 風格 fùng·gaak
subtitles 字幕 ji·mawk
suburb 郊區 gàau·kèui
subway 地鐵 day·tit
suffer 受苦 sau·fú
sugar 砂糖 sàa·tàwng
sugar cane juice 蔗汁 je·jàp
suitcase 行李箱 hàng·láy·sèung
sultana 葡萄乾 pò·tò·gàwn
summer 夏天 hua·tìn

sun 太陽 taai·yèung
sunblock 防曬油 fàwng·saai·yàu
sunburn 曬傷 saai·sèung
Sunday 星期日 sìng·kày·yat
sunglasses 黑眼鏡 hàak·ngáan·géng
sunny 天晴 tìn·chìng
sunrise 日出 yat·chèut
sunset 日落 yat·lawk
sunstroke 中暑 jung·séw
supermarket 超市 chìu·sí
superstition 迷信 mài·seun
supporter (politics) 支持者 jì·chì·jé
supporter (sport) 擁躉 yúng·dán
surf (waves) 滑(浪) waat (lawng)
surface mail 平郵 pìng·yàu
surfboard 滑浪板 waat·lawng·báan
surfing 滑浪 waat·lawng
surname 姓 sing
surprise ⓐ 驚訝 gìng·ngaa
sweater 冷衫 làang·sàam
Sweden 瑞典 seui·dín
sweet ⓐ 甜 tìm
sweets 糖 táwng
swim ⓥ 游水 yàu·séui
swimming (sport) 游泳 yàu·wìng
swimming pool 游泳池 yàu·wìng·chì
swimsuit 游泳衣 yàu·wìng·yì
Switzerland 瑞士 seui·sí
swollen 腫咗 júng·jáw
synagogue 猶太教堂
    yàu·taai·gaau·tàwng
synthetic 人做嘅 yàn·jo·ge
syringe 針筒 jàm·túng

T

table 台 tóy
tablecloth 台布 tóy·bo
table tennis 乒乓波 bìng·bàm·bàw
t'ai chi 太極 taai·gik
tail 尾 máy
tailor 裁縫 choy·fúng
take 攞走 láw·jáu
take a photo 影相 yíng·séung
talk ⓥ 傾偈 kìng·gái
tall 高 gò
tampon 棉塞 mìn·sàk
tanning lotion 助曬油 jawk·saai·yàu
Taoism 道教 do·gaau
tap ⓝ 水喉 séui·hàu
tap water 水喉水 séui·hàu·séui

tasty 好味 hó·may
tax 稅 seui
taxi 的士 dìk·sí
taxi stand 的士站 dìk·sí·jaam
tea 茶 chàa
teacher 先生 sìn·sàang
tea house 茶館 chàa·gún
team 隊 déui
tea pot 茶壺 chàa·wú
teaspoon 茶匙 chàa·chí
technique 技巧 gay·háau
teeth 牙齒 ngàa·chí
telegram 電報 dìn·bo
telephone ⓝ 電話 dìn·wáa
telephone ⓥ 打電話 dáa dìn·wáa
telephone box 電話亭 dìn·wáa·tìng
telephone centre 電話中心
    dìn·wáa jùng·sàm
telescope 望遠鏡 mawng·yéwn·geng
television 電視 dìn·si
tell 話俾 waa báy
temperature (fever) 發燒 faat·sìu
temperature (weather) 溫度 wàn·do
temple (shrine) 廟 miú
tennis 網球 máwng·kàu
tennis court 網球場 máwng·kàu·chèung
tent 營幕 yìng·maw
tent peg 營釘 yìng·dèng
terrible 可怕 háw·paa
test ⓝ 考試 háau·si
thank 道謝 do·je
that (one) 嗰個 gáw·gaw
theatre 劇場 kek·chèung
their 佢地嘅 kéui·day ge
there 嗰邊 gáw·bin
Thermos 暖水壺 léwn·séui·wú
they 佢地 kéui·day
thick 厚 háu
thief 賊 cháak
thin 薄 bawk
think 想 séung
third 第三 dai·sàam
(to be) thirsty 頸渴 géng·hawt
this (month) 呢個(月) lày·gaw (yewt)
this (one) 呢個 lày·gaw
thread 綫 sin
throat 喉嚨 hàu·lùng
thrush (health) 鵝口瘡
    ngàw·háu·chàwng
thunderstorm 雷雨 lèui·yéw
Thursday 星期四 sìng·kày·sai

ticket 票 piu
ticket collector 售票員 sau·piu·yewn
ticket machine 售票機 sau·piu·gay
ticket office 票房 piu·fawng
tide 潮流 chiu·làu
tight 緊 gán
time 時間 sì·gaan
time difference 時差 sì·chàa
timetable 時間表 sì·gaan·biú
tin (can) 罐頭 gun·táu
tin opener 開罐器 hòy·gun·hay
tiny 好細 hó·sai
tip (gratuity) 消費 siù·fai
tire 輪肽 lèun·tàai
tired 𤲟 gui
tissues 紙巾 jí·gàn
to (go to, come to) 到 do
toast 多士 dàw·sí
toaster 多士爐 dàw·sí·lò
tobacco 煙絲 yin·sì
tobacco kiosk 煙攤 yìn·tàan
tobacconist 煙店 yìn·dim
tobogganing 長橇運動 chèung·hiù wun·dung
today 今日 gàm·yat
toe 腳趾 geui·jí
tofu 豆腐 dau·fu
together 一齊 yàt·chài
toilet 廁所 chi·sáw
toilet paper 廁紙 chi·jí
tomato 番茄 fàan·ké
tomato sauce 茄醬 ké·jeung
tomb 墳墓 fàn·mo
tomorrow 听日 ting·yat
tomorrow afternoon 听日下晝 ting·yat haa·jau
tomorrow evening 听晚 tìng·máan
tomorrow morning 听朝 tìng·jiu
tonight 今晚 gàm·máan
too (expensive etc) 太 taai
tooth 牙齒 ngàa·chí
toothache 牙痛 ngàa·tung
toothbrush 牙刷 ngàa·cháat
toothpaste 牙膏 ngàa·gò
toothpick 牙籤 ngàa·chìm
torch (flashlight) 電筒 din·túng
touch 摸 mó
tour 旅游團 léui·yáu·tèwn
tourist 旅客 léui·haak
tourist hotel 旅店 léui·dim
tourist office 旅行社 léui·hàng·sé
towards 向 heung

towel 毛巾 mò·gàn
tower (telecom) 電訊塔 din·seun·taap
toxic waste 有毒廢物 yáu·duk fai·mat
toy shop 玩具店 wun·geui·dim
track (path) 山路 sàan·lo
track (sport) 田徑 tìn·ging
trade 行業 hàyng·yip
tradesperson 技工 gay·gùng
traffic 交通 gàau·tùng
traffic light 紅綠燈 hùng·luk·dàng
trail 小路 siú·lo
train 火車 fó·chè
train station 火車站 fó·chè·jaam
tram 電車 din·chè
transit lounge 轉機室 jéwn·gày·sàt
translate 翻譯 fàan·yip
transport 運輸 wun·sèw
travel 旅遊 léui·yàu
travel agency 旅行社 léui·hàng·sé
travellers cheque 旅行支票 léui·hàng jì·piu
travel sickness 暈船 wùn·sèwn
tree 樹 sew
trip (journey) 旅程 léui·chìng
trolley 手推車 sáu·tèui·chè
trousers 褲 fu
truck 貨車 fo·chè
trust 信用 seun·yung
try (attempt) 試圖 si·tò
T-shirt T恤 tì·sèut
tube (tyre) 內肽 loy·tàai
Tuesday 星期二 sìng·kày·yi
tumour 腫瘤 júng·làu
tuna 吞拿魚 tàn·làa·yéw
tune 曲調 kùk·diu
turkey 火雞 fó·gài
turn 轉身 jéwn·sàn
TV 電視 din·si
tweezers 鉗 kím
twice 兩次 léung·chi
twin room 雙人房 sèung·yàn·fàwng
twins 雙胞胎 sèung·bàau·tòy
two 二 yi
type 類型 leui·yìng
typical 通常 tùng·sèung
tyre 車肽 chè·tàai

ultrasound 超聲波 chiù·sìng·bàw
umbrella 雨遮 yéw·jè
uncomfortable 唔舒服 ǹg sèw·fuk

understand 明白 mìng·baak
underwear 底衫褲 dái·sàam·fu
unemployed 失業 sàt·yìp
unfair 唔公平 ǹg gùng·pìng
uniform ⓝ 工作服 gùng·jawk·fuk
universe 宇宙 yéw·jau
university 大學 daai·hawk
unleaded 不含鉛 bàt·hàm·yewn
unsafe 唔安全 ǹg ngàwn·chèwn
until 直到 jik·do
unusual 反常 fáan·sèung
up 上 séung
uphill 上山 séung·sàan
urgent 緊要 gán·yiu
urinary infection 尿道感染
  liu·do gám·yím
USA 美國 máy·gawk
useful 有用 yáu·yung

V

vacancy 空闕 hùng·kewt
vacant 有空闕 yáu hùng·kewt
vacation 假期 gaa·kày
vaccination 預防針 yew·fàwng·jàm
vagina 陰道 yàm·do
validate 確認 kawk·ying
valley 山谷 sàan·gùk
valuable 貴重 gwai·jung
value (price) ⓝ 價值 gaa·jik
van 小巴 síu·bàa
veal (beef) 牛肉 ngàu·yuk
vegetable ⓝ 蔬菜 sàw·choy
vegetable (leafy) ⓝ 青菜 chèng·choy
vegetarian ⓐ 食齋嘅 sik·jàai ge
vein 血脈 hewt·mat
venereal disease 性病 sing·beng
venue 地點 day·dím
very 好 hó
video recorder 錄影機 luk·yíng·gày
video tape 錄影帶 luk·yíng·dáai
view (scenic) ⓝ 景 gíng
villa 別墅 bit·séu
village 村 chèwn
vine (creeper) 攀藤 pàan·tàng
vinegar 醋 cho
vineyard 葡萄園 pò·tò·yèwn
virus 病毒 beng·duk
visa 簽證 chìm·jing
visit ⓥ 拜訪 baai·fáwng

vitamins 維他命／維生素
  wài·tàa·mìng/wài·sàng·so HK/China
vodka 伏特加 fuk·dak·gàa
voice 聲音 sìng·yàm
volleyball (sport) 排球 pàai·kàu
volume (sound) 聲量 sìng·leung
vote ⓥ 投票 tàu·piu

W

wage 薪水 sàn·séui
wait (for) 等 dáng
waiter 服務員 fuk·mo·yèwn
waiting room 等候室 dáng·hau·sàt
wake (someone) up 叫醒 giu·séng
walk ⓥ 行路 hàang·lo
wall (outer) 牆 chèung
want 要 yiu
war 戰爭 gin·jàng
wardrobe 衣櫃 yi·gwai
warehouse 貨倉 fo·chàwng
warm 暖 léwn
warn 警告 gíng·go
wash 洗 sái
wash cloth (flannel) 毛巾 mò·gàn
washing machine 洗衣機 sái·yì·gày
watch ⓝ 手錶 sáu·bìu
watch ⓥ 望 mawng
water 水 séui
water bottle 塑膠樽 sawk·gàau·jèun
water bottle (hot) 熱水袋 léwn·séui·dóy
waterfall 瀑布 buk·bo
watermelon 西瓜 sài·gwàa
waterproof 防水 fàwng·séui
water-skiing 滑水 waat·séui
wave 浪 lawng
way 路 lo
we 我地 ngáw·day
weak 弱 yeuk
wealthy 有錢 yàu·chín
wear 著 jeuk
weather 氣候 hay·hau
wedding 婚禮 fàn·lái
wedding cake 結婚蛋糕 git·fàn·dàan·gò
wedding present (red packet)
  結婚利市 git·fàn·lay·sí
Wednesday 星期三 sìng·kày·sàam
week 星期 sìng·kày
(last) week 上(個)
  seung(·gaw sìng·kày)

(this) week (呢個) 禮拜 (làygaw) láibaai

weekend 週末 jàumut

weigh 稱 ching

weight 重量 chúngleung

weights (in gym) 舉重 géuichúng

welcome ⊙ 歡迎 fùnyìng

welfare 福利 fùklay

well ⓐ 好好 hóhó

west 西 sài

wet ⓑ 濕 sàp

what 乜嘢 màtyé

wheel 車轆 chèlùk

wheelchair 輪椅 lèunyí

when 幾時 gáysì

where 邊度 bìndo

which 嚟個 gáwgaw

whisky 威士忌 wàisìgáy

white 白色 baaksìk

who 邊個 bingaw

wholemeal bread 全麥麵包 chewn màk mìnbàau

why 點解 dímgáai

wide 闊 fut

wife 老婆 lópò

win ⊙ 贏 yèng

wind (weather) ⓝ 風 fùng

window 窗 chèung

windscreen 擋風玻璃 dáwngfùng bàwlày

windsurfing 滑浪風帆 waatlawng fùngfàan

wine 葡萄酒 pòtòjáu

wings 翼 yìk

winner 贏家 yènggàa

winter 冬天 dùngtìn

wire 鐵線 titsín

wish ⊙ 祝 jùk

with 同埋 tùngmàai

within (an hour) (一個鐘頭) 之內 (yàt gaw jùngtàu) jìloy

without 之外 jìngoy

wok 鍋 wawk

woman 女人 léuiyán

wonderful 美妙 máymiu

wood 木 muk

woodblocks 木板 mukbáan

wool 羊毛 yèungmò

word 詞 chì

work ⓝ 工作 gùngjawk

work ⊙ 打工 dáagùng

work experience 工作經驗 gùngjawk gìngyìm

workout ⓝ 試用 siyung

work permit 工作簽證 gùngjawk chìmjing

workshop 工作室 gùngjawksàt

work unit 單位 dàanwái

world 世界 saigaai

World Cup 世界盃 saigaaibùi

worms 虫 chùng

worried 心急 sàmgap

worship ⊙ 崇拜 sùngbaai

wrist 手腕 sáuwún

write 寫 sé

writer 作家 jawkgàa

wrong 錯 chaw

WTO (World Trade Organisation) 世貿組織 saimau júkjìk

Y

year 年 lìn

(this) year (今) 年 (gàm) lìn

yellow 黃色 wàwngsìk

yes 係 hai

yesterday 琴日 kàmyat

(not) yet 重 (未) jung(may)

yoga 瑜伽 yèwgàa

yogurt 酸奶 sèwnláai

you 你 láy

you sg 你 láy

you pl 你地 láyday

young 年輕 lìnhèng

your 你嘅 láy ge

youth hostel 青年旅社 chìnglìn léuise

yum cha 飲茶 yámchàa

Z

zip/zipper 拉鏈 làailín

zodiac 星座 sìngjaw

zoo 動物園 dungmatyèwn

zucchini 西胡蘆 sàiwùló

This dictionary is arranged according to the number of strokes in the first character of the Cantonese word. The dictionary starts with 一 yàt 'one' (the character 一 yàt has one stroke), and ends with 鬱悶 wàt·mun (鬱 wàt has 29 strokes). As there are many characters with the same number of strokes, the characters within this number-of-strokes classification system are then ordered according to the form of the first stroke. The symbols ⓝ, ⓐ and ⓥ stand for noun, adjective and verb and have been added for clarity where necessary.

呢個係中英詞彙對照表，可以嚟幫呢位外國人明白佢想講嘅嘢。唔該你喺對照表左邊揾出相關嘅字，再喺右邊指出對應嘅英文。對照表嘅中文係按照筆劃數目順序編排。對照表採用標準中文字典嘅做法，凡筆劃數目相同嘅字，按部首編排，部首順序按部首筆劃數目編排。多謝你嘅熱心幫忙。

(Translation: This is a Chinese–English dictionary, which can be used to help this foreigner understand what you wish to say. Please find the relevant word from the list, and point to the corresponding English word in the far right. The Chinese words in the left are listed by number of strokes. As is standard practice in most Chinese dictionaries, characters with the same number of strokes are listed according to the number of strokes in their radical – the element which conveys the meaning of a word. Many thanks for your kind help.)

一劃 1 stroke

一 yàt one
一個人 yàt gaw yàn alone
一個都冇 yàt gaw dò mó none
一切 yàt·chai everything
一啲 yàt·dī few • little (amount) • some
一月 yàt·yewt January
一樣 yàt·yeung same
一次 yàt·chi once
一餐飯 yàt chàan fàan meal
一齊 yàt·chài together

二劃 2 strokes

七月 chàt·yewt July
九月 gáu·yewt September
二 yi two
二手 yi·sáu second-hand
二月 yi·yewt February
二等 yi·dáng second class
人 yàn people

人 yàn person
人力車 yàn·lìk·chè rickshaw
人做嘅 yàn·jo ge synthetic
人像速寫畫師 yàn·jeung chùk·sé wáa·sì portrait sketcher
人參 yàn·sàm ginseng
人權 yàn·kèwn human rights
入 yàp enter
入口 yàn·háu entry
入息稅 yàp·sìk·seui income tax
入場費 yap·chèung·fai cover charge
八月 baat·yewt August
八達通 baat·daat·tùng Octopus card
刀 dò knife
刀叉 dò·chàa cutlery
刀片 dò·pín razor blade
刀仔 dò·jái penknife • pocket knife
十一月 sap·yàt·yewt November
十二月 sap·yi·yewt December
十月 sap·yewt October
乜都冇 màt·dò·mó nothing
乜嘢 màt·yé what

三劃 3 strokes

三文魚 sàam·màn·yéw salmon
三月 sàam·yewt March
三輪車 sàam·lèun·chè pedicab
下(個月) haa (gaw yewt) next (month)
下午茶 haa·ńg·chàa afternoon tea
下巴 haa·pàa jaw
下身癱瘓 haa·sàn tàan·wun paraplegic
下面 haa·min below · down
下晝 haa·jau afternoon
(今日)下晝 (gàm·yat) haa·jau
  (this) afternoon
上 séung board (a plane, ship etc) ⓥ
上 séung up
上(個) séung(·gaw sìng·kày) (last) week
上山 séung·sàan uphill
上個 séung·gaw last (previous)
上海 séung·hóy Shanghai
上晝 séung·jáu aboard
乞依 hàt·yì beggar
叉 chàa fork
口信 háu·seun message
土地 tó·day land ⓝ
大 daai big · large
大自然 daai·ji·yìn nature
大衣 daai·yì coat · overcoat
大豆 daai·dáu soy
大使 daai·si ambassador
大使館 daai·si·gún embassy
大氣 daai·hay atmosphere (weather)
大堂 daai·tàwng foyer
大麻 daai·màa dope (drugs) ·
  marijuana · pot
大減價 daai·gáam·gaa sale
大道 daai·do avenue
大學 daai·hawk college (university)
大聲 daai·sèng loud
大麻煙 daai·jaap·wui hash (drugs)
女 léui daughter
女人 léui·yán woman
女士 léui·si Mrs
女王 léui·wawng queen
女仔 léui·jái girl
女同性戀 léui·tung·sing·léwn lesbian ⓐ
女性 léui·sing female
女朋友 léui·pàng·yáu girlfriend
女修道院 léui·sàu·do·yéwn convent
子宮帽 jí·gùng·mó
  diaphragm (contraceptive)
子宮頸癌預防檢查 jí·gùng·géng·ngàam
  yew·fàwng gím·chàa pap smear
小 síu little (size)

小巴 síu·bàa minibus
小姐 síu·jé Ms · Miss
小扁豆 síu·bín·dau lentil
小食 síu·sik snack ⓝ
小食店 síu·sik·dim snack shop
小販 síu·fáan street vendor
小童座 síu·tùng·jaw child seat
小路 síu·lo trail ⓝ
小說 síu·sewt fiction (novel)
小賣部 síu·maai·bo kiosk
小輪 síu·lèun ferry ⓝ
山 sàan mountain
山丘 sàan·yàu hill
山羊 sàan·yèung goat
山谷 sàan·gùk valley
山脈 sàan·mak mountain range
山頂 sàan·déng peak (mountain)
山路 sàan·lo path · track
山窿 sàan·lùng cave ⓝ
工作簽證 gùng·jawk chìm·jing
  work permit
工廠 gùng·cháwng factory
已婚 yí·fàn married
(一個鐘頭) 之內 (yàt gaw jùng·tau) jì·loy
  within (an hour)
之外 jì·ngoy without

四劃 4 strokes

不吸煙 bàt·kàp·yìn nonsmoking
不含鉛 bàt·hàm·yèwn unleaded
中午 jùng·ńg midday · noon
中心 jùng·sàm centre ⓝ
中風 jung·fùng stroke (health)
中草藥 jùng·chó·yeuk
  Chinese herbal medicine
中草藥醫生 jùng·chó·yeuk yì·sàng
  herbalist
中國 jùng·gawk China
中國人 jùng·gawk·yàn Chinese ⓑ
中暑 jùng·séw sunstroke
中華人民共和國
  jùng·wàa yàn·màn gung·wàw·gawk
  PRC (People's Republic of China)
中間 jùng·gàan between
中學 jùng·hawk high school
中醫 jùng·yì Chinese medicine doctor
互聯網 wu·lèun·máwng Internet
五月 ńg·yewt May
五金鋪 ńg·gàm·pó hardware store
今日 gàm·yat today
今晚 gàm·máan tonight

元旦 yèwn·daan New Year's Day
六月 luk·yewt June
公升 gùng·sìng litre
公斤 gùng·gàn kilo(gram)
公尺 gùng·chek metre
公仔 gùng·jái doll
公用 gùng·yung share ⓥ
公共 gùng·gung public ⓐ
公共汽車 gùng·gung hay·chè bus
公共電話 gùng·gung dìn·wáa phone box
公共電話 gùng·gùng dìn·wáa
  public telephone
公安局 gùng·ngàwn·gúk
  PSB (Public Security Bureau)
公里 gùng·láy kilometre
公寓 gùng·yew apartment (up market)
公廁 gùng·chi public toilet
公園 gùng·yéwn park • public gardens
公碗 gùng·wún communal bowl
公關 gùng·gwàan public relations
分開 fàn·hòy separate ⓐ
分鐘 fàn·jùng minute
午夜 ńg·ye midnight
午餐 ńg·chàan lunch ⓝ
反胃 fáan·wai nausea
反射療法 fàan·se liu·faat reflexology
天主教教堂 tìn·jéw·gaau gaau·tàwng
  cathedral
太陽 taai·yèung sun
太極 taai·gìk t'ai chi
少 síu less
尺碼 chek·máa size (general)
巴士 bàa·sí bus
巴士站 bàa·sí·jaam bus stop
巴士總站 bàa·sí·júng·jaam bus station
手 sáu hand
手工 sáu·gùng handmade
手工藝 sáu·gùng·ngai crafts •
  handicrafts
手巾 sáu·gàn handkerchief
手指 sáu·jí finger
手套 sáu·to glove(s)
手推車 sáu·tèui·chè stroller • trolley
手球 sáu·kàu handball
手袋 sáu·dóy briefcase • handbag
手提電腦 sáu·tài dìn·ló laptop
手腕 sáu·wún wrist
手槍 sáu·chèung gun
手機 sáu·gày mobile phone
手錶 sáu·bíu watch ⓥ
支票 jì·piu check • cheque (banking)
文具店 màn·geui·dim stationer

日出 yat·chèut dawn • sunrise
日記 yat·gay diary
日常 yàt·sèung daily
日期 yat·kày date (day) ⓝ
日落 yat·lawk sunset
日曆 yat·lìk calendar
日頭 yat·táu day
月 yewt month • moon
月台票 yewt·tòy·piu stand-by ticket
月經 yèwt·gìng menstruation
木 muk wood
木匠 muk·jeung carpenter
木板 muk·báan woodblocks
止痛藥 jí·tung·yeuk painkiller
比賽 báy·choy game (match, sport)
毛巾 mò·gàn face cloth • flannel •
  towel • wash cloth
毛筆 mò·bàt brush ⓝ
水 séui water ⓝ
水果 séui·gwáw fruit
水喉 séui·hàu faucet • tap
水喉水 séui·hàu·séui tap water
水痘 séui·dáu chicken pox
水稻田 séui·do·tìn rice paddy
火 fó fire ⓝ
火車 fó·chè train
火車站 fó·chè·jaam railway station
火腿 fáw·téui ham
火雞 fó·gài turkey
父母 fu·mó parents
父親 fu·chàn father
牙刷 ngàa·cháat toothbrush
牙科 ngàa·fò dentist
牙痛 ngàa·tung toothache
牙膏 ngàa·gò toothpaste
牙籤 ngàa·chìm toothpick
牛仔褲 ngàu·jái·fu jeans
牛奶 ngàu·láai milk
牛肉 ngàu·yuk beef • veal
牛油果 ngàu·yáu·gwáw avocado
冇牌經營 mó·paai gìng·ying
  speakeasy (restaurant with booths)
乒乓波 bìng·bàm·bàw table tennis
亞洲 ngaa·jàu Asia
亞麻布 a·màa·bo linen (material)
京劇 gìng·kek (Chinese) opera •
  classical Beijing opera
乘客 sing·haak passenger
乘涼 sìng·lèung enjoy the evening air
乾 gàwn dried • dry
乾淨 gàwn·jeng clean ⓐ

cantonese–english

五劃 5 strokes

世界 sai·gaai world
世界盃 sai·gaai·bùi World Cup
世貿組織 sai·mau juk·jik WTO
  (World Trade Organisation)
主婦 jéw·fú homemaker
以前 yí·chìn before
以後 yí·hau after • later
仔 jái son
兄弟 hìng·dai brother
冬天 dùng·tìn winter
出口 chèut·háu exit ⓝ
出世紙 chèut·sai·jí birth certificate
出去 chèut·heui go out (night out)
出生日期 chèut·sàng yat·kày
  date of birth
出生地 chèut·sàng·day place of birth
出發 chèut·faat departure
加油站 gàa·yàu·jaam service station
包 bàau bag • packet (general)
包裹 bàau·gáw package • parcel
北京 bàk·gìng Beijing
北邊 bàk·bin north
半 bun half
半熟 bun·suk soft-boiled
去 heui go
去世 heui·sai die
去滯 heui pò party (night out)
可以 háw·yí can (have permission)
可怕 háw·paa awful • terrible
唔可以 háw·yí can (be able)
可能 háw·làng maybe
古代 gú·doy ancient
古典 gú·dín classical
古典藝術 gú·dín ngai·seut
  classical Western art
古董 gú·dúng antique ⓝ
古董市場 gú·dúng sí·chèung
  antique market • fleamarket
右派 yau·paai right-wing
右邊 yau·bin right (direction)
叫 giu call ⓥ
叫醒 giu·séng wake (someone) up
台 tóy table
四月 say·yewt April
四肢癱瘓 sai·jì táan·wun quadriplegic
外公 ngoy·gùng grandfather (maternal)
外面 ngoy·min outside
外套 ngoy·to jacket
外國 ngoy·gawk foreign (goods)
外婆 ngoy·pò grandmother (maternal)

外幣兌換 ngoy·bai deui·wun
  currency exchange
失物 sàt·mat lost property
巨大 geui·daai huge
左邊 jáw·bin left (direction)
市中心 sí·jùng·sàm city centre
市場 sí·chèung market
平 pèng cheap
平安夜 pìng·ngàwn·ye Christmas Eve
平郵 pìng·yàu surface mail
幼稚園 yau·ji·yéwn childminding •
  crèche • kindergarten
打 dàa dozen
打 dáa play (cards)
打(電話) dáa (din·wáa) ring (phone) ⓥ
打工 dáa·gùng work ⓥ
打火機 dáa·fó·gày lighter (cigarette)
打風 dáa·fùng storm
打針 dáa·jàm injection
打掃 dáa·so clean ⓥ
打電話 dáa din·wáa telephone ⓥ
打獵 dáa·lip hunting
未婚夫 may·fàn·fù fiancé
未婚妻 may·fàn·chài fiancée
民主制 màn·jéw·jai democracy
民謠 màn·yiu folk music
玉 yuk jade
瓜 gwàa melon
瓜子 gwàa·jí watermelon seeds
生日 sàang·yat birthday
生意人 sàang·yi·yàn business person
生薄人 sàang·bó·jàn stranger
白色 baak·sìk white
白粉 baak·fán cocaine • heroin
白酒 baak·jáu spirits (Chinese alcohol)
白痴 baak·chi idiot
目的地 muk·dìk·day destination
石油 sek·yàu oil

六劃 6 strokes

交通 gàau·tùng traffic
交通地圖 gàau·tùng day·to road map
任何 yum·hàw any
光 gwàwng light ⓝ
先生 sin·sàang Mr • teacher
全麥麵包 chewn mak min·bàau
  wholemeal bread
共和國 gung·waw·gawk republic
共產主義 gung·cháan·jéw·yi
  communism
再次 joy·chi again

再見 joy·gin **goodbye**
冰 bìng **ice**
冰箱 bìng·sēung **fridge**
印度 yan·do **Hindu**
危險 ngàih·hím **dangerous**
同伴 tung·bun **companion**
同志 tùng·ji **comrade**
同志 tung·ji **gay** ③
同志吧 tung·ji·bàa **gay bar**
同事 tùng·sì **colleague**
同性戀 tung·sing·léwn **homosexual**
同埋 tùng·màai **and · with**
吊床 diu·chàwng **hammock**
名 méng **first name**
名勝古蹟 ming·sing gú·jìk
  historical (site)
合同 hap·tung **contract**
地址 day·jí **address** ⑩
地板 day·báan **floor** ⑩
地球 day·kàu **Earth**
地圖 day·tò **map**
地震 day·jan **earthquake**
地鐵 day·tit **metro (train) · subway**
地鐵站 day·tit·jaam **metro station**
多 dàw **more**
好 hó **good**
好多 hó·dàw **(a) lot · many**
好好 hó·hó **well**
好痛 hó tung **painful**
好極 hó·gik **excellent · great (fantastic)**
好運氣 hó·wan·hay **lucky**
好逼 hó·bìk **crowded**
字幕 ji·mawk **subtitles**
安全 ngàwn·chèwn **safe** ⓐ
安全性交 ngàwn·chèwn sing·gàau
  safe sex
安全帶 ngàwn·chèwn·dáai **seatbelt**
安眠藥 ngàwn·mìn·yeuk **sleeping pills**
年 lìn **year**
(今)年 (gàm) lìn **(this) year**
年輕 lìn·hèng **young**
年齡 lìn·lìng **age** ⑩
收音機 sàu·yàm·gày **radio**
收費公路 sàu·fai gùng·lo
  motorway (tollway)
收銀機 sàu·ngán·chew **cash register**
收據 sàu·geui **receipt**
早 jó **early**
早餐 jó·chàan **breakfast**
曲奇 kùk·kày **cookie**
有 yáu **have**
有可能 yáu háw·làng **possible**
有用 yáu·yung **useful**

有冷氣嘅 yáu láang·hay ge
  air-conditioned HK
有空調嘅 yáu hùng·tiù ge
  air-conditioned China
有空閒嘅 yáu hùng·kewt **vacant**
有病 yáu·beng **ill**
有暖氣 yáu léwn·hay **heated**
朱古力 jèw·gù·lìk **chocolate**
死水 sái·séui **still water**
死咗 sái·jáw **dead**
污糟 wù·jò **dirty**
灰色 fui·sìk **grey · grey**
百 baak **hundred**
百分比 baak·fan·báy **per cent**
百姓 baak·sing **common people**
百貨公司 baak·fo gùng·sì
  department store
百萬 baak·maan **million**
竹 jùk **bamboo**
米 mái **rice (raw)**
米酒 mái·jáu **rice wine**
老太太 ló·taai·táai
  old woman (respectful)
老伯 ló·baak **old man (respectful)**
老坑 ló·hàang **old man (derogatory)**
老婆 ló·pò **wife**
而家 yì·gàa **present (time)**
耳仔 yí·jái **ear**
自從 (五月) ji·chùng (ńg·yewt)
  since (May)
自然保護區 ji·yìn bó·wu·kèui
  national park
自然療法 ji·yìn liù·faat **naturopathy**
虫 chùng **worms**
血型 hewt·yìng **blood group**
血液 hewt·yik **blood**
血壓 hewt·ngaat **blood pressure**
行人 hàng·yàn **pedestrian**
行公司 hàang gùng·sì **go shopping**
行李 hàng·láy **baggage · luggage**
行李洛卡 hàng·láy làwk·káa
  luggage lockers
行李寄存 hàng·láy gay·chèwn
  left luggage
行李寄存處 hàng·láy gay·chèwn chew
  left luggage (office)
行李認領處 hàng·láy ying·líng·chew
  baggage claim
行李標簽 hàng·láy biù·chìm **luggage tag**
行李箱 hàng·láy·sèung **suitcase**
行程表 hang·chìng·bíu **itinerary**
行路 hàang·lo **walk** ⓥ
西 sài **west**

住 jew **live (somewhere) • stay (at a hotel)**
但係 daan·hai **but**
你 láy **you sg**
你哋 láy·day **you pl**
你嘅 láy·ge **your sg**
伯爺婆 baak·yè·pó **old woman (derogatory)**

七劃 7 strokes

佛 fat **Buddha**
佛寺 fat·jí **monastery (Buddhist)**
佛教 fat·gaau **Buddhism**
佛教徒 fat·gaau·tò **Buddhist**
兌現 deui·yin **cash (a cheque)** ⓥ
兌換率 deui·wun·léut **exchange rate**
免費 mín·fai **free (gratis)**
免費行李 hàng·láy **baggage allowance**
冷衫 làang·sàam **jumper • sweater**
冷氣 làang·hay **air-conditioning**
別墅 bit·séui **villa**
助聽器 jawk·ting·hay **hearing aid**
助曬油 jawk·saai·yàu **tanning lotion**
听日 ting·yat **tomorrow**
听日下晝 ting·yat·ha·jau **tomorrow afternoon**
听晚 ting·máan **tomorrow evening**
听朝 ting jiu **tomorrow morning**
妊娠檢測 yam·san gím·chàak **pregnancy test kit**
屁股 pay·gú **bottom (body)**
尿片 liu·pín **diaper • nappy**
尿道感染 liu·do gám·yím **urinary infection**
尿褲疹 liu·fu·chán **nappy rash**
床 chàawng **bed**
床單 chàawng·dàan **bed linen • sheets**
床墊 chàawng·din **mattress**
快 faai **fast • quick • soon**
我 ngáw **I • me**
我哋 ngáw·day **we • us**
我哋嘅 ngáw·day ge **our**
我嘅 ngáw ge **my**
抗菌素 kawng·kún·so **antibiotics**
找錢 jáau·chín **change (coins)** ⓝ
投訴 tàu·so **complaint**
更衣室 gàng·yì·sàt **changing room (in shop)**
村 chèwn **village**
步行路徑 yéwn·jùk lo·ging **hiking route**
步行靴 yéwn·jùk·hèu **hiking boots**
每（日）muí·(yat) **per (day)**

每次 muí·chi **always • every**
每個 muí·gaw **each**
每個人 muí·gaw·yàn **everyone**
沙斯 sàa·sì **SARS (virus)**
沙漠 sàa·mawk **desert** ⓝ
沖涼 chùng·lèung **bath** ⓝ
沖涼房 chùng·lèung·fàwng **bathroom • shower**
汽水 hay·séui **soft drink**
汽車出租 hay·chè chèut·jò **car hire**
汽車旅館 hay·chè léui·gún **motel**
汽油 hay·yàu **gas • petrol**
汽油站 hay·yàu·jaam **petrol station**
男人 làam·yán **man**
男仔 làam·jái **boy**
男朋友 làam·pàng·yáu **boyfriend**
私人 sì·yàn **private**
罕見 háwn·gin **rare (uncommon)**
肝炎 gàwn·yìm **hepatitis**
肚痛 tó·tung **stomachache**
肚痾 tó·ngàw **diarrhoea**
見 gin **meet**
走廊 jáu·làwng **aisle (on plane)**
身份證 sàn·fán·jing **identification card (ID)**
車 chè **car**
車主所有權 chè·jéw sáw·yáu·kèun **car owner's title**
車房 chè·fàwng **garage**
車站 chè·jaam **station**
車牌 chè·pàai **number plate**
車牌號碼 chè·pàai ho·máa **licence plate number • car registration**
車鎖 chè·sáw **bike lock**
車軨 chè·lùk **wheel**
車鏈 chè·lín **bike chain**
車胎 chè·tàai **tire • tyre**
防止 fàwng·jí **stop • prevent**
防水 fàwng·séui **waterproof**
防曬油 fàwng·saai·yàu **sunblock**
佢 kéui **he • she • it**
佢哋 kéui·day **they**
佢哋嘅 kéui·day ge **their**
佢嘅 kéui ge **her • his**

八劃 8 strokes

到達 do·daat **arrive**
取消 chéui·siù **cancel**
受傷 sau·sèung **injured**
味精 may·jìng **MSG**
咖啡屋 gaa·fè·ngùk **café • coffee house**
和平 waw·ping **peace**

和尚 wàw·séung **monk (Buddhist)**
呢度 lày·do **here**
呢個 lày·gaw **this (one)**
呢個(月) lày·gaw (yewt) **this (month)**
夜晚 ye·maan **night**
夜晚活動 ye·maan wut·dung **night out**
夜總會 ye·júng·wúi **nightclub**
妹妹 mùi·múi **sister (younger)**
姑姐 gù·jè **aunt (father's sister)**
姓 sing **family name • surname**
季節 gwai·jit **season**
宗教 jùng·gaau **religion**
岳父 ngawk·fú **father-in-law**
岳母 ngawk·mó **mother-in-law**
幸運曲奇 hang·wun kùk·kày
  fortune cookies
店 dim **shop**
底 dái **bottom (position)**
底衫褲 dái·sàam·fu **underwear**
底褲墊 dái·fu gin **panty liners**
(簽證)延期 (chìm·jing) yìn·kày
  extension (visa)
房 fáwng **room**
房東 fàwng·dùng **landlady**
房號 fáwng·ho **room number**
所有嘅 sáw·yáu ui **all**
招待所 jiù·doy·sáw **boarding house**
拔火罐 bat·fó·gun **cupping**
  (traditional therapy)
拋錨 pàau·làau **broken down**
  (car/vehicle)
拍拖 paak·tàw **go out with**
抵達 dái·daa **arrivals**
明白 mìng·baak **understand**
服務 fuk·mo **service**
服務員 fuk·mo·yèwn **waiter**
服務費 fuk·mo·fai **service charge**
服裝店 fuk·jàwng·dim **clothing store**
朋友 pàng·yáu **friend**
東方 dùng·fàwng **east**
武術 mó·seut **martial arts**
歧視 kày·si **discrimination**
注射 jew·se **inject**
法律 faat·leut **law**
泊(車) paak·(chè) **park (a car)**
炒 cháau **fry (stir-fry)**
爸爸 baa·bàa **dad**
牧師 muk·sì **priest**
玩得開心嘅 wáan dàk hòy·sàm dì
  have fun
的士 dìk·sí **taxi**
的士站 dìk·sí·jaam **taxi stand**
盲公狗 màang·gùng·gáu **guide dog**

盲眼 màang·ngáan **blind**
直到 jik·do **until (Friday, etc)**
社會主義 sé·wúi·jéw·yi **socialism**
社會主義者 sé·wúi·jéw·yi·jé **socialist**
社會福利 sé·wúi fûk·lay **social welfare**
空 hùng **empty**
空氣 hùng·hay **air**
空郵 hùng·yàu **airmail**
空調 hùng·tiù **air-conditioning**
空闕 hùng·kewt **vacancy**
肥皂 fày·jo **soap**
肥皂劇 fày·jo·kek **soap opera**
臥鋪 ngaw·pò **sleeping berth**
臥鋪車廂 ngaw·pò chè·sèung
  sleeping car
花名 fàa·méng **nickname**
近 kán **near**
長城 chèung·sìng **Great Wall**
長途汽車 chèung·tò hay·chè
  intercity bus
長褲 chèung·fu **pants (trousers)**
長襪 chèung·mat **stockings**
阿姨 a·yì **aunt (mother's sister)**
阿斯匹靈 a·sì·pàt·lìng **aspirin**
阿媽 a·màa **mum**
阿爺 a·yèh **grandfather (paternal)**
阿嫲 a·màa **grandmother (paternal)**
附近 fu·gan **nearby**
雨衣 yéw·yì **raincoat**
雨遮 yéw·jè **umbrella**
青口 chèng·háu **mussel**
青年旅社 chìng·lìn léui·se **youth hostel**
青椒 chèng·jiù **capsicum • pepper (bell)**
青菜 chèng·choy **leafy vegetable**

九劃 9 strokes

信 seun **letter (mail)**
信用卡 seun·yung·kàat **credit card**
便利店 bin·lay·dim **convenience store**
保險 bó·hím **insurance**
保險箱 bó·hím·sèung **safe**
係 hai **yes**
前日 chìn·yat **(the) day before yesterday**
南 làam **south**
咬 ngáau **bite (dog/insect)**
城市 sìng·sí **city**
屋 nguk **house**
屋企 nguk·káy **home**
巷仔 hawng·jái **alleyway**
度 do **degrees (temperature)**
後 hau **rear (seat etc)**
後日 hau·yat **(the) day after tomorrow**

後面 hau·mín **behind**
後邊 hau·bín **back (position)**
急傷車 gau·sèung·chè **ambulance**
指甲鉗 jí·gaap·kím **nail clippers**
指南 jí·làam **guidebook**
指南針 jí·làam·jàm **compass**
政府 jing·fú **government**
政治 jing·jí **politics**
春天 chèun·tìn **spring (season)**
春節 chèun·jit **Spring Festival**
星 sìng **star**
星座 sìng·jawk **horoscope • zodiac**
(四)星級 (say)·sìng·kàp **(four-)star**
星期 sìng·kày **week**
星期一 sìng·kày·yàt **Monday**
星期二 sìng·kày·yí **Tuesday**
星期三 sìng·kày·sàam **Wednesday**
星期四 sìng·kày·sai **Thursday**
星期五 sìng·kày·ńg **Friday**
星期六 sìng·kày·luk **Saturday**
星期日 sìng·kày·yat **Sunday**
某人 máu·yàn **someone**
毒品 duk·bán **drug(s)**
洗 sái **laundry (clothes)** ⊙ • **wash** ⊙
洗衣店 sái·yì·dim **launderette •
  laundry (place)**
洗衣房 sái·sàam·fàwng **laundry (room)**
洗衣機 sái·yì·gày **washing machine**
洗頭水 sái·tàu·séui **shampoo**
玻璃 bàw·lày **glass (drinking)**
皇后 wàwng·hau **empress**
皇帝 wàwng·dai **emperor**
相 séung **photo**
相機 séung·gày **camera**
相機鋪 séung·gày·pó **camera shop**
秋天 chàu·tìn **autumn • fall**
穿梭巴士 chèwn·sàw bàa·sí **shuttle bus**
紀念品 gay·lim·bán **souvenir**
紀念品店 gay·lim·bán·dim
  souvenir shop
紀念碑 gay·lim·hày **monument**
約會 yeuk·wui **date (appointment)** ⓝ
美食廣場 máy·sik gwáwng·chèung
  food court
背囊 bui·làwng **backpack**
英文 yìng·man **English (language)**
英文教師 yìng·man gaau·sì
  English teacher
要 yiu **want**
訂 deng **book (make a booking)**
訂滿 deng·mún **booked out**
面 mìn **face** ⓝ
面子 mìn·jí **face (social standing)** ⓝ

音樂 yàm·ngawk **music**
音樂店 yàm·ngawk·dim **music shop**
風水 fùng·séui **feng shui**
風俗 fùng·juk **custom**
風景區 fùng·gíng·kèui **scenic area**
飛行時差反應
  fày·hàng sì·chàa fáan·ying **jet lag**
飛翔船 fày·chèung·sèwn **hydrofoil**
飛機 fày·gày **aeroplane •
  airplane • plane**
飛機場 fày·gày·chèung **airport**
飛翼船 fày·yik·sèwn **jetfoil**
食 sik **eat**
食物 sik·mat **food**
食煙 sik·yìn **smoke** ⊙
食齋嘅 sik·jàai ge **vegetarian**
首相 sáu·seung **prime minister**
香水 hèung·séui **deodorant**
香港 hèung·gáwng **Hong Kong**
香煙 hèung·yìn **cigarette**
厘米 lày·mái **centimetre**

十劃 10 strokes

借 je **borrow**
修女 sàu·léui **nun**
修車店 sàu·chè·dim **bike shop**
凍 dung **(to be) cold**
原子筆 yèwn·jí·bàt **pen (ballpoint)**
哥哥 gàw·gàw **(elder) brother**
唔安全 ǹg ngàwn·chèwn **unsafe**
唔係 ǹg·hai **not**
唔得 ǹg·dàk **no**
夏天 hua·tìn **summer**
娛樂指南 yèw·lawk jí·làam
  entertainment guide
孫 sèwn **grandchild**
家姐 gàa·jè **(elder) sister**
家庭 gàa·tìng **family**
宮內節育器 gùng·loy jit·yuk·hay
  IUD (contraceptive)
宮殿 gùng·dín **palace**
座位 jawk·wái **seat (place)**
旁邊 pàwng·bìn **beside • next to**
旅行支票 léui·hàng jì·piu
  travellers cheque
旅行社 léui·hàng·sé **tourist office •
  travel agency**
旅行團 léui·hàng·tèwn **guided tour**
旅店 léui·dim • **tourist hotel**
旅客 léui·haak **tourist**
旅游團 léui·yàu·tèwn **tour** ⓝ
旅程 léui·chìng **trip (journey)**

旅遊 léui·yàu travel ⓥ
旅遊巴 léui·yàu·bàa coach (bus)
時事 sì·sí current affairs
時差 sì·chàa time difference
時間 sì·gaan time
時間表 sì·gaan·bíu timetable
時髦 sì·mò fashion
書 sèw book
書店 sèw·dim book shop
核子 hat·jí nuclear
核試 hat·si nuclear testing
核電 hat·din nuclear energy
核廢物 hat·fai·mat nuclear waste
梳 sàw comb
栗子 leut·jí chestnut
桑那 sàwng·làa sauna
桃 tó peach
冧酒 làm·jáu rum
氣 hay chi
氣氛 hay·fàn atmosphere
氣候 hay·hau weather
氣墊船 hay·din·sèwn hovercraft
氧氣 yéung·hay oxygen
浪 lawng wave ⓝ
浪漫 lawng·maan romantic
消毒劑 siù·duk·jài antiseptic ⓝ
消費 siù·fai tip (gratuity)
海關 hóy·gwàan customs (immigration)
特別行政區 dak·bit hàng·jing·kèui
    SAR (Special Administrative Region)
留喺 làu·hái stay in (one place)
疾病 jat·beng disease
病 beng sick
紙巾 jí·gàn tissues
紙幣 jí·bai banknote
胸 hùng chest (body)
胳膊 sáu·bay arm
航班 hàwng·bàan flight
蚊 màn mosquito
蚊香 màn·hèung mosquito coil
蚊帳 màn·jeung mosquito net
起泡 háy·pàwk blister
送 sung give
迷幻劑 mài·waan·yeuk ecstasy (drug)
酒吧 jáu·bàa bar · pub
酒店 jáu·dim hotel
酒店業 jáu·dim·yip hospitality
酒料 jáu·liú (alcoholic) drink ⓝ
酒精 jáu·jìng alcohol
酒樓 jáu·làu restaurant
酒瓶 jáu·pó bottle shop · liquor store
針筒 jàm·túng needle · syringe
針線 jàm·sin needle and thread

除夕 cheut·jik New Year's Eve
高速公路 gò·chùk gùng·lo highway

十一劃 11 strokes

雪櫃 sewt·gwai fridge
俾錢 báy·chín pay
停 ting stop (bus, tram, etc) ⓝ
停止 ting·jí stop (cease) ⓥ
停車場 ting·chè·cheung car park
假期 gaa·kày holiday(s) · vacation
偏頭疼 pin·tàu·tung migraine
商場 sèung·chèung shopping centre
啱 ngàam right (correct)
問 man ask (a question)
問題 màn·tài question ⓝ
售票員 sau·piu·yèwn ticket collector
售票機 sau·piu·gay ticket machine
婚姻狀況 fàn·yàn jawng·fawng
    marital status
崩潰 bàng·kui break down
常用語手冊 sèung·yung·yéw sáu·chàak
    phrasebook
帶 daai bring
帶狀泡疹 dáai·jawng bàau·chán
    shingles (illness)
強奸 kèung·gàan rape ⓝ & ⓥ
得閒 dàk·hàan free (available)
從 chùng from
從未 chùng·may never
情感 chìng·gám feeling (physical)
捲煙紙 géwn·yìn·jí cigarette papers
掛號 gwaa·ho (by) registered mail/post
推拿 tèui·làa shiatsu
推遲 tui·chì delay ⓝ
排隊 pàai·déui queue ⓥ
救生衣 gau·sàang·yì life jacket
救傷用品 gau·sèung yung·bán
    first-aid kit
晚飯 máan·faan dinner
望 mawng watch ⓥ
望遠鏡 mawng·yéwn·geng binoculars
望遠鏡 mawng·yéwn·geng telescope
殺人 saat·yàn murder ⓥ
殺人犯 saat·yàn·fáan murder ⓝ
毫米 hò·mái millimetre
涼鞋 lèung·hàai sandal
現金 yin·gàm cash ⓝ
痕 hàn itch ⓝ
眼睛 ngáan·jing eye(s)
眼藥水 ngáan·yeuk·séui eye drops
眼鏡 ngáan·géng glasses (spectacles)
票 piu coupon · ticket

票房 piu·fàwng **ticket office**
票價 piu·gaa **admission (price) • fare**
移民 yì·màn **immigration**
細佬 sai·ló **brother (younger)**
細節 sai·jit **details**
細路仔 sai·lo·jái **child • children**
船 sèwn **boat • ship**
許可證 héui·háw·jing **permit** ⓝ
販毒 fáan·duk **drug trafficking**
責任 jàak·yam (someone's) **fault**
軟臥 (飛) yéwn·ngaw (fày)
   soft-sleeper (ticket)
軟盤 yéwn·pún **disk (floppy)**
通常 tùng·sèung **typical**
通過 tùng·gaw **pass** ⓥ
連接 lìn·jip **connection**
連襪褲 lìn·mat·fu **pantyhose**
速度 chùk·do **speed (velocity)**
速度表 chùk·do·bíu **speedometer**
速遞 (信) chùk·dai (seun) **express (mail)**
(寄) 速遞信 (gay) chùk·dai seun
   (by) express mail
部份 bo·fan **part (component)**
都 dò **also**
陰道 yàm·do **vagina**

十二劃 12 strokes

勞動節 lò·dung·jit **Labour Day**
博物館 bawk·mat·gún **museum**
喺 hái **at • on**
喺……前面 hái … chìn·mín **in front of**
喺……裡面 hái … léui·mìn **in**
單 dàan **bill (restaurant etc)**
單人 dàan·yàn **single (person)**
單人房 dàan·yàn·fáwng **single room**
單車 dàan·chè **bicycle • bike**
單程 dàan·chìng **one-way (ticket)**
報紙 bo·jí **newspaper**
報攤 bo·tàan **newsagency • newsstand**
帽 mó **hat**
幾多 gáy·dàw **how much**
幾時 gáy·sì **when**
廁所 chi·sáw **bathroom • toilet**
廁紙 chi·jí **toilet paper**
復活節 fuk·wut·ji **Easter**
悶 mun **bored**
插頭 chaap·táu **plug (electricity)**
換 wun **exchange** ⓥ
換錢 wun chín **change (money)** ⓥ
揾到 wún·dó **find**
揾笨 wán·ban **rip-off**

普通話 pó·tùng·wáa
   Mandarin (language)
景 gíng **view (scenic)** ⓝ
晾衫繩 lawng·sàam·síng **clothesline**
晾乾 lawng·gàwn **dry (clothes)** ⓥ
朝早 jìu·jó **morning**
棉塞 mìn·sàk **tampon**
港口 gáwng·háu **harbour • port**
游水 yàu·séui **swim** ⓥ
游水衣 yàu·séui·yì **bathing suit**
游水護眼鏡 yàu·séui wu·ngáan·geng
   goggles (swimming)
游泳池 yàu·wíng·chì **swimming pool**
煮飯 jéw·faan **cook** ⓥ • **cooking** ⓝ
痢疾 lay·jat **dysentery**
痛 tung **hurt** ⓥ • **pain** ⓝ • **sore** ⓐ
登革熱 dàng·gaap·yit **dengue fever**
登記 (口) dàng·gay·(tóy) **check-in (desk)**
登機口 dàng·gày·háu **gate (airport, etc)**
登機卡 dàng·gày·kàat **boarding pass**
登機關口 dàng·gày jaap·háu
   departure gate
硬臥 (飛) ngaan·ngaw·(fày)
   hard-sleeper (ticket)
硬幣 ngaan·bai **coins**
稅 seui **tax** ⓝ
窗 chèung **window**
等 dáng **wait (for)**
等候室 dáng·hau·sàt **waiting room**
菜單 choy·dàan **menu**
街 gàai **street**
街市 gàai·sí **street market • market**
象棋 jeung·káy **chess (Chinese)**
貴 gwai **expensive**
買 mǎai **buy**
買嘢 mǎai yé **shop** ⓥ
超市 chìu·sí **supermarket**
跌 dit **lose**
逮捕 dai·bo **arrest** ⓥ
週末 jàu·mut **weekend**
郵 yàu **mail (postal system)**
郵局 yàu·gúk **post office**
郵政編碼 yàu·jing pìn·máa **postcode**
郵票 yàu·piu **stamp**
郵費 yàu·fai **postage**
鄉下 hèung·háa **countryside**
開 hòy **open** ⓥ
開心果 hòy·sàm·gwáw **pistachio**
開支 hòy·jì **budget**
開車 hòy·chè **drive** ⓥ
開放 hòy·fawng **open** ⓐ
開瓶器 hòy·pìng·hay **bottle opener**
開創性 hòy·chawng·sing **original**

開頭 hòy·chí **start** ⓥ
開罐器 hòy·gun·hay **tin opener**
隊 déui **team**
階級制度 gāai·kùp jai do **class system**
陽具 yèung·geui **penis**
集會 jaap·wúi **rally** ⓥ
雲 wún **cloud**
順勢療法 seun·sai lìu·faat **homeopathy**
飯 faan **rice (cooked)**
飲 yám **drink** ⓥ
飲料 yám·líu **drink** ⓝ
飲茶 yám·chàa **yum cha**
黃瓜 wàwng·gwàa **cucumber**
黃色 wàwng·sīk **yellow**
黃豆 wàwng dáu **soy bean**
黃金 wàwng·gàm **gold**
黑白 (片) hàak·baak(·pín) **B&W (film)**
黑色 hàak·sīk **black**
黑眼鏡 hàak·ngáan·géng **sunglasses**
黑暗 hàak·ngam **dark**
睇 tái **look • see**
睇法 tái·faat **opinion**
睇書 tái·sèw **reading**

十三劃 13 strokes

傳真 chèwn·jàn **fax machine**
傳統藝術 chèwn·túng ngai·seut
　　classical Chinese art
傾偈 kìng·gái **chat • talk** ⓥ
傷 sēung **injury**
傷風 sēung·fùng **feel cold • have a cold**
傷殘 sēung·chàan **disabled**
嗌 ngaai **shout** ⓥ
嗰個 gáw·gaw **that (one) • which**
嗰邊 gáw·bìn **there**
園丁 yèwn·dìng **gardener**
圓 yèwn **round** ⓐ
圓環交叉路口 yèwn·wàan gàau·chàa lo·háu
　　roundabout
塞 sàk **plug (bath)**
塞咗 sàk·jáw **blocked (toilet)**
塑像 sawk·jeung **sculpture**
塑膠 sawk·gàau **plastic**
塑膠樽 sawk·gàau·jèun **water bottle**
塔 taap **pagoda**
塊 faai **piece**
奧運會 au·wun·wúi **Olympic Games**
媽媽 màa·màa **mother**
幹部 gawn·bo **communist party official**
幹道 gawn·do **main road**
微波爐 may·bàw·lò **microwave (oven)**

微笑 mày·siu **smile** ⓥ
意大利 yi·daai·lay **Italy**
意外 yi·ngoy **accident**
意粉 yi·fán **pasta**
感光度 gám·gwàwng·do **film speed**
感冒 gám·mo **flu**
感冒 gám·mo **influenza**
感染 gám·yím **infection**
感情 gám·chìng **feelings**
感激 gám·gìk **grateful**
想 séung **think**
想念 séung·lìm **miss (feel absence of)**
愛 ngoy **love** ⓥ
愛人 ngoy·yàn **lover**
愛情 ngoy·chìng **love** ⓝ
愛滋病 ngoy·jì·beng **AIDS**
愛滋病毒 ngoy·jì·beng·duk **HIV**
愛爾蘭 ngoy·yí·làan **Ireland**
搞笑 gáau·siu **funny**
搭順風車 daap·seun·fùng·chè **hitchhike**
搖滾 yìu·gún **rock (music)**
搖滾樂隊 yìu·gún ngàwk·déui
　　rock group
新 sàn **new**
新加坡 sàn·gàa·bàw **Singapore**
新西蘭 sàn·sài·làan **New Zealand**
新聞 sàn·màn **news**
新鮮 sàn·sìn **fresh**
暈船 wùn·sèwn **seasick** ⓐ •
　　travel sickness
暖 léwn **warm** ⓐ
暖水壺 léwn·séui·wú **flask • Thermos**
暖氣 léwn·hay **heating**
暖爐 léwn·lò **heater**
會議 wui·yí **conference**
極標子 gik·lìk·jí **clutch (car)**
椰子 yè·jí **coconut**
椰菜花 yè·choy·fàa **cauliflower**
溫度 wàn·do **temperature (weather)**
滑浪 waat·lawng **surf (waves)**
滑水 waat·séui **waterskiing**
滑板 waat·báan **skateboarding**
滑浪 waat·lawng **surfing**
滑浪板 waat·lawng·báan **surfboard**
滑浪風帆 waat·lawng fùng·fàan
　　sailboarding • windsurfing
滑雪 waat·sewt **ski**
滑雪 waat·sewt **skiing**
滑雪板 waat·sewt·báan **snowboarding**
滑雪護眼鏡 waat·sewt wu·ngáan·geng
　　goggles (skiing)
準時 jéun·sì **on time**
準備 jéun·bay **prepare**

準備好 jéun·bay·hó **ready**
溜冰 làu·bìng **skate (ice)** ⓥ
煎鍋 gìn·wawk **pan**
煙灰缸 yìn·fèui·gàwng **ashtray**
煙肉 yìn·yuk **bacon**
煙店 yìn·dim **tobacconist**
煙絲 yìn·sì **tobacco**
煙攤 yìn·tàan **tobacco kiosk**
煤氣 mui·hay **gas (for cooking)**
照顧 jiu·gu **look after**
煲 bò **saucepan**
瑞士 sèui·sj **Switzerland**
瑞典 sèui·dín **Sweden**
瑜伽 yèw·gàa **yoga**
痲疹 màa·chán **measles • mumps**
矮 ngái **short (height)**
碗 wún **bowl**
筷子 faai·jí **chopsticks**
節日 jit·yat **festival**
節目 jit·muk **gig • program**
節奏 jit·jau **rhythm**
粵語流行曲 yewt·yéw·làu·hàng·kùk
　　Cantopop (music)
經前緊張 gìng·chìn·gán·jèung
　　premenstrual tension
經常 gìng·sèung **often**
經理 gìng·láy **manager**
經痛 gìng·tung **period pain**
經絡按摩 gìng·lawk ngawn·mò
　　pressure point massage
經濟艙 gìng·jai·chàwng **economy class**
經驗 gìng·yim **experience**
罪犯 jeui·fáan **prisoner**
聖人 sing·yàn **saint**
聖經 sing·gìng **Bible**
聖誕日 sing·daan **Christmas Day**
聖誕節 sing·daan·jit **Christmas**
腰果 yiù·gwáw **cashew**
腰袋 yiù·dóy **bumbag**
腸胃炎 chèung·wai·yìm **gastroenteritis**
腳 geui **foot**
腳按摩 geui ngawn·mò **foot massage**
腳踏 geui·daap **pedal**
腳腕 geui·jàang **ankle**
腫瘤 júng·làu **tumour**
腫咗 júng·jáw **swollen**
腺熱 sin·yit **glandular fever**
落 (車) lawk(·chè) **get off (a train, etc)**
落山 lawk·sàan **downhill**
落雨 lawk·yéw **rain**
落單 lawk·dàan **order** ⓝ
葉 yip **leaf**
葬禮 jawng·láy **funeral**

葡提子 pò·tài·jí **raisin**
葡萄 pò·tò **grapes**
葡萄柚 pò·tò·yáu **grapefruit**
葡萄酒 pò·tò·jáu **wine**
葡萄乾 pò·tò·gàwn **sultana (raisin)**
葡萄園 pò·tò·yèwn **vineyard**
號碼 ho·máa **number**
蜂蜜 fùng·mat **honey**
裙 kùn **skirt**
補液鹽 bó·yik·yìm **rehydration salts**
裡面 léui·min **inside**
解放軍 gáai·fawng·gùn
　　PLA (People's Liberation Army)
試 si **try** ⓥ
試用 si·yung **workout**
試圖 si·tò **try (attempt)** ⓥ
詩歌 sì·gàw **poetry**
話俾 waa báy **tell**
賊 cháak **thief**
資本主義 jì·bún·jéw·yi **capitalism**
賈第虫病 gáa·dik·chùng·beng **giardiasis**
賄賂 kuí·lo **bribe** ⓥ
跟 gàn **follow**
路 lo **road • way**
路仔 lo·jái **footpath • path**
路線 lo·sin **route**
跳 tiu **jump** ⓥ
跳虱 tiu·sàt **flea**
跳舞 tiu·mó **dance** ⓥ
跳線 tiu·sin **jumper leads**
較剪 gaau·jín **scissors**
農民 lùng·màn **farmer**
農田 lùng·tìn **crop (field)**
農地 lùng·day **farm** ⓝ
農曆年 lùng·lik·lìn **New Year (Chinese)**
運氣 wan·hay **luck**
運動員 wan·dung·yèwn **sportsperson**
運輸 wun·sèw **transport**
遊行 yàu·hàng **protest** ⓝ
道教 do·gaau **Taoism**
道謝 do·je **thank** ⓥ
逼力 bìk·lìk **brakes**
過去 gaw·heui **past** ⓥ
過夜 gaw·ye **overnight**
過重 (行李) gaw·chúng
　　excess (baggage)
過氣 gaw·hay **stale**
過敏 gaw·mán **allergic**
過量 gaw·leung **overdose**
過濾 gaw·leui **filtered**
過癮 gaw·yán **interesting**
鉗 kím **tweezers**
鉛筆 yèwn·bàt **pencil**

雷雨 lèui·yéw **thunderstorm**
電 dın **electricity**
電用品店 dın·jí yung·bán·dim **electrical store**
電子狂歡舞會 dın·jí kàwng·fùn mó·wúi **rave** ⓝ
電子游戲 dın·ji yàu·hay **computer game**
電子郵件 dın·jí yàu·gín **email**
電池 dın·chì **battery**
電車 dın·chè **tram**
電流 dın·làu **current (electricity)**
電風扇 dın·fùng·sin **fan (machine)**
電訊塔 dın·seun·taap **tower (telecom)**
電梯 dın·tài **elevator · escalator · lift**
電船 dın·sèwn **motorboat**
電單車 dın·dàan·chè **motorbike · motorcycle**
電報 dın·bo **telegram**
電筒 dın·túng **flashlight · torch**
電視 dın·si **television · TV**
電暖爐 dın·léwn·lò **radiator**
電腦 dın·ló **computer**
電話 dın·wáa **phone · telephone** ⓝ
電話卡 dın·wáa·kàat **phone card**
電話簿 dın·wáa·bó **phone book**
電影 dın·yíng **film (cinema) · movie**
靴 hèu **boots (footwear)**
預防針 yew·fàwng·jàm **vaccination**
預定 yew·deng **reservation (booking)**
鼓 gú **drum**

十四劃 **14 strokes**

僱主 gu·jéw **employer**
僱員 gu·yèwn **employee**
凳 dang **chair**
匱 gui **tired**
嘈 cho **noisy**
圖書館 tò·sèw·gún **library**
圖章 tò·jèung **personal seal**
夢 mung **dream** ⓝ
寧願 lìng·yéwn **prefer**
瘕日 kàm·yat **yesterday**
對 deui **pair (couple)**
對方付款 deui·fàwng fu·fún **collect call (reverse charge)**
對面 deui·mın **opposite**
慢 maan **slow**
慢慢 maan·máan **slowly**
摘水果 jaak séui·gwáw **fruit picking**
摸 mó **feel · touch**
榛果仁 jèut·gwáw·yàn **hazelnut**
歌手 gàw·sáu **singer**

歌曲 gàw·kùk **song**
歌劇 gàw·kek **opera (Western)**
演出 yín·chèut **performance**
演員 yín·yewn **actor**
滿 mún **full · no vacancy**
漆器 chàt·hay **lacquerware**
熊貓 hung·màau **panda**
瘧疾 yeuk·jat **malaria**
監察點 gàam·chaat·jàam **checkpoint**
監獄 gàam·yuk **jail · prison**
睡房 seui·fáwng **bedroom**
睡袋 sheui·dóy **sleeping bag**
碟 díp **dish (of food) · plate**
福利 fùk·lay **welfare**
種花 jung·fàa **gardening**
種族歧視 júng·juk kày·sì **racism**
稱 ching **weigh**
算命佬 sewn·meng·ló **fortune teller**
綠色 luk·sìk **green**
綠茶 luk·chàa **green tea**
緊 gán **tight**
緊急意外 gán·gàp yi·ngoy **emergency**
緊要 gán·yiu **urgent**
網 máwng **net**
網吧 máwng·bàa **Internet café**
網球 máwng·kàu **tennis**
綿羊 mìn·yéung **sheep**
維生素 wài·sàng·so **vitamins**
維他命 wài·tàa·ming **vitamins**
綳帶 bàng·dáai **bandage**
罰款 fat·fún **fine (penalty)** ⓝ
膀胱 pawng·gwàwng **bladder**
膀胱炎 pawng·gwàwng·yìm **cystitis**
膊頭 bawk·tàu **shoulder**
腿 téui **leg**
舞蹈 mó·do **dancing**
蒙古 mùng·gú **Mongolia**
蒜 sewn **garlic**
蜜桃 mat·yewt **honeymoon**
蜜糖 mat·tò **nectarine**
蜜蜂 mat·fùng **bee**
蜘蛛 jì·jèw **spider**
製作 jai·jawk **make**
語言 yéw·yìn **language**
說明書 sewt·ming·sèw **brochure**
賓館 bàn·gún **guesthouse**
輕 hèng **light (not heavy)**
輕瀉劑 hìng·se·jài **laxative**
辣椒 laat·jìu **chilli**
辣椒醬 laat·jìu·jeung **chilli sauce**
遠 yéwn **far**
遠足 yéwn·jùk **hike · hiking**
遙控 pìn·pìk **remote control**

酸奶 sèwn·láai **sour cream · yogurt**
酸梅湯 sèwn·mùi·tàwng **sour plum drink**
銀 ngàan **silver**
銀包 ngàn·bàau **purse**
銀行 ngàn·hàwng **bank**
銀行賬戶 ngàn·hàwng jeung·wu **bank account**
需要 sèui·yiu **need** ⓥ
領事館 lǐng·si·gún **consulate**
領導 líng·do **leader**
餃 gáau **dumpling**
(煮) 餃 (jéw) gáau **(boiled) dumpling**
(煎) 餃 (jin) gáau **(fried) dumpling**
(蒸) 餃 (jing) gáau **(steamed) dumpling**
餅店 béng·dim **cake shop**
餅乾 béng·gàwn **biscuit · cracker**
鼻 bay **nose**

十五劃 15 strokes

價值 gaa·jik **value** ⓝ **· price**
價錢 gaa·chìn **cost** ⓝ **· price**
劇 kek **play (theatre)**
劇場 kek·chèung **opera house · theatre**
劍擊 gim·gìk **fencing (sport)**
嘴唇 jéui·sèun **lips**
墳場 fàn·chèung **cemetery**
墳墓 fàn·mo **grave · tomb**
審核 sám·hat **review** ⓝ
寫 sé **write**
層 chàng **floor (storey)**
廢氣 fai·hay **exhaust (car)**
廢墟 fai·hèui **ruins**
廚房 chèw·fáwng **kitchen**
廚師 chèw·sì **chef · cook** ⓝ
廟 miú **shrine · temple**
廣告 gáwng·go **advertisement**
廣東 gwáwng·dùng **Guangdong**
廣東話 gwáwng·dùng·wáa **Cantonese (language)**
廣場 gwáwng·chèung **square (town)**
彈 tàan **play (guitar)**
彈弓 dàan·gùng **spring (coil)**
影 yíng **shade · shadow**
影相 yíng·séung **take a photo**
德國 dàk·gawk **Germany**
德國麻疹 dàk·gawk màa·chán **rubella**
慶祝 hing·jùk **celebration**
撞車 jawng·chè **crash** ⓝ
撥號音 but·ho·yàm **dial tone**
樓 láu **building · flat (apartment)**
樓梯 làu·tài **stairway**

樂隊 ngawk·déui **band (music)**
歐元 ngàu·yèwn **euro (currency)**
歐洲 ngàu·jàu **Europe**
醬 jeung **sauce**
潔牙線 git·ngà·sin **dental floss**
潛水 chìm·séui **diving (sport) · snorkelling**
潛水裝備 chìm·séui jàwng·bay **diving equipment**
潮流 chìu·làu **tide**
潤滑油 yeun·waat·yáu **lubricant**
熟食店 suk·sik·dim **delicatessen**
熟食檔 suk·sik·dawng **cooked food stall**
熱 yit **heat** ⓝ **· hot** ⓐ
熱水 yit·séui **hot water**
熱水袋 léwn·séui·dóy **(hot) water bottle**
瘤 láu **lump**
瘦肉 sau·yuk **muscle**
瘡口貼 chòng·háu·tip **Band-Aid**
賙低 fan·dài **lie (not stand)**
賙覺 fan·gaau **sleep · sleeping**
確切 kawk·chit **exactly**
確定 kawk·dìng **confirm (a booking)**
確認 kawk·ying **validate**
窮 kùng **poor · poverty**
箱 sèung **box · carton**
編輯 pìn·chàp **editor**
線 sin **thread**
罷工 bàa·gùng **strike** ⓝ
膝頭 sàt·tàu **knee**
膠水 gàau·séui **glue**
蔗汁 je·jàp **sugar cane juice**
蓮 lìn **lotus**
蔬菜 sàw·choy **vegetable**
蝴蝶 wù·díp **butterfly**
蝦 hàa **prawn**
蝸牛 wàw·ngàu **snail**
衛生巾 wai·sàng·gàn **sanitary napkin**
請求 chéng·kàu **ask (for something)**
請客 chéng·haak **invite** ⓥ
請願 chíng·yewn **petition**
調味料 tiu·may·liú **herb (cooking)**
調情 tiu·ching **chat up**
調解器 tiu·gáai·hay **modem**
豌豆 wún·dau **pea**
豬 jèw **pig**
豬肉 jèw·yuk **pork**
豬肉佬 jèw·yuk·ló **butcher**
賬單 jeung·dàan **account · bill · check**
賭 dó **bet** ⓥ
賭場 dó·chèung **casino**
賭錢 dó·chín **gamble**

賣 maai **sell**
質量 jàt·leung **quality**
踢 tek **kick** ⓥ
踩單車 cháai dàan chè **cycle** ⓥ
輪椅 lèun·yí **wheelchair**
輪胎 lèun·tàai **tire · tyre · drunk**
醋 cho **vinegar**
醃菜 yip·choy **pickles**
銷售稅 siu·sau·seui **sales tax**
鞋 hàai **shoe(s)**
鞋店 hàai·dim **shoe shop**
餓 ngaw **(to be) hungry**
駛…… chìn cost ⓥ
駕駛執照 gaa·sái jàp·jiu **drivers licence**
骷髏頭 fù·lò·tàu **skull**
髮型屋 faa·yìng·ngùk **hairdresser**
鬧交 naau·gàau **argue**
鬧鐘 law·jùng **alarm clock**
靚 leng **pretty**

十六劃 16 or more strokes

壁虎 bìk·fú **lizard**
壁球 bìk·kàu **squash**
學 hawk **learn**
學生 hawk·sàang **student**
學校 hawk·haau **school**
學歷 hawk·lìk **qualifications**
導游 do·yàu **guide (person)**
導演 do·yín **director (film)**
戰爭 gin·jàng **war**
擁躉 yúng·dán **supporter (sport)**
擋風玻璃 dáwng·fùng bàw·lày
  windscreen
操作員 chò·jawk·yèwn **operator**
樽 jèun **bottle**
橙 cháang **orange**
橙汁 cháang·jàp **orange juice**
橙色 cháang·sìk **orange (colour)**
橙醬 cháang·jeung **marmalade**
樹 sew **tree**
樹蔭 sew·yam **shade**
橄欖 gaam·láam **olive**
橄欖油 gaam·láam·yàu **olive oil**
橋 kiù **bridge**
機場稅 gày·chèung·seui **airport tax**
機會 gày·wui **chance**
機器 gày·hay **machine**
歷史 lik·sí **history**
澳大利亞 ngo·daai·lay·a **Australia**
澳式橄欖球 ngo·sìk gaam·láam·kàu
  Australian Rules Football

燒傷 siu·séung **burn** ⓥ
燒燶 siu·lùng **burnt**
燈膽 dàng·dáam **light bulb**
燕麥 yin·mat **oats**
燙斗 tawng·dáu **iron (for clothes)**
燜 màn **braise**
積分牌 jìk·fàn·páai **scoreboard**
穆茲利 muk·ji·lày **muesli**
穆斯林 muk·sì·làm **Muslim**
糖 tàwng **sweets**
糖尿病 tàwng·liu·beng **diabetes**
糖果 tàwng·gwáw **candy · lollies**
蕩失路 dawng·sàt·lo **lost (disoriented)**
螞蟻 máa·ngái **ant**
褲 fu **trousers**
貓 màau **cat**
辦公室 baan·gùng·sàt **office**
選擇 séwn·jaak **choose**
選舉 séwn·géui **election**
遲到 chì·do **late**
遺跡 wài·jìk **relic**
錯 chaw **wrong**
錯誤 chaw·ng **mistake**
錢 chín **money · payment**
錫 sek **kiss** ⓥ
錄 luk **record** ⓥ
錄音 luk·yàm **recording**
錄音帶 luk·yàm·dáai **cassette**
錄音導游 luk·yàm do·yàu **guide (audio)**
錄影帶 luk·yíng·dáai **video tape**
錄影機 luk·yíng·gày **video recorder**
錦標賽 gám·biù·choy **championships**
霍亂 fawk·lewn **cholera**
靜坐 jing·jawk **meditation**
頸渴 géng·hawt **thirsty (to be)**
頸鏈 géng·lín **necklace**
頭 tàu **head**
頭巾 tàu·gàn **scarf**
頭皮 tàu·pày **scalp**
頭刷 tàu·cháat **hairbrush**
頭蝨 tàu·sàt **lice**
頭按摩 tàu ngawn·mò **head massage**
頭痛 tàu·tung **headache**
頭盔 tàu·kwài **helmet**
頭等艙 tàu·dáng·chàwng
  business class · first class
頭暈 tàu·wàn **dizzy**
頭髮 tàu·faat **hair**
餐巾 chàan·gàn **napkin · serviette**
餐卡 chàan·kàa **dining car**
餡餅 háam·béng **pie**
鴨 ngaap **duck**

壓力 ngaat·lìk **pressure**
嬰兒食品 yìng·yì sìk·bán **baby food**
尷尬 gaam·gaai **(very) embarrassed**
幫助 bàwng·jaw **help** ⓝ
戲院 hay·yéwn **cinema**
戲劇 hay·kek **drama**
檢疫站 gím·yìk·jaam **quarantine**
氈 jìn **blanket**
氈酒 jìn·jáu **gin**
濕 sàp **wet** ⓐ
濕疹 sàp·chán **eczema**
營地 yìng·day **camping ground**
營釘 yìng·dèng **tent peg**
營業時間 yìng·yìp sì·gaan
   opening hours
營幕 yìng·maw **tent**
牆 chèung **wall (outer)**
環境 wàan·gíng **environment**
癌症 ngàam·jìng **cancer**
縫紉 fùng·yan **sew (not mend)**
總統 júng·túng **president**
翼 yìk **wings**
聲音 sìng·yàm **voice** ⓝ
聲量 sìng·leung **volume**
聰明 chùng·mìng **brilliant (clever)**
臨時工 làm·sì·gùng **casual work**
臨時保姆 làm·sì bó·mó **babysitter**
舉重 géui·chúhng
   weights (for workout)
薪水 sàn·séui **salary • wage**
薄 bawk **thin**
薑 gèung **ginger**
薯仔 sèw·jái **potato**
螺絲開瓶器 làw·sì hòy·pìng·hay
   corkscrew
講 gáwng **say • speak**
講師 gáwng·sì **lecturer**
講笑 gáwng·siú **joke** ⓝ
賽車 choy·chè **racing bike**
賽場 choy·chèung **racetrack**
避孕用品 bay·yan yung·bán
   contraceptives
避孕套 bay·yan·to **condom**
避孕藥 bay·yan·yeuk **(the) pill**
鍵盤 gìn·pún **keyboard**
鍊 lín **chain**
鍋 wawk **frying pan • wok**
鍋 wawk **wok**
錘 chéui **hammer**
闊 fut **wide**
隱形眼鏡 yán·yìng ngáan·géng
   contact lens

隱形眼鏡水 yán·yìng ngáan·géng séui
   contact lens solution
霜 sèung **frost**
點 dím **point** ⓝ
點心 dím·sàm **dim sum**
點菜 dím·choy **order** ⓥ
點解 dím·gáai **why**
點樣 dím·yéung **how**
櫃 gwai **cupboard**
櫃枱 gwai·tóy **counter (at hotel)**
檸檬 lìng·mùng **lemon • lime (fruit)**
檸檬汁 lìng·mùng·jàp **lemonade**
檸檬味 lìng·mùng·may **lime (flavour)**
檯球 tóy·kàu **pool (game)**
瀑布 buk·bo **waterfall**
禮物 lái·mat **gift • present**
禮拜 lái·baai **mass (Catholic)**
(呢個) 禮拜 (lày·gaw) lái·baai **(this) week**
簡單 gáan·dàan **simple**
簡歷 gáan·lìk **résumé • CV**
糧食 lèung·sìk **provisions**
翻譯 fàan·yìk **interpreter** ⓝ •
   translate ⓥ
舊貨鋪 gau·fo·pó **second-hand shop**
藍色 làam·sìk **blue**
蟲 chùng **bug (insect)**
轉身 bawng·sàn **turn** ⓥ
轉換插頭 jéwn·wun chaap·làu **adaptor**
轉機室 jéwn·gày·sàt **transit lounge**
醫生 yì·sàng **doctor**
醫院 yì·yéwn **hospital**
醫學 yì·hawk
   medicine (study, profession)
醫藥 yì·yeuk **medicine (medication)**
醬 jeung **dipping sauce**
鎊 bàwng **pound (money, weight)**
鎖 sáw **lock** ⓝ & ⓥ
鎖 sáw **padlock**
鎖咗 sáw·jáw **locked (door)**
離婚 lày·fàn **divorced**
離開 lày·hòy **depart (leave)**
雜技 jaap·gay **circus**
雜紙 jaap·ji **magazine**
雜貨 jaap·fo **grocery**
雙人 sèung·yàn **double**
雙人床 sèung·yàn·chàwng **double bed**
雙人房 sèung·yàn·fàwng
   double room • twin room
雙周 sèung·jàu **fortnight**
雙胞胎 sèung·bàau·tòy **twins**
雙程 (飛) sèung·chàng (fày)
   return (ticket)

嚟 lài **come**
雞 gài **chicken**
雞尾酒 gài·máy·jáu **cocktail**
雞蛋 gài·dáan **egg (chicken)**
雞蛋果 gài·dáan·gwáw **passionfruit**
顏色 ngàan·sìk **colour**
騎 kè **ride** ⊙
騎馬 kè·máa **horse riding**
騎樓 kè·láu **balcony**
鬆 sùng **loose**
鯉魚 láy·yéw **carp**
鵝 ngáw **goose**
鵝口瘡 ngàw·háu·chàwng **thrush (health)**
壞 waai **bad**
壞咗 waai·jáw **broken • out of order**
懷孕 wàai·yan **pregnant**
懶惰 láan·daw **lazy**
攀岩 pàan·ngàam **rockclimbing**
攀藤 pàan·tàng **creeper (plant) • vine**
瀕臨滅絕物種 pàn·làm mìt·jewt
   mat·júng **endangered species**
簽名 chìm·méng **signature**
簽證 chìm·jing **visa**
繩 síng **rope**
繩 síng **string**
羹 gàng **spoon**
藝術 ngai·seut **art**
藝術家 ngai·seut·gàa **artist**
藝術館 ngai·seut·gún **art gallery**
藥方 yeuk·fàwng **prescription**
藥片 yeuk·pín **pill**
藥材 yeuk·chòy **herb (medicine)**
藥房 yeuk·fàwng **chemist • pharmacy**
藥劑師 yeuk·jài·sì **chemist (person)**
證件 jing·gín **identification**
證明 jing·mìng **certificate**
贈券 jang·gewn **complimentary (free)**
邊 bìn **ledge**
邊度 bìn·do **where**
邊界 bìn·gaai **border**
邊個 bìn·gaw **who**
鏡 geng **mirror**
鏡片 geng·pín **lens**
關 gwàan **close** ⊙
關心 gwàan·sàm **care (for someone)**
關門 gwàan·mùn **closed**
關係 gwàan·hai **relationship**
難 làam **difficult**
難民 laan·màn **refugee**
類 leui **class (category)**
類型 leui·yìng **type** ⑪
饅頭 màan·tàu **steamed bun**

騙子 pin·jí **liar**
騙局 pin·guk **cheat** ⊙
嚴肅 yìm·sùk **serious**
懸崖 yewn·ngàai **cliff**
爐 ló **stove**
礦泉水 kawng·chewn·séui
   mineral water
籃 láam **basket**
籃球 làam·kàu **basketball**
蘑菇 màw·gù **mushroom**
蘆筍 lò·séun **asparagus**
蘋果 ping·gwáw **apple**
蘋果酒 pìng·gwáw·jáu **cider**
蘇克蘭 sò·gaak·làan **Scotland**
蠔 hò **oyster**
議會 yí·wúi **parliament**
警告 gíng·go **warn**
警察 gíng·chaat **police (officer)**
警察局 gíng·chaat·gúk **police station**
贏 yèng **win** ⊙
贏家 yèng·gàa **winner**
鐘 jùng **clock**
鐘頭 jùng·tàu **hour**
饑荒 gày·fàwng **famine**
騷擾 sò·yíu **harassment**
鹹魚 hàam·yéw **sardine**
鹹魚罐頭 hàam·yéw gun·táu
   herring (salted in a can)
麵包 mìn·bàau **bread • roll**
麵包店 mìn·bàau·dim **bakery**
麵店 mìn·dìm **noodle house**
麵粉 mìn·fán **flour**
麵條 mìn·tìu **noodles**
黨 dáwng **party (politics)**
黨員 dáwng·yèwn
   communist (party member)
獼猴桃 mày·hàu·tò **kiwifruit**
攝影 sip·yíng **photography**
攝影家 sip·yíng·gàa **photographer**
櫻桃 yìng·tò **cherry**
爛咗 laan·jáw **spoiled**
蠢 chéun **stupid**
蠟燭 laap·jùk **candle**
襪 mat **sock(s)**
護士 wu·si **nurse**
護照 wu·jiu **passport**
護照號碼 wu·jiu ho·máa
   passport number
護膚膏 wu·fù·gò **moisturiser**
護髮素 wu·faat·so **conditioner (hair)**
鐵線 tit·sín **wire** ⑪
露營 lo·yìng **camp** ⊙

露營用品店 lo·yìng yung·bán·dim **camping store**

露營地點 lo·yìng day·dím **campsite**

鶴嘴鋤 hawk·jéui·chàwk **pickaxe**

攞 láw **get (fetch)**

攞走 láw·jáu **take**

權力 kèwn·lìk **power**

歡迎 fūn·yìng **welcome**

癮君子 yán·gùn·jí **drug user**

聽 tèng **listen (to)**

聽到 tèng·dó **hear**

讀 duk **read**

鬚後水 sò·hau·séui **aftershave**

攪拌 gáau·bun **mix** ⊙

曬傷 saai·sèung **sunburn**

蘿蔔 làw·baak **radish**

變質 bin·jàt **off (spoiled)**

驚訝 gìng·ngaa **surprise**

驗血 yìm·hewt **blood test**

驗眼師 yìm·ngáan·sì **optometrist**

體育 tái·yuk **sport**

體育用品店 tái·yuk yung·bán dim **sports store/shop**

體育館 tái·yuk·gún **stadium**

體操 tái·chò **aerobics • gymnastics**

癲癇 dìn·gáan **epilepsy**

癲嘅 dìn·ge **crazy**

罐 gun **pot (ceramics)**

罐頭 gun·táu **can • tin**

靈氣按摩 lìng·hay ngawn·mò **reiki**

鷹嘴豆 yìng·jéui·dáu **chickpea**

鹽 yìm **salt**

觀景臺 gùn·gíng·tòy **lookout**

鑰匙 sáw·sì **key**

纜車 laam·chè **cable car • chairlift (skiing)**

鬱悶 wàt·mun **sad**

INDEX

254